BASIC ACTING

The Modular Acting Process

Sabin R. Epstein
John D. Harrop

Original Illustrations by Linda Sarver

Allyn and Bacon, Inc.
Boston • London • Toronto • Sydney • Tokyo • Singapore

Editor-in Chief, Humanities: Joe Opiela
Series Editor: Carla Daves
Editorial Assistant: Mary Visco
Marketing Manager: Karon Bowers
Composition and Prepress Buyer: Linda Cox
Manufacturing Buyer: Aloka Rathnam
Cover Administrator: Suzanne Harbison
Production Administrator: Deborah Brown
Editorial-Production Service: P. M. Gordon Associates

"Fool for Love," copyright © 1983 by Sam Shepard, from FOOL FOR LOVE AND
OTHER PLAYS by Sam Shepard. Used by permission of Bantam Books, a division of
Bantam Doubleday Dell Publishing Group, Inc.

Library of Congress Cataloging-in-Publication Data

Epstein, Sabin R.
   Basic acting : the modular acting process / Sabin Epstein, John
Harrop : original illustrations by Linda Sarver.
      p.   cm.
   Includes bibliographical references and index.
   ISBN 0–205–18338–7
   1. Acting.   I. Harrop, John.   II. Title.
PN2061.E68   1996
792'.028—dc20   95-37909
                                                                 CIP

Printed in the United States of America
10 9 8 7 6 5 4 3 2 1   00 99 98 97 96 95

CONTENTS

Coda   303

ACKNOWLEDGMENTS

All acting process and actor training are essentially eclectic and derivative, building upon the past and adapting to the needs of the future. In this context we freely acknowledge our debt to the great teachers, directors, actors, and colleagues who have helped to formulate and mentor the ideas expressed in this book. Thank you Konstantin Stanislavski, Viola Spolin, Rudolf Laban, Michel St. Denis, Michael Chekhov, Keith Johnstone, Edward De Bono, Cicely Berry, William Ball, Allen Fletcher, Edward Hastings, Larry Hecht, John C. Fletcher, and Jimmy Listenbee, with a special acknowledgment to Vicki Harrop. We would also like to thank our reviewers, Terry Allen of the University of Wisconsin at Eau Claire, Martha LoMonaco of Fairfield University, and Alan Wade of George Washington University.

ABOUT THE AUTHORS

Sabin R. Epstein was associated with the American Conservatory Theater in San Francisco for twenty years as an actor, director, and teacher, including three years as Conservatory Director. He has taught acting at such institutions as Cal/Arts in Los Angeles and S.U.N.Y. Purchase in New York. His work as a director has been seen at the Kennedy Center in Washington as well as the Oregon, Utah, and Georgia Shakespeare festivals. He is currently Resident Director at A Noise Within in Los Angeles and Associate Artist at the Georgia Shakespeare Festival, and he teaches acting privately. He is the co-author, with John Harrop, of *Acting with Style.*

John D. Harrop worked in the theater for more than thirty years. As an actor, he appeared professionally in London; toured California in productions of works by Pinter, Beckett, and Brecht; and worked in resident theaters in Knoxville and Philadelphia, and in Los Angeles at A Noise Within. He served as professor of drama and head of the Bachelor of Fine Arts acting program at the University of California at Santa Barbara, and taught acting in England, Australia, and San Francisco. He also directed productions in San Francisco, Santa Barbara, and Utah.

This book is dedicated to the memory of John Harrop.

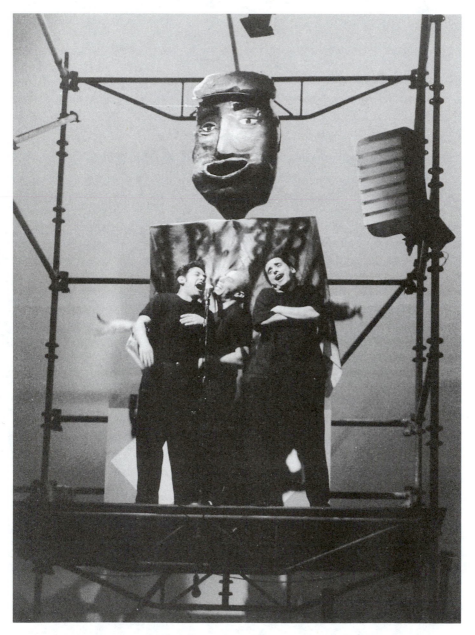

Radio Mambo: Culture Clash Invades Miami, written and performed by Richard Montoya, Ric Salinas, and Herbert Siguenza; directed by Jose Luis Valenzuela; at the Colony Theater, Miami, Florida.
Photograph © Miami Herald/Roberto Koltun.

PROLOGUE

Much contemporary actor training still smacks of the bottomless samovar of tea shared at the Slavic Bazaar restaurant in 1897 by Konstantin Stanislavski and Nemirovich-Danchenko. As a result of their all-night meeting the Moscow Art Theatre was born, and the Stanislavski Acting System gradually evolved.

The System was spread, in the United States, after the visit of the Moscow Art Theatre in 1923. Richard Boleslavsky, an actor/director with the company, stayed in the United States and taught his version of the System, which was later adopted by the Group Theatre in the 1930s. When the group dissolved in the 1940s the New York Actor's Studio emerged in 1947. Lee Strasberg began to teach there in 1950. Strasberg successfully parlayed his understanding of Stanislavski's system into "the Method," which has been the most influential acting process, particularly in the United States, for the past forty years. The Method reflects the social and cultural dynamics of the 1940s, 1950s, and early 1960s and became, for its time the TRUTH of the nature of acting and the actor's process.

The Method was particularly suited to the realistic and naturalistic theatre of the 1940s and 1950s, and it gained worldwide influence through the essentially realistic medium of film, where many of Strasberg's protégés, including James Dean and Marlon Brando, made their name and fortune. Realism, however appealing to the average man and woman who liked to watch their everyday lives being worked out on stage and screen, made for a limited form of theater that dealt with the world of the 1950s, with its basic nuclear family of one dog, two parents, three children, and a fourth wall. This realistic world was essentially white and male-headed, domestically run by the mother, who most likely stayed at home. The whole family would have had a strong belief in the Constitution and the moral values handed down from the eighteenth century by the Founding Fathers. Though the world outside had changed significantly in philosophy and social values since the eighteenth century, even from 1897, these changes had yet to penetrate the right little, tight little, white little structure of realism for which the Method was suited.

The Method held firmly to its belief in the consistent individuated self with its rational throughline of character and its vision of action that connected point A with point B with point C in an equally straightforward and rational way. It could see itself and its confusions mirrored whether it looked at the stage, the screen, or out of the window of its own house.

But, already by the 1950s, "Reality ain't what it used to be." In 1897 Einstein had yet to publish his theory of relativity, whereby space bent, and, therefore, Stanislavski's psychological throughlines could not be held sacrosanct any more. Marshall McLuhan had yet to publish his treatise that declared "the Medium is the Message," confirming not only that the world was round, but that images outpowered intellectual ideas, and images spoke louder than words in the new global media village.

Philosophically, Sartre and existentialism helped to make ideas and essences less significant than actions and practice. Then came deconstruction and chaos theory in which everything is relative, but dependent upon everything else (one famous chaotic image: the fluttering of a butterfly's wings in Brooklyn can affect the weather in Alaska). These ideas finally sounded the death knell of realism's values around the 1970s, after the social revolution of the 1960s had finally brought the philosophical, structural, and political values of realism under an attack that it could no longer avoid. Psychiatry had an earlier dawn and by the 1950s was well established, but it was soon to be taken over by the Method and its adherents and used for personal as well as for theatrical purposes as an interesting, quirky bend in the straight and narrow yellow brick road of realism.

This is not to say there were not individuals in the theater during this time period who recognized or intuited that all the newer elements of philosophy and physics, of political and social change, must be reflected and incorporated into theater work. It was many years before they were to become remotely mainstream, as little by little they insinuated their structural and aesthetic elements into realism itself—or stood on the fringes and threw their contemporary firecrackers at largely unsuspecting audiences.

There were those like Jacques Copeau who started the Vieux Colombier in 1913 to explore nonrealistic staging on bare stages, and who then added a school in 1926. There was his nephew, Michel St. Denis, who opened the London Theatre Studio in 1936 and then went on to schools in Canada and Juilliard in New York to "rediscover style," i.e., theater that had more to say than could be heard or seen through the peephole of the fourth wall. There was Rudolf Laban, who has come as close as anyone yet to evolving a system based upon the iconography of physical action of the body. There were Peter Brook and Jerzy Grotowski, who both looked at the strenuous physical preparation of actors for a Theatre of Cruelty, a theater that ripped away the realistic patina used by the post-Stanislavski actor and revealed the raw, transcendental passion beneath the realistic mask.

These are some of the great teachers who have tried to keep actors prepared to deal with the dynamics of a changing world that realism and its Method acting process has largely ignored, or been unable to deal with. There also have been some directors whose iconic productions have marked the progress of the new world created since 1897, or even 1950. Jerzy Grotowski's *The Constant Prince*; Richard Schechner's *Dionysos in 69*; a deconstruction of *The Bacchae*; Peter Brook's *Marat/Sade*, a combination of Grotowski's physicality and Brecht's alienation; Robert Wilson's *Einstein on the Beach*, a self-creation of media and visual images; the work of the Wooster Group; the Shakespearean deconstructions of Arianne Mnouchkine; and the wholesale deconstruction of Peter Sellars. Meanwhile, realism and the Method went marching on: it will always be with us (though film and television may take it over) because we narcissistically need to confirm our own existence and see a reflection of what we think of as our "normality." It is easy, but it is no longer enough. We now need an acting process to deal with the world as it is today, almost a century since the then-crucial and necessary founding of the Moscow Art Theatre.

Not only have media broken down boundaries between cultures that now can be brought in instant touch with each other in McLuhan's global village, but the physical breaking down of long-established barriers is now occurring. For almost a thousand years (since 1066) the English Channel had protected England from invasion by other countries, and had compartmentalized it from Europe. In 1994 the Chunnel was opened beneath England's watery moat, which now can be crossed by rail in thirty minutes; London, Paris, and Berlin, the capitals of countries that had been at war with each other many times during many centuries, are connected with barely the trouble of changing trains. (Unless you want to visit Disneyland in Paris!)

Though yet to be connected to the mainland by a tunnel, Hawaii, in 1959, became the first of the United States not to have a population of essentially European descent. The white population of California will be in a minority by the early part of the twenty-first century (already 90 non-English languages and dialects are spoken in Los Angeles' schools); by 2030 less than sixty percent of total immigration to the United States as a whole will be by whites or those of European background. No more will immigrants be bringing the remnants of Western culture with them, nor will they be familiar with the Greek, Renaissance, Enlightenment, and democratic industrial capitalist cultures upon which the United States was founded. Ellis Island saw the last of that. The changing face of America now will be crossing its southern and western borders (reflecting the Pacific Rim). As the first country built by immigrants, the United States will be the first country to adapt to an essentially postmodern culture. No one will be able to hide from it. What change your next door neighbor doesn't introduce you to, the media will.

Already twenty million people around the world are hooked up to electronic bulletin boards. We are facing a five-hundred channel television future. Consistency will be an assortment of inconsistencies, a Chinese menu approach to clothing and style taken by young people, dictated by mood, as eclectic as the world they live in: punk one day, new romantic the next; grunge, preppy, funk, thrift store, after that mix and, maybe, match; not kept consistent by any Constitution or Method. Culture "pops" with flash bulb swiftness, or the flick of the thumb on the channel changer.

The legacy of 1897 will no longer entirely be enough for the actor of 1997 and beyond, in a world that bends, is multicultural, is nonnuclear in living situations, and in which there may be many different truths that fit different occasions. The breaking down of traditional forms in life and theater (for the theatrical process, although conservative, is finally inextricable from the contemporary sensibility that surrounds it) is forcing humankind to explore its multifaceted world, and multifarious, multicultural self. A mirror held up to nature today will not reveal any one discrete reflection. Today's mirror will show the many faces of the postmodern world, and the many-masked selves of contemporary men and women.

So how to train the actor for a world that is no longer based upon rational throughlines and discrete characters? A world no longer based upon the fourth wall and white western-based nuclear family structure, but one that includes gays, women in positions of power, and the kaleidoscope of multiculturalism? After years of gestation, we, the authors of this book, finally met at a cafe in Los Angeles in 1992, and arrived at the *Modular Acting Process* (*MAP*).

The acronym MAP is no accident. It does in fact connect this new process with perhaps the most distinctive principle of Stanislavski's system: that a text is a map to action. But, unlike Strasberg's Method derivative, it is outward—not inward—looking and action—not character—driven. Action is genderless and raceless. If the actor finds the journey of action that the map of the script provides, then the essence and spirit of his or her intention will be communicated to the audience.

One of the interesting connections among nonrealistic productions (by whatever name or whatever director) of the past forty years is that they have been outward looking, not dealing with inner character processes. They have used the body as a sign and instrument and mask as an interchangeable persona, not a singular psyche. What was needed was a training process that focused upon these factors, that was essentially action and physically based, that was flexible and embraceable by the new multiculturalism that would mark the acting community in the next century. This process had to be flexible enough to include gay, African-American, and feminist theater and gays, African-Americans, and feminists all in the same production, while at the same time have enough structure to make a practical theatrical statement possible while riding the curve of Einstein's bent space, and catching the breadth of the butterfly's wings of chaos theory.

A modular process, based upon action, body, and mask and the premise that culture isn't color, seemed to be the answer. The principles developed in this book are that a text is a map of action, that the map is broken down into modules of action that do not necessarily have to follow a simple narrative throughline, and that character is a complex of masks that equally do not have to contain a singular throughline and consistency. Discovering and playing action is not necessarily a rational process leading from points A to B to C, but it can stem from a nucleus including points A, B, and C, and not necessarily in that order.

The map of the text is a series of modules of action. These may be dealt with by actors in any order. The modules are flexible; they may be moved around and mixed and matched, allowing for the possibilities of deconstruction and allowing for any problem of action to be dealt with in any order. Actors may enter the journey of the map at any point. The selection of the problem can be arbitrary. Any problem will trigger a series of solutions, which will lead to new, more specific problems to be solved. Once the modules of action have been dealt with, actors may still examine and explore the nucleus of the action, which contains the spirit or truth of the journey they have set out upon.

Shakespeare said that "Action is eloquence." It is also per se colorless and raceless. All great theater work deals in its heart with the issues of humanity and the problems common to the soul of any culture. Whatever color or shape they may take, they touch and are recognizable to the spiritual inheritance derived from Adam and Eve, no matter when or where we may have been born. The real issues of humanity are common to us all and are carried in the nucleus of the spirit of dramatic action whatever outward form or shape it may take. Life no longer "goes on" with Aristotle and Stanislavski. It "goes around" like Shakespeare's Globe, and McLuhan's global village.

Life is now seen as multilayered and multifaceted. Theater requires an acting process that is geared to the multicultured dimensionality of the postmodern world and the demands it makes upon the actor. This is what the *Modular Acting Process* does. Its distinctive feature is that it responds to the variegated nature of life today, and to the increasingly accepted idea that the human being does not have one unique and distinct self, but acts with different masks in different situations. Eugene O'Neill, a major American playwright of the realistic period, had this intuition fifty years ago. In his essay "On Masks" he said that the use of masks will be discovered eventually to be the freest solution to the modern dramatist's problems. The British playwright Howard Barker also has referred to the "permanent disruption of character... the instability of motive"[1] in the work of contemporary theater.

Many years ago the human body as an autonomous self "enslaved by its own magic" was broken down by cubism. The postmodern map of theater uses modules and masks to suit its nonprescriptive purposes. Theater work today demands of the actor that he or she can look in many directions at the same time. Wear many faces in many places. Relativity, deconstruction, cubism, chaos theory. Nothing is straightforward, separate, and rational. As Robert Lewis, one of the earliest members of the Group Theatre and associate of the Method, has said, "playwriting and performance has changed. Plays have become fragmented like cubism. The whole business of introducing a character and developing it consistently doesn't exist any more. We have to arrange our training to suit our performance needs."[2] This is what a *Modular Acting Process* does.

Notes

1. H. Barker, *Guardian*, 22 August 1988, R. 34.
2. R. Lewis, "Dialogue with Robert Lewis"; in *Directing the Action*, Charles Marowitz, New York, Applause Theatre Books, 1986, p. 91. It should be added that Mr. Lewis was one of the first to adopt Stanislavski's system and one of the first to criticize Strasberg's Method, in *Method or Madness*, New York, Samuel French, 1958.

PART ONE

THE MAP

Brecht's *Good Person of Setzuan* at La Jolla Playhouse, San Diego, California.
Photograph © 1995 by Ken Howard.

ON THE ACTING PROCESS

A play is a fiction of time, place, and action. The audience collaborates with the story tellers—the playwright, designers, director, and actors—to create the illusion of the play; once the audience suspends its disbelief and validates the play's action by recognizing it as true, the event known as theater begins. Actors and audience then cross a threshold together, uniting in a journey through shared time, space, and imagination.

In this journey, acting is the process of wearing the mask of character; the actors convince the audience that they are other than who they really are.

Every act of creation, every attempt to make the invisible visible, involves the creation of an illusion. For the actor, the process of theatrical illusion begins with an impulse.

An impulse is a movement forward, towards doing. The impulse transforms and leads to an image. The image is lodged within the actor's own experience, or within the actor's ability to imagine experience. The image leads to the physical manifestation of the impulse, action. Action is tangible, malleable, and capable of transformation.

In life, action is spontaneous. In the theater, an audience witnesses structured action, action that is calculated to create the illusion of spontaneity, yet which is nonetheless predetermined. The predetermined score of action is organized and structured by intent—what the character wants. The intent gives action a target, or direction.

Playing targeted action involves rebalancing the character's relationships. The actor is always in relationship with herself (through the use of the inner voice, which is the tangible manifestation of the self); in relationship with the environment (where we are, when we are, and, in response to the rules, customs, and context of our culture, how we are); and in relationship with people and objects in that environment (who we are).

Targets are used to motivate action, propelling us forward in time as we plan what we intend to do, or to justify action, looking back in time to rationalize what we've done. Targets are always stated in the form of infinitive verbs attached to the phrase "I want," such as "I want you to smile," or "I want you to forgive me." Targets create forwardness in action. They are positive, immediate, and obtainable. Targets lead to action that is tangible and affords immediate gratification.

A character has a target in every act, scene, and frame—or unit of action—within a play. Targets form into patterns of logical consistency when they are linked together from moment to moment by a magnet. The magnet is always the character's secret; it pulls the character forward because it involves what the character ultimately intends for himself.

Endowments create the context for action. They are the way things are— the facts—before the action begins. Endowments exist in and affect the use of time and space. They condition, tone, and affect how you act, what you can and cannot do, and the way in which you can and cannot do it.

Endowments include the character's emotional and psychological state-of-being up to the moment of the play's action (the character's biography); the physical and sensory conditions of the environment (incorporating the political, economic, cultural, and social conditions of the play's context); and the state of balance of the character's relationships before the action starts. Endowments are the rules of the game. These rules are contained within the text and must be agreed upon by all the players.

Shared endowments establish a balance between the characters, so that the level and degree of tension that exists in the relationships before the action begins—the gap—can change.

Characters always change their status during the course of a scene. Status is the moment-to-moment positioning that creates the gap. Although it can be linked to power, status is not necessarily about power or control. Status deals exclusively with where characters stand in relation to one another. Every transaction, or action exchange, involves a change of status and a change in the gap.

A character does not always hit his target in every scene. But the character always initiates, engages in, and completes each frame of action in pursuit of the target.

Every target has a hurdle, which is used to block effort. The bigger the hurdle, the greater the effort required to get over, under, or around it. When the effort is strong the action becomes more intense and specific and the actor engages on a deeper level.

Every action involves tension. Tension is not necessarily a negative factor; tension becomes negative only when it is excessive and overloaded. Tension requires an expenditure of energy, known as effort.

Effort is measured by observing the four effort factors in operation. In every action:

1. the weight of an effort varies from light to strong;
2. the time of an effort varies from quick to sustained;
3. the focus in space of an effort varies from direct to indirect; and
4. the combination of time, weight, and space produces flow, which varies from open to bound. Flow moves through and links effort into patterns of action.

Effort may be inhibited or it may be released. Released effort involves surrender and leads to greater forwardness in action. Inhibited effort leads to a closing down of the creative impulse.

Character is physicalized in the form of shape. Shape transforms into mask when it becomes the tangible expression of the character's inner life. The mask is determined physically by the character's age, occupation, environment, social status, biography, and effort patterns. The mask is determined verbally through the character's use of language.

Language is thought in action. Thirty percent of communication is based on language; the other seventy percent is a combination of physical and verbal expression, inflection, pitch, rhythm, and intonation. Every character has its own way of speaking, its own verbal life, and its own verbal pattern that extends thought into space.

Flow becomes bound when the stakes of a relationship are at their highest and when the characters are most vulnerable because they stand either to win—to hit or miss their target. Flow opens when tension is released.

There is always a margin in performance that allows the actor to respond to the impulse of the moment with fellow actors and with the audience. Playing is the factor that accounts for this margin of flexibility.

Playing allows the player to remain spontaneous within the fixed structure—the set sequence—of the action, and it gives the actor permission to manipulate the endowments and adjust and adapt effort for maximum effect.

The training process centers on the single but essential premise that the impulse for creativity is formed through problem solving, and that problem solving demands doing. What you do is how you solve the problem; how well you do it is how well you play.

Inherent in this premise is the belief that we are all capable of solving problems. The training, therefore, is skills oriented: developing skills for the actor/player in defining specific problems to be solved, be it in an improvisational or textual context, as well as developing the skills of communication necessary for solving problems creatively, effectively, and economically.

The training, by necessity, focuses on expanding the player's awareness of her range, potential, and ability by engaging the full use of the instrument in solving each problem. The process is predominantly visceral; it stresses direct experience through participation and encourages self-discovery through insight and evaluation.

The aim of the MAP is the development of a technique that is tangible and specific for each actor/player. The initial phase of the training focuses on releasing inhibition—tension—in order to physicalize and verbalize the player's impulse. Once the impulse is externalized, the player molds and shapes it into a score of action that is repeatable. The player then confronts the specific problems involved in playing that score from moment to moment.

The process, then, is aimed at training creative actors who are capable of working individually as well as collaboratively with other theater artists. The training is complementary to any other form of theater training and is not exclusive; it is aimed at helping actors diagnose their own problems and encourages them to seek additional training and technique in order to solve those problems. Therefore, additional voice and movement work, approaches to characterization and style, and continued study in textual analysis and interpretation are all vital to the full development of the actor.

The initial steps of the MAP use improvisation and theater games to release inhibition and free impulse. The energy release is high, imaginations are stimulated, and actors begin to experience playing. Gradually the problems to be solved in the improvisational exercises become more specific and the games become increasingly complex, requiring the full use of communicative skills. Throughout, the concept of dramatic action is examined and brought into focus. As the players become more adept at problem solving, the problems become more difficult and sophisticated until, inevitably, a text is used as a focus for the actor. The problems of the text are defined by and solutions through improvisation and experimentation are sought by the individual players. A score of action is developed and then refined. The players are then required to play the score precisely, moment to moment. The final steps of the training deal with the problems of playing in performance—playing a fixed score of actions in front of an audience while retaining the original freshness and spontaneity that lead to the creation of the score.

ON THE MAP PROCESS

The Modular Acting Process—MAP—is a practical guide to the actor's art and focuses on developing skills in four overlapping fields of study: Shaping, Playing, Structuring, and Performing the Action.

In Shaping the Action the player develops an awareness of the manipulation of the outer to trigger the inner. Shaping studies the movement from the intuitive to the analytical and then, from the analytical to the intuitive. Skills involved focus on releasing, organizing, and arranging patterns of energy and tension.

In Playing the Action players focus on the creative process. Playing examines the conditions and contexts that affect action. By learning to identify and associate rules of behavior with contexts the player learns to improve the quality of his play.

In Structuring the Action players examine the fundamental principles that govern outward focus and interaction. Players develop skill in the formation of creative boundaries, as well as develop skill in the creation of narrative voice, which gives the action direction, momentum, and purpose.

In Performing the Action players focus on applying shape and structure to expand and intensify scores of action. Performance skills include the integration of language and mask to create character.

These four areas of training are interwoven into each exercise and together form the structural grid of the MAP.

The grid works 1) horizontally, progressing from individual exercises to partner exercises to group exercises; 2) vertically, moving from shaping exercises to playing exercises to structural exercises to performance exercises; and 3) laterally, in any and all directions, by exercising skills in problem solving technique.

It is possible to use one single exercise to illustrate any or all of the concepts in the training process; therefore it is possible to spend one training session on a single area of attention or, by combining two or three areas of attention, to examine one concept from multiple points of view. The grid pattern is open to as many possibilities of arrangement as is imaginable.

Each of these four fields of study—shape, play, structure, and performance—focuses on three separate aspects of dramatic action. Combined, all twelve aspects—or modules—represent twelve different ways of seeing action. Each module isolates a different facet of the process and examines it in depth:

In Shaping the Action players focus on:
> physical **Shape**—developing skill in directing attention to the outer;
> **Release,** developing awareness of stress and inhibition;
> **Flow,** developing skill in the experience of engagement.

In Playing the Action players focus on:
> **Transformation**—developing skill in moving from "point to point" and linking "points" together;
> **Patterns**—developing skill in defining boundaries and applying rules of play;
> **Endowments**—developing skill in "bridging," devising ways to link the player and the world of the play.

In Structuring the Action players focus on:
> **Status**—developing skill in perceiving and manipulating balance in relationships;
> **Targets**—developing skill in directing attention to create action with forward motion;
> **Hurdles**—developing skill in provoking and stimulating the imagination to intensify playing.

In Performing the Action players focus on:
> **Masks**—developing skill in merging outer and inner to create character;
> **Language**—developing skill in transforming thought into action;
> **Set Sequences**—developing skill in heightening effort to intensify patterns of action and play.

The initial phases of MAP training use improvisation and theater games to release inhibition. Gradually the problems to be solved in the improvisational exercises become more specific and the games increasingly complex, requiring the full use of communicative skills. As players become more adept at problem solving, the problems become more sophisticated until, inevitably, a text is used as a focus for the training.

A training session usually follows a set sequence, beginning with individual work to focus attention, remove inhibition, and "tune" the instrument. The session then progresses to interactive drills between two or three players, focusing on the quality of play and the dynamics of action. The session ends with a large group problem, quite often a performance game, which enlarges the circle of attention to include the role of an audience in the process.

Players move from experiencing the fundamental rules of play and the basic patterns of action—through structured games—to creating patterns of action from their own life experience through improvisation; to recreating patterns of action through cloning, imitating, and interpreting scores of action; and finally to rehearsing and performing these created scores of action.

The final phase of the training process moves into application of all the skills by focusing on rehearsing and performing a scene from a contemporary American play. The world of the play is created through improvisation and exercise, stressing endowments, targets, hurdles, analysis of patterns and status, and the creation of the mask through the integration of shape and language. Once a score of action is determined and designed, it is performed and then reworked for specificity and spontaneity.

As skills strengthen, more and more complex scores and texts will be used as the basis of continued study. Players will eventually move on to the creation of scenes from plays involving other times and other places, expanding their range of experience, integrating research into the work process, and learning how to approach plays of heightened language and style.

MAP training, by necessity, focuses on expanding the player's awareness of his or her range, potential, and ability by engaging the use of the full instrument in solving every problem. The process is predominantly visceral; it stresses direct experience through participation and encourages self-discovery through insight and evaluation.

NOTES TO THE PLAYER

Actions speak louder than words.

Your body doesn't lie.

You may have a wonderful imagination, but if you don't have the skills and tools necessary for translating your imagination into action you will be forever trapped inside your mind.

Focus your attention on developing your sense of physicality in order to expand and translate the potential of your imagination into action.

All of the exercises, games, structures, and activities in the MAP are metaphors for understanding and experiencing the concepts and principles of action. As you train, your perception will move from the general to the specific. Play first and talk after. Your perception of action must be experiential rather than theoretical and intellectual. The more you see, and see clearly, the easier it will be for you to do.

Once you have experience stored in your body you can name it and connect it to its underlying concept. Then it is yours for life. Everyone works and grows at their own rate. There is no predicting when you will stumble into "insight" and connect physical experience with intellectual understanding. This process of kinesthetic learning can only happen when you play first and talk afterward. Give yourself over to the doing. Sometimes the understanding happens long after the experience. When you do "insight" you will know it with your sense of intuitive rightness.

Although you want to play well, give up your sense of being perfect, especially as you begin to learn to play. Process means that the work is going to evolve, shift, change, develop, and grow. There is a technique to the process of playing, just as there is a technique involved with the process of acting.

Mastery of technique evolves over a long period of time. Usually it is imperceptible. Suddenly you are able to do things you've been struggling with; you don't know how or when you've changed, you just have. Your awareness and perception develop as your technique improves. You see more, because suddenly there is more to see. Everything always becomes clear with hindsight. Playing combines physical as well as mental skill. Skill is something that can be strengthened by drill and improved by technique.

Technique provides structure. It gives you clear boundaries. Within defined boundaries you gain vision and, with vision, perception. You know what you are looking at, and what you are looking for. Every drill involves developing a vocabulary for seeing. The point of the drill is to increase your perception and strengthen your involvement by building your sense of engagement in playing action.

There is a pattern involved in the structure of every game. Once you see the pattern, the playing will be easier. Patterns are the architecture of action.

The first stage of the process focuses on finding ways to discover and see the pattern. The second stage of the process focuses on setting the pattern into motion, moving it out of your head and into your body in space. The third stage of the process focuses on making the playing of the pattern interesting, dynamic, and dramatically engaging. The fourth stage of the process focuses on performing the pattern in front of an audience to complete the acting cycle.

When you are lost or confused in the middle of an exercise, use someone else as a model. Give yourself a visual and physical reference that allows you to continue playing; don't be afraid to imitate. You do not have to be original, creative, or unique at every moment. Using a model is a deliberate provocation to trigger your imagination and get you moving when you are blocked.

When you become so set or rigid in your way of looking at things that you stop having new or stimulating ideas, you need to deliberately provoke yourself into breaking out of your habits in order to expand your perception. All training is a form of provocation. As you become aware of a pattern that is stifling you, deliberately break it in order to create a new one. Every creative idea is born out of provocation. Every "offer" is a deliberate provocative device used to stimulate your imagination. It forces you to respond spontaneously, without predetermination or forethought. A provocation opens the window for inspiration.

Relationships are the heart and soul of every scene. If the audience doesn't understand who you are to one another physically, in space, as well as in verbal intent, they will never surrender to the scene. The words and the pictures must always mesh. No matter how clever you are in your playing, an audience always knows when you are not telling the truth.

Always respond positively to your partners. This keeps the energy circulating between you and makes it possible to collaborate. Rejecting inhibits the creative response, denies participation, and undermines effort. If you can accept every idea you are offered and build on it, new and better ideas will emerge. When you all work together as an ensemble you can create ideas larger than the sum of the individual parts.

Each time you start to work you must define the problem to be solved. Focusing on a problem gives you a point of entry into a scene. It stimulates your imagination and clarifies your target—where and how to direct and focus the intent of your effort.

A specific point of entry gives you purchase and leads you forward towards active playing and dynamic choices. The selection of the point of entry can be arbitrary. Because a scene will have several problems to be solved, and most problems are interrelated, any solution will work if it stimulates and engages your imagination.

Work within precise rules. Pressure too can be provocative. Work quickly, within a fixed time limit. This overloads the imagination with so many choices that you will respond without any censoring. Or do the opposite, and work with an unlimited amount of time to remove pressure and creative tension. This enhances the process of transformation, allowing ideas to change and grow gradually.

Changing points of view and working with opposites opens alternatives and stimulates perception. Approach a scene as your partner's character in order to better understand the total action of the scene.

Exaggerate in order to define action. Exaggeration leads to clearer images and working with images helps structure the pattern involved with inner flow. As the physical action develops you must find the corresponding inner image and add it into your inner score of action. Use hurdles to trigger stronger images. The stronger the effort the more tangible the action. When you feel no stimulus, do nothing. Doing nothing eliminates the artificial pressure to constantly perform and also shifts the burden of responsibility off of yourself and on to your partner, who must work to trigger your imagination.

When searching for an idea, jiggle or toss ideas back and forth with your partner. Play with an idea arbitrarily until your energy begins to flow and your imagination is released. The energy exchange heightens the dynamic and strengthens the creative endeavor.

After working, evaluate your achievements and process. Avoid value judgments; focus on how to create clearer working images. Understanding how a problem is solved and receiving positive and constructive feedback will help you define and refine the process the next time you play.

Once you understand the rules that create context, you are well on the way to discovering the style of a scene. Style is a **series of consistencies.** As you develop your physical imagination you can shape, mold, and design action to be "in sync" with its environment and context, so that the inner and outer worlds "fit." Growth and perception are cumulative experiences. The MAP is also cumulative.

It takes time, patience, and practice before the process begins to reveal itself and make analytical sense. Stay with it and don't give up, even if results are not instantaneous. The quality of your playing will change; learn to trust your sense of intuitive rightness, and let that guide you until the pieces of the puzzle begin to fit together.

Throughout the training, the concept of dramatic action is examined and brought into focus. MAP training starts with the single but essential premise that the impulse for dramatic action is found through problem solving, and that problem solving demands doing. What you do is how you solve the problem; how you do it is how you play.

Inherent in this premise is the belief that the instinctive player intuitively knows how to act and how to create. MAP training seeks to remove any inhibiting factor that stifles the creative spirit. Once that spirit has been released, the player learns to give it voice by developing skill, and freedom of expression by developing technique.

Most players know when they have successfully solved a problem. Intuitive rightness takes over and the player feels inspired, having lost all sense of self-consciousness or self-awareness.

The structure of action remains when "inspiration" fades. If the player repeats the intuitively discovered action often enough, even without knowing why he or she did what they did or what it means, only knowing that it "feels right," the action will gradually take on dimension, meaning, and structure.

Through repetition, the intuitive response eventually merges with analytical thinking, and the two processes synthesize to create action that has forwardness in motion and purpose. The MAP examines this creative process; it is a way of seeing, interpreting, arranging, and organizing the components of action that engage the body and, through the body, the imagination.

The aim of the MAP is to discover and develop physical, imaginative, and creative flexibility. The training stresses playing as a means of integrating mind and body. The playing moves from physical experience to intellectual perception—from the outer to the inner—and then from intellectual perception back to physical experience—from the inner to the outer. With the MAP players learn to release the creative impulse, act on the impulse and then rediscover the impulse anew.

The first stage of the MAP involves participation—engaging in and learning through doing. The second stage of the process involves perception—the ability to see and identify a concept or principle of action. The third stage of the process involves practice—developing proficiency, flexibility, and dexterity with the skills.

The player continues to practice the drills until the skill is integrated into the body on a subconscious level, ready to be used when necessary.

Participation, perception, and practice are the cornerstones of the MAP. Technique is the foundation of communicable creative expression. It is the basic vocabulary that enables the player to express him/herself cogently, coherently, and creatively.

By studying the physical signs that govern and condition action—observing and analyzing patterns of action as well as engaging in them—the player develops a specific, active, and experiential vocabulary. This vocabulary evolves through trial and error during each MAP training session. It is crucial that everyone speaks the same language and shares a common thread of experience. In MAP this new vocabulary defines the expenditure of energy in action. By identifying the various effort factors, and observing how they work, it is possible for players to identify their own patterns of action and their acting habits. Once the pattern is identified, the player can seek alternative solutions to expand his or her range of creative possibilities.

Provocation is a deliberate tool in MAP that is used to expand the player's imagination of action.

NOTES TO THE TRAINER

Always begin every session with a physical warmup that engages the spine and the pelvis. Use physical activity to focus the player's attention by identifying and releasing held or inert body parts. Stretch to increase flexibility and break down resistance.

Develop a vocabulary for coaching using active words to help players adjust and adapt their effort while playing: words such as "strong," "light," "quick," or "sustained," as well as directions involving, withholding, and releasing energy.

Coaching helps the players engage in the activity and then intensify the experience once they are engaged. As an observer stay objective and on the alert; monitor the overall design and shape of the playing.

Never tell a player what to feel. You create the boundaries of an exercise by explaining the rules and guide the nature of the player's experience by cuing the effort factors.

Make individual corrections and/or suggestions to the players while they are playing. Be direct in your suggestions to help focus the playing. The games/exercises/activities are structures to be filled with interaction between the players.

Shift the focus often within a session. Move from physical warmups to outer-focus activities to games involving other players to a large group effort.

Solo work always involves inner flow and near space—the immediate and close circle around the player. Players will need to bridge when they develop relationships with the environment or with the other players.

Shifting focus helps players stay alert and off guard. They can't fall back on predictable play patterns. Focus on discovering the habitual play patterns of each player. Coach them to increase and intensify the quality of the play, moving them into a less self-conscious and more spontaneous state. Deepen the quality of the flow by intensifying physical involvement.

Encourage the sense of forwardness, of playing with a purpose. Help players stay forward on action, rather than attitude or emotion.

The exercises always involve a surrender of control, either to the mask or to the playing partner. Any desire for one player to enforce her own will in the creative process and block her partner's suggestions inhibits creative flow.

Be on the alert for this tendency and encourage players to risk not knowing where they are going for a period of time in order to break free of restrictive habits.

The outer is the major guideline in coaching. The outer always triggers the inner. Players are to be reminded continually to engage physically. They are not talking heads. They must play the scenes they create by engaging their bodies in action. The body will continually recharge the imagination.

The more alert, alive, and present the player is physically, the easier it will be for them to stay stimulated, engaged, and involved in the action of the scene.

Your primary goal is to move players into fully committed, fully engaged playing. The playing must have purpose, intent, and forward direction in space. Use hurdles to fuel and increase effort involvement and to feed spontaneity.

At the same time, keep players within the boundaries and perimeters of the structure of the game or scene. They must be encouraged to maintain the ongoing discipline of playing within the rules. Quality of play increases as players become familiar and comfortable with rules. As the comfort increases, make the rules more complex and challenging.

The basic rules of playing—offer, accept, offer, the status see-saw, the manipulation of the effort factors—are a constant. They are always present in every context and situation. They form the substructure for the development of the narrative voice of a scene. They are to be honed, exercised, and drilled to form the spine of the MAP. They exist to aid and affect the player's perception, to help him "see" what needs to be done in any given situation and to provide the player with the tools necessary to do whatever needs to be done.

As the playing progresses you can focus more on bridging from the player's world to the creation of a fictive world. Players will shift focus playing out of their own private experience to creating a mask and playing someone else's private experiences.

Developing the imagination allows the player to exercise curiosity, to wonder why and how. The player can then translate these questions into problems to be solved in rehearsal.

The paradox of the mask is that as the player moves into a fictive persona the mask conceals and helps reveal the player's true personality at the same time. The mask is a device to free spontaneity and originality.

By releasing instinct and the sense of intuitive rightness the player engages his true self in creating the foundation for the score of action. The mask is an exercise in releasing protective devices and revealing vulnerability.

Bridge into the mask through physical work in shape. Use keys, leads, cloning, and perfect and imperfect covers to give the players an opportunity to wear masks in nonthreatening ways.

When players start to play each other, by cloning, they bridge into character based on physical observation. Leads, keys, effort patterns, and basic action drives (BADs) all trigger and stimulate the imagination and enhance the inner life of the character.

Once engaged, the mask transforms and evolves into its own persona, moving away from its initial model and into its own sense of self. This is the time to add more boundaries, rules, and hurdles. The mask will define its own restrictions, intentions, obsessions, and patterns of behavior.

Scoring action with set sequence games integrates the various individual components into a cohesive pattern. As players become more familiar with scoring they will be able to drill and practice the rehearsal process. Players must always work with a specific point of focus and a specific point of entry into the score. They must always have a specific target to take them forward, and specific hurdles to make hitting the target difficult, challenging, and engaging. Create boundaries and rules to guide, control, and condition the play. Repetition and focus are keys to increase specificity and spontaneity.

The scores are always built out of the player's imagination and experience. Once they are cloned they become scripts to be expanded, developed, and fleshed out by the other players.

The sessions are always cumulative. They build a vocabulary and then reference the vocabulary through repetition and use. Because it is crucial that all the players speak the same language and have common experiential reference points, use the sessions as the experiential reference points. They provide the context for defining concepts through practice, through engagement, and through insight and evaluation after the doing.

Evaluation and discussion are crucial to the process. Players must articulate their experiences in order to connect activity with concept. Once a player has had an insight by linking the discovered concept with his/her physical activity, the player owns the concept for life.

The evaluation is also a form of feedback, an opportunity for the coach to hear what has worked and what hasn't, where the players got stuck and where there was flow, and how to adapt and adjust the coaching.

It is important to continually remind players that growth and perception are cumulative experiences. The MAP is also cumulative. It takes time, practice, patience, and persistence before the process begins to reveal itself and make analytical sense.

Flow is the connective element within every session. Every session will have its own flow pattern, depending on the sequence of exercises and activities used. Players can work for a sustained period of time if they have coaching to guide and move them along, shifting their focus to new points of attention along the way.

Effort must always transform and change in each session. Players may work within the specific "frames" of an activity to keep the effort even and constant. In order to do so they must focus on withholding the urge to change. This takes players into insight and understanding about the use of hurdles, how they condition playing, and the overwhelming desire to play with many changes of effort.

Players also respond to rapid changes of effort. Use games that vary the effort patterns, triggering different responses. Opposites become crucial in modulating the quality of the play; use "freeze/go" for sudden shifts or refocusing a session.

Keep the players off guard to increase spontaneity in a session. They should never be able to predict or predetermine their responses to the work.

At times coaches must provoke and challenge the player to break and change their patterns of perception. Always follow a provocation with a suggestion for an alternative approach to solving a problem. Players love to cling to old beliefs—they're familiar and comfortable.

The aim of the coaching is to create an environment in which players can develop new perceptions about problem solving and experiment with and improve their skills in playing, creating, and acting with confidence. This can only happen in a safe, open environment, one that rewards risk-taking and views "failure," i.e., an exercise not working, as an opportunity for discovery.

The experience of failure manifests itself in inhibition and the shutting down of flow. Creative energy stays trapped inside the body and won't move. The player needs to be coached into refocusing and releasing the energy to return to the pattern with alternative solutions. Focus on the process, not the result. Always acknowledge and reward the effort.

PART TWO

MAP MODULES

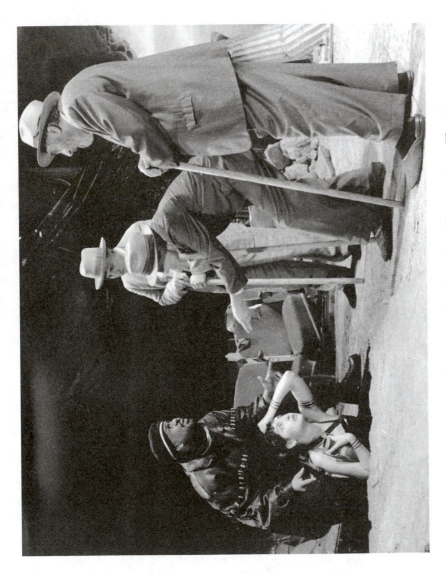

Sophocles' *Antigone*, 1993 production at the American Conservatory Theater, San Francisco, California.
Photograph © 1993 by Larry Merkle.

FIRST TRIAD: SHAPING THE ACTION

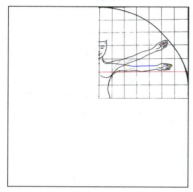

In the first triad of the MAP you will focus on physicalizing action.

You will expand your physical awareness through exercise to create flexibility and mobility in approach, play, and performance.

By developing your body, you will expand the potential of your imagination. The physical process works to connect the inner with the outer for a full and dynamic release of energy.

You will be developing an experiential vocabulary, one based on your own use of effort and energy. By working with a shared vocabulary, you will be able to communicate and collaborate with your partners in defining the rules and principles that govern play.

You will then apply these rules by playing within structured activities that expand your perception and strengthen your skills in communicating. You will develop additional tools for shaping the design of your effort, giving it dynamic life and tension.

As you expand your awareness of physicalized action, you will be able to identify the flow of energy through your body and isolate and unlock trapped and inflexible body parts. You will then connect the parts within the body to observe and create patterns of action. You will focus on the physical processes of initiating, engaging, and completing action.

In this first triad you will focus your attention on three factors of physicality: release, shape, and flow.

In Release you will become aware of patterns of stress and tension, and see how these patterns inhibit the free flow of energy—your physical, creative, and emotional energy.

You will develop tools for releasing this energy and directing it forward, into action. You will use direct focus-in-space to bridge with your environment and the other players in your environment.

In Shape you will examine the physical axes and planes of your body and experiment with how to design your outer—your body—to influence and at the same time reflect your inner—the psychological core of character.

In Flow you will learn how to read your body, developing an awareness of your flow patterns and how negative tension inhibits these patterns.

You will also focus on developing tools to increase synchronicity, or co-coordination, in your playing and how to manipulate energy to create action.

In this triad you will expand your awareness through observation and experimentation. You will begin this process by isolating your focus and observing your self in action. As you become aware of your patterns you will expand your attention to include those of your partners.

Finally, you will expand your focus and create fictive identities—masks—that embody and use different flow patterns, body types, and body shapes to create character.

Throughout, you will be given instructions about how to adjust and adapt your playing by changing your use of effort to trigger different reposes. You will never be told what to feel; you will only be given instructions about what to do.

RELEASE

The first area of focus in the MAP is release. Release deals with the tension, stress, and inhibition that close down, shut off, and limit your flow of physical and creative energy. Tension either opens or binds, it expands or it contracts, it holds or it releases. Holding is a protective device against fear and creates negative tension. You will examine negative physical tension, which shuts down your body's response to stimuli. You also will examine the factors involved in negative creative tension, which inhibits the flow of your imagination and drains spontaneity from your playing.

Release requires surrender—a gradual letting go, a movement forward into action. Release is a state of receptivity, openness, and awareness. It does not signal the absence of tension; rather, it means preparedness, the ability to move into action from a committed, neutral base. Release leads to a merger of the outer and the inner in order to create this connected center. Synchronicity is the process of balancing the outer and the inner energies. As you work on releasing, you will be developing an awareness of your resistance patterns.

With the MAP you either surrender to the pattern, gradually chipping away at it through deliberate provocation, or you detour around, over, or under it to create alternative approaches to stimulate growth and change. MAP seeks to identify your comfortable and habitual stress patterns, and encourages you to experiment with alternative choices in order to broaden your range of creative possibilities.

In this module you will begin to experience positive stress to add weight to your work. Stress produces strong response; strong response leads to definition, specificity, and clarity in playing.

Release

1. Neutral Stance
2. Balloon Breathing
3. The Elevator
4. Solo Stretch
5. The Calendar
6. Scissors
7. Scrape the Bowl
8. The Whip
9. Gooseneck Stretches
10. Duet Stretch
11. Massage
12. Spinal Walk Down
13. Spinal Float
14. Back Elevator
15. Slide Stretches
16. Seated Knee Press
17. Ensemble Breathing
18. Rope Trick
19. Circle Elevator

Neutral Stance

This is the basic position for all physical work:

1. Stand with your arms at your sides.
2. Keep your focus at eye level.
3. Separate your feet until they are as wide as your shoulders.
4. Place your weight slightly forward towards the balls of your feet. Lift your insteps up off the ground, shifting your weight to the outside edges of your feet.
5. Bend your knees to unlock your legs.
6. Release your pelvis forward to lengthen your lower spine.
7. Keep your hips parallel to the floor.
8. Lift your breast bone and elongate your upper spine.

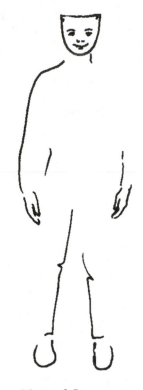

Neutral Stance

Observations.   This position may feel different from your everyday posture. It **is** different. You may experience difficulty in releasing your pelvis,
keeping your hips parallel, or lengthening your spine. These all improve
with time and practice.

Your ankles, knees, hips, and shoulders should be parallel to the floor.
You hold and retain tension in your body; these "held" points become evident when you start to work with body symmetry. Do not be discouraged
when you discover where you are holding your tension; the point is not to
be "perfect" but to work at, and experience, change within your body. Most
importantly, remember to breathe.

Balloon Breathing

Use this exercise to stimulate your imagination and trigger an inner image:

1. Stand in a wide Neutral Stance.
2. Imagine your arms as balloons.

3. As you inhale, imagine filling your arms with air and swing your arms up, over your head.
4. Drop your shoulders into your spine and hold your breath for a count of five. Hold a giant imaginary globe between both hands.
5. As you exhale, press your arms down through space until they return to the sides of your body.
6. Repeat five times, slowing your breathing each time.
7. At the peak of the inhalation, hold your arms above your head and sip in an extra bit of air.
8. Breathe without using your arms. Imagine them moving.

Effort: Sustained and very light.

Observations. Use this activity after quick and strong work. It will help you to return to neutral.

Ballooning gives you a mental focus and a specific visual reference. Link the physical with the mental. Use the balloon image and its associated physical action to trigger your breathing pattern.

Sigh often when you breathe. Fill your lungs and release the breath with sound. See if this makes a difference in the quality of your release.

The Elevator

This exercise is for coordination and physical control.

1. Begin in the Neutral Stance.
2. Shift your weight onto your right leg.
3. Imagine you are standing in sand. With your left foot, draw a semi-circle behind your right leg.
4. Retrace the drawing with your left foot and return to the Neutral Stance.
5. Repeat, shifting your weight to your left leg.
6. Repeat again, shifting your weight back to your right leg.
7. After drawing the semi-circle with your left foot, keep your left foot behind you. Lower your entire body down to the ground. Sit with both hips touching the ground. Your right leg should cross your left leg and your right knee should face the ceiling.
8. Without using your hands, rise to a standing position.
9. Repeat on the opposite side.

Effort: Sustained and light.

Observations. Do not use your arms or your torso to control your balance.

Work slowly; control the movement by engaging your spine and your pelvis. When your spine and pelvis are aligned, the movement and the effort are simplified.

Use two images: a straight line and a curved line. Your spine, moving vertically up and down, makes the straight line. Your pelvis, moving spatially, back, and forth, makes the curved line. Your pelvis also defines your relationship with gravity. As you near the floor, shift your focus from making the straight line to making the curved one.

Solo Stretch

This is a passive stretch, in which your body weight does most of the work. You will experience greater release if you use less effort.

1. Begin in the Neutral Stance.
2. Use The Elevator to sit on the floor. Keep both hips level and on the ground. Sit forward on your pelvis. Elongate and lengthen your spine.
3. Straighten your legs onto the floor. Your knees should face the ceiling.
4. Open your legs into a wide V.
5. Place your hands behind your back. Only your fingertips should touch the floor.
6. Flex your feet—push your heels forward, and stretch through your Achilles tendon to flatten your foot, as if you are pushing against an imaginary wall. Your heels will lift up off the floor.
7. Using your fingertips, push yourself up and off the floor until your heels touch the ground.
8. Point your toes and sit down on the floor.
9. Repeat steps 5, 6, & 7 twice. Remember to sit on top of your pelvis; do not sink or collapse your spine.
10. Breathe for one minute in this stretched position.
11. With your palms on the floor, walk your hands away from the center of your body.
12. If you can, place your elbows, then your chest, on the ground.
13. Rest in this position for one minute. Inhale. Lengthen your spine and sit up. Exhale.
14. Inhale. Keep both hips flat on the floor and turn toward your right leg.
15. Exhale. Release forward, over your right knee, and lengthen your spine. Place your chest on top of your thigh. Your right knee should face the ceiling.
16. Inhale. Lengthen your spine and return to the center seated position. Exhale.
17. Repeat on the left side.
18. Flex your feet and draw them together. Keep your knees elongated. You will feel this movement deep in your hip socket.
19. Exhale and release forward, over your knees. Lengthen your chest onto your thighs.

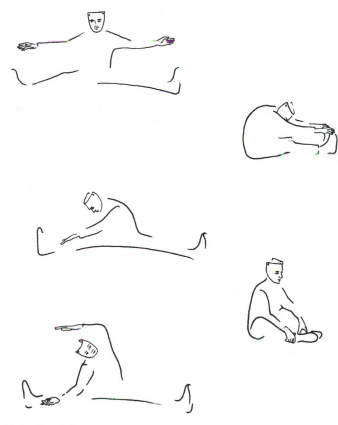

Solo Stretch

20. Inhale. Return to the center seated position.
21. Draw your knees into your chest. Touch the soles of your feet together; let your knees fall open into the "frog leg" position.
22. Hold onto your ankles. Elongate your spine. Exhale; sit forward on your pelvis.
23. Gently stretch your knees down to the floor. Lengthen your chest onto the ground.
24. Inhale. Elongate your spine and return to the center seated position.
25. Exhale.
26. Repeat the entire stretch sequence a second time.

Effort: Sustained and light.

Observations.   You will initially feel pain in your hamstrings behind your knees. You may want to back away and release the pain by letting it out with sound or a sigh. Your inhibition about acknowledging pain abates as you move through the pain with sound.

Always elongate your spine each time you return to the center seated position. This is the counter-stretch to balance rounding in the "forward" parts of the exercise.

There is no way you can force the stretch to happen. All you can do is release. When you release, you do less. The less you do, the more you will stretch. Your body weight will do most of the work for you. Make sure both of your hips touch the ground at all times. Breathe. Working on the breath is the most important element of the exercise.

When you repeat the exercise for the second time, you should be able to stretch further. You already know the sequence of the stretch, where to focus your attention, and when to release. Take enough time to work deeply and thoroughly.

The Calendar

This gentle stretch releases held energy by further articulating the separation between pelvis and spine.

1. Lie on the floor on your back with your palms face down and legs straight. Your shoulders should touch the ground.
2. Bend your right knee. Move it in towards your chest.
3. With your left hand, reach to the outside of your right knee. Cross your right knee over your left leg until it touches the floor. The toes on your right foot should touch your left knee.
4. Turn your head to your right. Keep both shoulders on the floor.
5. Breathe for one minute in this position.
6. Release your knee. Roll your right hip back onto the floor. Pull your right leg up towards your chest. Place your leg on the floor.
7. Repeat on the opposite side.
8. Work with a partner. While you stretch, your partner will be alongside you.
9. If you are kneeling beside your partner, place one hand on your partner's hip, the other on the shoulder. As your partner twists and crosses the knee to the floor, hold the shoulder down on the ground and gently move the hip in the direction of the knee.
10. Once your partner has made the full twist, release your hands and let your partner roll onto the back.
11. Repeat on the opposite side.

Effort: Sustained and light.

The Calendar

Observations. If you do nothing and allow your body to find its own counter-weight, you will maximize the separation involved in the stretch.

You will notice the effects of the stretch after working one side of your body. It will feel longer and more released. As soon as you experience the length of your right side, balance it by stretching the left.

Scissors

Use this strengthening sequence to build coordination and endurance.

1. Lie on your back. Keep your arms at your sides, your legs together and stretched forward.
2. Lift your head up off the floor. Push through your abdomen to flatten the small of your back onto the floor. Exhale. Continue to roll up your spine. Keep the small of your back on the floor.
3. Exhale. Roll your spine down onto the floor. Bend your knees slightly and tilt your pelvis forward. Your hips should face the ceiling (keeping the small of your back flat).
4. Repeat this sequence three times.

5. Repeat once more. As you tilt and round your spine up off the floor, lift your legs up and bend your knees and bring them into your chest.
6. Wrap your arms around your knees. Balance on your tailbone. Make sure you breathe.
7. Inhale. Extend your legs straight out. Lift your arms above your head. Your arms and legs should form angles diagonal to the floor, making a giant V. Exhale and return to the wrapped, curled position. Balance on your tailbone.
8. Uncurl. Lengthen your arms and legs onto the floor. Move your arms and legs in the same tempo as your spine.
9. Repeat the sequence three times.
10. Roll up into the wrapped, curled position. Open into the extended diagonal stretch and separate your legs into a wide V. Open and close your arms and legs like a giant scissors.
11. Bring your arms and legs together rapidly. Pull into the curl before elongating onto the floor.
12. Repeat the entire sequence three times.

Effort: Sustained and strong.

Observations.   This exercise is difficult and challenging. As you become more familiar with the structure of the activity work for greater control by slowing down. To make the exercise more engaging, give yourself a reason for having to extend out or pull in. Engage your imagination by using someone else in the room as a point of focus.

See if your balance improves when you have an outward focus as a point of release.

Variation.   Work with your eyes closed.

Scrape the Bowl

This excellent warm-up activity for your lower and middle spine uses physical action to trigger an image. You'll work from the outer to the inner and then transform the inner to affect and color the outer.

1. Begin in a wide Neutral Stance.
2. Imagine a large bowl suspended upside down from the ceiling.
3. Using both hands, hold an imaginary spoon directly in front of you, extending out from the middle of your breast bone.
4. Use the spoon to scrape the sides of the bowl. Stir its contents.
5. Alternate directions. First scrape to the right, then to the back, to the left, and finally, forward.

6. Repeat, reversing direction.
7. Throughout the entire rotation, keep your pelvis and hips in place, parallel to the floor. Never let them move.

Effort: Moderately quick and strong.

Observations.   Reach and stretch in all directions, especially behind you.

You may want to hold your hands fairly close to your body. Instead, exaggerate your reach forward, to the sides, and backward. Keep you eyes open, and focus on the direction you are moving in. When you are working behind, your breastbone should face directly up to the ceiling.

Change the substance in the bowl whenever you want. A change in the substance will create a change in your energy and how you exert effort.

Focus on the movement of your spine and not the degree of elasticity in your hamstrings. Flexibility will develop over a period of time. Do not compete to see who can stretch the farthest and fastest. Work at your own rate of development and measure your growth over a period of weeks and months.

Sound helps release held breath as well as pain. Once you work with sound your stretch will improve, and you will be able to have more fun with these exercises.

The Whip

This spinal warm-up requires highly focused effort in space.

1. Begin in a wide Neutral Stance.
2. Use your right hand to point to a fixed spot opposite you.
3. Rotate your arm to your right, then behind you, to your left, and back to center.
4. During the rotation move your eyes, head, and upper torso in tandem with your right arm. Your arm leads the movement. Your lower body remains immobile.
5. Find a new focal point. Reverse directions with your right hand; move to your left, then backwards; to your right, then center.
6. Change arms. Circle with the left, swinging first to your left, then backwards; to your right, then center.
7. Change focal points and directions with your left hand; right, back, left, center.
8. Gradually increase the tempo until you are whipping around. Add sound.

Effort: Quick and strong.

Observations.   As you begin The Whip, you may lose your balance and fall forward. Allow yourself to do this. Losing control will let you find a natural and spontaneous way to recover control.

The Whip lets you begin to develop your physical sense of adjust and adapt. Vary the tempos as you play. Make the movement as rhythmical as possible. Use each other as focal points. Justify the action at all times.

Gooseneck Stretch

This is a short/long stretch; actively long on one side, passively short on the other. Focus on the flexibility and mobility of your spine.

1. Begin in the Neutral Stance.
2. Roll down your spine; release your head forward, and let gravity pull you down. End the roll down with your palms touching the floor. Keep your eyes open. Make your breathing slow and steady.
3. Reverse directions and roll up the length of your spine. Bend your knees first. Release your pelvis forward as you straighten your legs. Lift your spine, vertebra by vertebra. Sit directly on top of your pelvis. Let your head float up to sit on top of your spine.
4. Inhale. Elongate your spine. Exhale. Drop your head backward.
5. Inhale. Lift your head. Let it float on top of your spine.
6. Repeat. When you release your head backwards, engage your shoulders and then your midback into the move. Lift the center of your breastbone to face the ceiling. Bend your knees and release your pelvis forward, to provide a counterbalance for the shift of direction in your spine.
7. Inhale and lift up onto the Neutral Stance.
8. Exhale. Release your head to the right. Tilt your head, resting your right ear on top of your right shoulder. Keep your hips parallel to the floor.
9. Slowly release your weight to the right, as if you are carrying a heavy suitcase in your right hand. Keep your pelvis center and your hips still parallel to the floor.
10. Use your left hand to reach up and over your head. Point your elbow directly up to the ceiling. Turn your head to look through your elbow to the ceiling.
11. Exhale. To extend the stretch, release your pelvis out to your left side. Hold this position one minute.
12. Shift your pelvis back into center. Slowly lift your spine back into the Neutral Stance.
13. Repeat stretching to the left.
14. Repeat the entire sequence.

Effort: Sustained and light.

Observations. The release will be gradual in this stretch. You will first feel the tightness and some tension through the hamstrings, and perhaps some shortness of breath.

Keep your eyes open at all times. Look in the direction you are moving, especially when you move backwards. Release with sound.

Use an image of a gooseneck lamp. Your pelvis forms the base of the lamp; your spine is the coiled electrical column and your head is the light bulb. The image will help maximize the bending and stretching in the sequence.

Duet Stretch

Use this activity to give up control and surrender. Allow yourself to be guided by your partner.

1. Select a partner of the same size and weight. Decide who will be A and who B. Stand front to back, your arms around each other.
2. Breathe together for one minute.
3. A: Drop your arms and bend your knees, as if you are collapsing.
4. B: Catch your partner under the arms and seat him down gently on the floor. Kneel and support your partner's weight against your legs, abdomen, and chest.
5. A: Pull your legs together into a parallel position and then open them into a wide V.
6. Pause. Breathe together for one minute.
7. Inhale together. B: Place your hands under your partner's armpits and gently lift up to elongate your partner's spine. A: Make sure both your hips are touching the ground. Let yourself be moved by your partner. Exhale together.
8. B: Still elongating your partner's spine, place your partner forward, so that your partner's spine is now between their legs.
9. Slide your body up the length of your partner's spine. Rest your chest on the curve of your partner's back.
10. Breathe together. Release forward, into the stretch. A: Think of releasing into your lower spine. B: Gradually release your weight onto your partner's back. Help your partner move closer towards the ground.
11. Inhale together. B: Lift your partner back into the seated center position. Breathe together again.
12. Together, stretch in a similar manner, over the right leg. Return to center. Pause. Breathe. Stretch over the left leg. Return to center.
13. A: Draw your legs together into the forward parallel position. Together, stretch over center once again. Return to a seated center position.
14. A: Bring the soles of your feet together. Open your knees into a "frog" position. Together, stretch over center. Continue to support your part-

ner's weight on your back. B: Continue, in all of the stretches, to gradually and gently release your weight against the curve of your partner's
back. Inhale together. Return to center.

15. A: Open your legs into a wide V.

16. Repeat the entire sequence, moving rapidly from one position to the
next.

Duet Stretch

17. B: Maintain contact with your partner—keep one hand on your part-
    ner's back. Stand. Come around in front of your partner; take both
    wrists, and help your partner to a standing position by counter-balanc-
    ing them as they rise.
18. Take a moment and talk about the activity. What felt good? What didn't?
    When were you together? When were you apart? Did you observe any
    changes in either yourself or your partner during the course of the exer-
    cise?
19. Reverse roles, and repeat the entire sequence.

Effort: Sustained and strong.

Observations. Fear is the primary hurdle in this exercise. Fear that you
will hurt your partner or that you will be hurt. Fear that you will stretch too
far, too fast. That you have no control.

If, at any time, you feel a sharp pain or a deep burning sensation, tell
your partner. Find a way to let your partner know when to release the weight.
Usually, at the point of surrender, you will both experience a sudden drop in
the lower spine. When that happens, return to the seated center position.

Find the stretch through the breath. Your breathing patterns are your
connective links to one another. Breathing should be your point of focus.
When you repeat the entire sequence, you may find your stretch to be deeper
and the breathing more fluid.

Keep your eyes open. Don't drift. Stay connected with your partner and
to the energy and dynamic in the room.

Massage

This is a variation of a classic stress reduction technique. It is an excellent
activity for breaking down personal spatial barriers, moving from near to
intermediate reach space.

1. Sit front to back on the floor. Decide who will be A and who B. Breathe
   together for one minute. Work without talking.
2. B: Sit behind your partner and support your partner's weight against
   your chest. Use long strokes with your fingers and massage your partner
   from:

   > Forehead to temples
   > Eyebrow to temples
   > Under the eyebrows to temples
   > Across the eyelids
   > Nose to under eyes, along the cheekbone to upper and lower jaw

Upper lip

Lower lip

Behind the ear to the center of head to neck, along corners of the head

Sides of the head, including scalp, pulling the hair up and away
from the scalp

Back of head, where the spine meets the cranium

Neck to shoulders, pulling elbows down

Knead the neck and shoulders, as if they were bread dough

3. Muscle pinch: Hold the top of the shoulders between your thumb and two fingers. Slowly squeeze and pinch the trapezius muscle (the large muscle at the top of the shoulders) while your partner exhales. Repeat, adding a little more pressure to the pinch. Repeat a third time, using still more pressure. Hold the pinch a little longer.

4. Continue the body massage: up and down the sides of the spine with your fingers. Use your knuckles to massage the base of the spine, through the waist, the small of the back, and the kidneys.

5. Rework the shoulders and the neck.

6. Pause. Breathe together. Maintain contact with your partner, one hand on the spine, and come around in front of your partner. Holding your partner's wrists, use the see-saw to come to a standing position.

7. Take a moment to talk about the activity: What felt good? What didn't? When were you working together and when were you apart? Did you notice any physical changes in either yourself or your partner in the course of the activity?

8. Reverse positions, and repeat the entire sequence.

Effort: Sustained and strong.

Observations.   Nothing should come as a surprise during the massage.

You need to be prepared for The Pinch. It will be uncomfortable at first. If you are being pinched, know it is coming and release your breath with sound. If you are pinching, work slowly, carefully, and with great awareness of what you are doing. Though it will be uncomfortable at first, you will experience a release of tension within 30 seconds after the pinch.

Massage in silence. Focus on maintaining an even and shared breathing pattern. Sigh whenever possible. Sighing affords the maximum amount of release. Work as a coach with your partner. Direct and guide, during the course of the activity, through body language and nonverbal communication.

Spinal Walk Down

This is another activity to release stored or trapped energy in the lower spine.

1. Select a partner of the same size and weight. Decide who will be A and who B. Stand front to back, your arms around one another. Breathe together.
2. If you are A, drop your arms and release your head forward; rest your chin on your chest. If you are B, keep one arm wrapped around your partner's waist. Take one step back and to the side. Place your free hand on the top of your partner's head.
3. B: Use two fingers of your free hand and "walk down" the length of your partner's spine. Walk down the sides of the spine, not directly on top of it. Walk down from the tip of the head to the base of the tailbone.
4. A: Drop a release forward wherever you feel you partner's fingers "walking." You should end the walk down rounded over, with your knees bent, your arms dangling, and your eyes open.
5. B: When your partner is rounded over, open the palm of your hand and rest it against your partner's tailbone. Start at the base of your partner's spine and slide your hand all the way up to your partner's head. Don't be afraid to exert some pressure during the slide.

Spinal Walk Down

6. A: Keep your knees bent, your spine rounded, and your eyes open. Remember to breathe. Try not to move your spine while your partner is "sliding."
7. Repeat The Slide three or four times.
8. B: Start at the base of your partner's spine and, with two fingers, slowly walk up the length of your partner's spine. Walk along the side of the spinal cord, not on top of it.
9. A: Round your pelvis under. Slowly come up onto your vertical axis as your partner continues to walk up the length of your spine.
10. Once you are standing up, turn to face your partner.
11. Take a moment and talk to one another about the activity: What felt good, what didn't? Did you notice any physical changes during the activity?
12. Trade roles and repeat.

Effort: Sustained and light.

Observations.   When you are B, don't be afraid to exert pressure as you walk down, slide, and walk up your partner's spine. Your partner will resist if you are too forceful. Support your partner's weight with your hand around their waist. This provides an extra measure of security during the exercise.

As B, you are the active, guiding partner. Work to direct your partner's attention by the quality of your touch. As A, you must yield to the nonverbal commands of your partner. Surrender your sense of control. Allow yourself to be guided.

As in most physical stretches, you will feel the greatest release in your lower spine. Tension carried in your neck and shoulders will also ease.

Breathing is the most important component in the exercise. Use your breath to link with your partner and to stay connected with one another throughout the activity.

Spinal Float

This is a passive stretch. Surrender and give up control. Let your partner do all the work.

1. Select a partner of the same size and weight. Decide who will be A and who B. Stand back to back.
2. If you are A, rest your armpits on your partner's shoulders. If you are B, stand in a very wide stance. Bend your knees so that your partner's buttocks fits comfortably into the small of your back. Wrap your arms around your partner's waist.

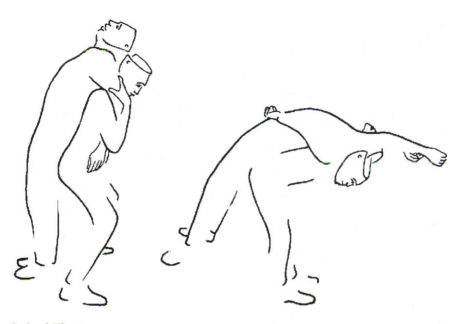

Spinal Float

3. B: Straighten up and lean forward. Balance your partner along the length of your back. Make sure your spines are touching.
4. Breathe in this position for one minute.
5. A: Stretch your arms above your head and continue to hang. The image is of a cloud, floating.
6. B: When you are ready to come down, either continue to wrap your hands around your partner's waist or take hold of their wrists. Bend your knees slightly. Slowly straighten until you are standing back to back.
7. Reverse roles and repeat.
8. Repeat the entire sequence three times.

Effort: Moderately sustained and moderately light.

Observations.   If, for any reason, either of you feels off balance during any part of the exercise, then stop, return to the starting position, and begin again.

Once you are in the lift, release. Focus on doing nothing. Let gravity and your own body weight do most of the work.

Remember to breathe together during the exercise and keep your eyes open at all times. Extending your arms over your head opens up your chest and gives you a deeper stretch.

Back Elevator

This variation of The Elevator is good for balance and surrendering control of your partner.

1. Select a partner of the same size and weight. Stand back to back.
2. Without talking or using your hands, move simultaneously and sit on the floor. Your spines must touch at all times.
3. You are not seated until both your hips touch the ground. Your knees should be bent and your feet flat on the ground.
4. Without talking, stand up.
5. Move up and down until you balance one another comfortably.

Effort: Moderately quick and moderately light.

Observations.   You will want to talk during the course of this exercise. Make your body do the talking. Develop nonverbal signals to heighten your communication.

Work to maintain the vertical axis between you. The vertical will make the move easier, and help you work with equal effort throughout the exercise.

Let your partner do most of the work. Release and let go of the need to be responsible for "making" this exercise happen.

Slide Stretches

These lower spinal stretches involve surrendering and becoming aware of holds and blocks within your body.

Stretch No. 1:

1. Select a partner of the same size and weight. Decide who will be A and who B. Stand back to back. Use the Back Elevator to sit on the floor.
2. If you are A, lengthen your legs and extend them so they are in a parallel position on the floor. If you are B, keep you legs bent and your knees close to your chest.
3. B: Use your feet to push yourself up off the floor. Exhale and slide your spine along the length of your partner's spine. Your spines should be touching each other.
4. A: Exhale and stretch forward. Use your partner's weight on your back to help stretch and lengthen your lower spine.
5. Inhale. Return to a seated position.
6. Reverse roles and repeat.

Effort: Sustained and moderately light.

Stretch No. 2:

1. Repeat Slide Stretch No. 1.
2. B: Extend your arms above your head and, as you slide up your partner's spine, reach for and hold on to your partner's feet. Increase the amount of time you use for the stretch.
3. Inhale. Return to a seated position.
4. Reverse roles, and repeat.

Effort: Sustained and moderately light.

Stretch No. 3:

1. Repeat Slide Stretch no. 2.
2. Work in your own amount of time. Sustain the stretch until you reach the point of surrender.
3. Reverse roles, whenever it is appropriate.
4. Work in silence.

Effort: Sustained and light.

Observations. When you are on top, you may want to hold on, to protect your partner underneath. But the only real protection you need throughout is a strong sense of surrender and a willingness to let go.

You may reach the point of surrender in the second or third round of the exercise. The first round is for discovering the pattern of the exercise—what it is you are to do. The second round is for practicing how to do it. The third round is for releasing into the pattern and letting go. At the moment of surrender, you will experience a slight release in your lower spine. This is when the true stretch begins.

If the stretch is too intense in your hamstrings, bend your legs, or separate them into a modified V.

You may feel warm or flushed after this activity. Occasionally, you will feel lightheaded. The energy flow is strong because you are releasing a tremendous amount of energy stored in your lower spine.

Seated Knee Press

This gentle stretch requires sustained focus and gradual release.

1. Sit with your partner on the floor, front to back. Decide who is A and who is B.
2. If you are A, sit with the soles of your feet together, in the frog position. Roll your pelvis forward and lengthen your spine.

3. B: Stand behind your partner. Place your hands on top of your partner's shoulders.
4. Very carefully place the instep of your right foot onto the middle of your partner's right thigh.
5. Shift your weight onto your hands. Press down onto your partner's shoulders. With your left foot, step onto the middle of your partner's left thigh.
6. Once you are balanced, gently rock back and forth, from right to left, for thirty seconds. Step off your partner's legs.
7. Repeat the entire sequence.
8. Reverse roles and repeat the entire sequence.

Effort: Sustained and strong.

Observations.   You control your weight distribution by the placement of your hands on your partner's shoulders. Actual leg/foot contact is minimal.

Verbal communication is an important part of this activity. Voice your needs—and responses—so that you and your partner have a sense of control.

Release with sound. Keep breathing.

You will feel this stretch deep in your hip sockets. Do not move rapidly after the stretch. Take your time in bringing your legs together and in standing up.

Ensemble Breathing

This activity develops synchronicity and spatial awareness.

1. Begin in the Neutral Stance with eyes closed. Establish a sustained, even breathing pattern.
2. Open your eyes. Turn and face a partner. Embrace your partner. Place your hands on your partner's lower back, just above the waist. Close your eyes.
3. Gently inhale through your nose for three counts. Hold your breath for a count of twelve. Slowly exhale through your mouth for six counts.
4. Take one step back from each other. Maintain the same breathing pattern. Make sure you are still in contact with your partner. Breathe together with the same 3-12-6 pattern.
5. Continue to move apart until you lose contact with one another.
6. Open your eyes. Form into a group of 4.
7. Stand in a circle, your arms linked around one another's waists. Inhale through your nose, exhale through your mouth. Close your eyes. Slowly separate and sustain contact with your partners. Open your eyes when communication is broken.

8. Repeat in groups of 8.
9. Repeat with everyone in one circle.

Effort: Sustained and light.

Observations. Breathe into your lower back. By placing your hands on your partner's lower back you can monitor and check one another's breathing. As you become more comfortable with the 3-12-6 breathing pattern, you will expand and increase the amount of space you use when you separate from one another.

You may feel like laughing when you first enter into the embrace. Work through it until you are comfortable standing and holding your partner and sustaining the pattern through space.

The task is compounded as you add more players. Focus on the signals you are receiving from your right and left. This overload takes the focus off you and places it onto your partners. Use the outer focus as a point of release.

Rope Trick

This activity exercises awareness of pelvic/spinal separation as well as group coordination.

1. Sit in a circle on the floor. Your feet should touch the floor. Pull your knees into your chest. Wrap your arms and hands lightly around your knees.
2. Sit forward. Elongate your spine without shortening your neck.
3. Release your arms and hands. Roll the small of your back onto the floor.
4. As soon as you make contact with the floor, stop. Reverse direction and sit forward.
5. Repeat. Roll down to the middle of your back. Stop. Reverse direction. Sit forward.
6. Repeat. Roll down until your entire spine is touching the floor. Reverse direction. Lift your head first, tucking it forward slightly. Lift your spine off the floor. Return to the seated position.
7. Repeat the entire sequence. Work with a partner, someone opposite you. Imagine a rope between you. Release the rope to roll down, pull the rope to roll up.
8. Work as a group to roll down and roll up at the same time. Use an image of ropes crisscrossing through the circle.
9. End the activity resting on the floor. Bend your knees. Place your feet on the floor, so the small of your back makes contact with the floor.

Effort: Sustained and strong.

Observations.   Using a rope focuses your mental effort and your attention. Physical technique is easier and less strenuous when you engage your imagination.

Remember to breathe when you work. Singing, especially if you are holding one position for a long period of time, is an easy form of release and helps open your lungs.

Engage your entire spine in this activity. Your feet must remain on the floor throughout, with your knees bent and apart. Direct the effort away from the lower part of your body. Control comes from engaging the abdominal muscles and holding them down onto the floor.

Use your partner to help with the activity. Motivate and justify the action by creating a specific relationship between the two of you. Enlarge the focus of the relationship to include the entire group.

Circle Elevator

Focus on balancing individually, yet stay a part of the group.

1. Stand in a circle, equidistant from one another.
2. Hold each other's wrists. Bend your elbows and hold them in by the sides of your rib cage. You must be able to support your own weight.
3. Together, shift your weight to your right. Use The Elevator to move down to the floor. Make sure both hips touch the floor once you are seated.
4. Once seated, use The Elevator to stand.
5. Repeat, shifting the weight to your left.

Effort: Sustained and light.

Observations.   You may have difficulty rising on your own from the floor. Avoid the temptation to use another player for support.

Using sustained time forces a stronger, more deliberate focus. Use the focus as a point of release. As your focus strengthens you will exert more effort and work with more physical control.

Variation.   Work with your eyes closed.

SHAPE

After release, the second component in the MAP deals with **shape.** In shape you will focus your attention on the creation of the outer. You will learn how to read your body and develop a basic physical vocabulary to describe the various combinations of the axes and planes within your body.

Body shape is a combination of physical dimensions and planes in space. There are three basic dimensions in your body: the vertical (up and down) dimension, the horizontal (side to side) dimension, and the sagittal (forward and back) dimension. These dimensions combine to form planes. A plane is a two-dimensional, flat surface. Each plane has a primary dimension and a secondary dimension. When you combine planes and dimensions you create shape. Shape makes action visible and meaningful in space.

You will become aware of how your energy moves through, holds, or blocks specific body parts from engaging in action. You will develop a technique for recognizing and circumventing the effects of this inhibition.

You will examine the relationship of body parts by isolating and sequencing them to create synchronicity. You will expand your awareness of shape by experiencing shapes and space. You will begin to observe yourself and your partners in **reach space,** expanding or contracting your attention as you define your relationship with your environment. As you create Body Shape, you will begin to use your outer as the conduit to your inner.

Shape

1. Parallel and Perpendicular
2. The Tree
3. Curve, Straight, Arch
4. The Worm
5. Body Shape
6. The Dolly
7. Kinetic Sculpture
8. Blind Offers
9. Living Doll
10. Melted Architecture

Parallel and Perpendicular

Use this neutral body exercise as the starting point for all shape work.

1. Stand in place, with your feet apart.
2. Lift the middle of your breastbone and lengthen your spine.
3. Release your knees to unlock your legs.
4. Rotate your pelvis forward to unlock the base of your spine.
5. Float your head on top of your spine.
6. Imagine your spine as a vertical line perpendicular to the floor. Cross that perpendicular line with five horizontal lines parallel to the floor:

a line through your ankles
a line through your knees
a line through your hips
a line through your shoulders
a line through your ears

7. Move around the playing space. Keep all five parallel lines symmetrical to the floor. Do not swing your hips, bob your head, lean forward or back with your torso, or compensate with any body part in any direction.

Effort: Sustained and light.

Observations.   Walking while maintaining the images of perfectly perpendicular and perfectly parallel leads to tight, constricted, and highly bound playing at first.

Maintaining symmetry is particularly difficult because all of us are slightly asymmetrical. We tend to hold the right side of our body either higher or lower than the left.

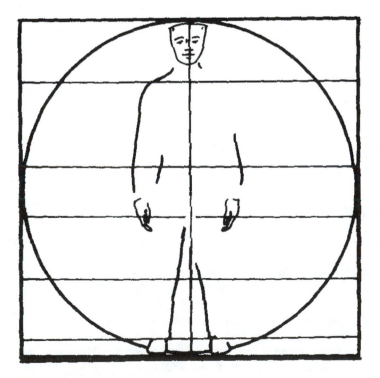

Parallel and Perpendicular

Maintain the image of the shape and use less effort. Think yourself long (perpendicular) and think yourself wide (parallel). You don't need to work as hard as you think you do.

The Tree

This exercise will help you develop an awareness of your vertical plane. You also will begin to discover how your spine and pelvis interact to create balance.

1. Begin in the Neutral Stance.
2. Shift your weight off the central axis of your body and onto your left leg. Keep your hips parallel to the floor.
3. Bend your right knee and turn it out to your right side. Rest your right foot on the inside of your left knee. Your right instep will fit snugly into the right side of your left knee.
4. Separate your hands. Raise your right arm above your head. Hold your left arm out to your left side. Imagine yourself a tree, rooted in the earth, extending up and out to the sky.
5. Once you've found your balance, bring your hands together, palms touching one another, fingers pointing up in front of your breastbone in a "prayer" position.
6. Balance and close your eyes. Imagine yourself a tree in the wind; rooted in the earth, yet flexible.
7. Open your eyes. Return to the "prayer" position. Regain your balance. Return to the Neutral Stance.
8. Repeat the entire exercise, reversing arms and legs.

Effort: Sustained and light.

Observations. Find your balance through your pelvis, not through your arms.

Variation. Divide into two teams. One half observes while the other half does The Tree. Reverse. Observe and use one another as models. Using a model takes the pressure off yourself to be perfect from the beginning. Seeing others struggle to find balance is reassuring. You all work at different rates and levels.

Curve, Straight, Arch

This exercise strengthens awareness of spine/pelvis coordination and uses the physical axes and planes of your body to create abstract shape.

1. Begin in the Neutral Stance. Release your head forward onto your chest.
2. Roll down the length of your spine. Do not release your midback, waist, or pelvis.
3. Breathe for one minute in this "rolled down" position.
4. Release your waist, then your pelvis. Hang down.
5. To make the curve tuck your pelvis under your spine, rounding and lengthening your back. Lift your abdomen and try to flatten it against your back. In profile, your shape is like an inverted C.
6. Release your pelvis. Return to the hang down position.
7. Repeat the curve three times.
8. To make the straight line, begin by rounding into the curve. Release your pelvis. Elongate your spine until it is parallel to the floor. Raise your arms

Curve, Straight, Arch

and press them along the side of your head, your elbows by your ears, reaching forward. Your spine will form a straight line parallel to the floor.

9. Round your pelvis. Tuck it under the spine, rounding your lower back into the Curve.
10. Release into the hang down position.
11. Repeat the Straight and the Curve three times.
12. Elongate into the Straight line.
13. To make the Arch begin in the Straight line, lift the middle of your breast bone up towards the ceiling and dip your lower spine.
14. Release the Arch into the Straight line. Round the Straight line into the Curve. Drop down into the hang down position.
15. Repeat all three shapes, Curve, Straight, and Arch, three times.
16. Roll up into the Neutral Stance.

Effort: Moderately sustained and light.

Observations.   Remember to breathe and use sound to help release stored tension.

The Arch is the most difficult shape in the sequence because it involves a triple stretch—through the hamstrings, the lower spine, and the upper spine.

Maximize the effect of the sequence by changing the shapes rapidly. Catch yourself off guard. Once you know the pattern of the exercise, work to keep your playing spontaneous.

Continue to work on the shapes; repetition affords the opportunity to refine your playing skills and improve the quality of your play.

This sequence should always be followed by quick and light activities in which you move through space.

The Worm

This is a good activity for developing flexibility, stamina, and coordination.

1. Begin in the Neutral Stance.
2. Roll your knees forward, then your pelvis. Use your spine as a counterweight in these movements.
3. Move your pelvis back swiftly. Round your spine forward, releasing your neck and head.
4. As you round your spine forward swing your arms behind your body and forward over your head. The swing will add momentum to the forward thrust as you pull your pelvis back.
5. Repeat until this movement feels fluid and easy. The image is of a current of electricity running through your body, from the floor up to the top of your head.

6. Select a partner. Decide who will be A and who B.
7. If you are A, lie down on the floor, face down. Repeat this "wave" on the floor, with the palms of your hands under your shoulders. The wave should have the shape and feel of a horizontal undulation.
8. If you are B, coach your partner.
9. Trade roles. The image is of a worm slinking through the earth.

Effort: Moderately sustained and moderately light.

Observations.   You cannot force the flow in this activity.

Discover the image through the physical action. Paradoxically, the physical action helps define the image, by making it more specific and playable.

Activate your lower spine when working on the floor. Do this by using your knees, lifting your pelvis, and rounding your back.

Working as a coach allows you to break down and analyze the movement in order to teach it. Information can be absorbed, digested, and recycled without overintellectualization.

Body Shape

Use this activity to investigate the relationship between shape and personality type.

When we combine planes and dimensions, we create shape.

People who are primarily up and down, with some side to side movement, are primarily vertical. Think of someone standing in a doorway, arms and legs outstretched into the door frame; this is a vertical person. Vertical people are "doors": they tend to be ordered, logical, upright (primary vertical dimension), flexible, and open to give and take (secondary horizontal plane). They tend to be thinkers and idea people.

People who are primarily side to side, with some forward and back, are primarily horizontal. Think of someone sitting at a table in a swivel chair, turning around and around, trying to take it all in; this is a horizontal person. Horizontal people are "tables": they take in everything around them (primary horizontal plane) and have a sense of purpose (secondary sagittal plane). They are good observers and good communicators.

People who are primarily forward and back, with some side to side are primarily sagittal. Think of someone in perpetual motion, always doing something, intent on getting it done; this is a sagittal person. Sagittal people are "wheels": they have strong forward drive (primary sagittal plane) and are good observers (secondary horizontal plane). They are doers and reactors.

When working as a team, you want all three "shapes" working together: the "door" to think of the idea, the "table" to sell it, and the "wheel" to set it in motion.

Body Shapes

When you work with Body Shapes start with a Perpendicular and Parallel to balance all three dimensions—ready to go forward, ready to take it all in, ready to think. Readiness is your preparation for infinite possibilities.

Walk around the playing space and move into and out of each Body Shape. The one that feels most uncomfortable is the one shape you should work with most.

Try playing scenes consciously using a different Body Shape. Let the shape trigger the dynamic of the action. If you change the inner in the course of the scene, change the outer as well.

The Dolly

This activity uses the basic principles of nonverbal communication to investigate physicalizing relationships through shapes in space.

No. 1

1. Divide into two teams. Select a partner in the opposite team. Stand on opposite sides of the room, facing your partner.
2. Use your hands to form a frame, or viewfinder. Look at your partner through the frame.

3. Keeping your partner "in frame," move in, or "dolly," towards one another.
4. Keeping your partner "in frame," dolly away from one other, back to your starting position.

Effort: Quick and light.

Observations. The frame, or viewfinder, is a device to focus your attention. Your partner is your only focus; you want to lose everything else, including your peripheral vision.

No. 2

5. Standing opposite your partner, abandon the viewfinder. Focus on your partner.
6. Begin to dolly in toward one another. Take two steps toward each other. Freeze.
7. Stand in a neutral position. Without adjusting or adapting, see if your positions in space suggest a relationship to you. Do you know who you are to one another? Note any images that come to mind.
8. Take three steps towards each other. Freeze.
9. Who are you to one another?
10. Take a half-step toward each other. Stand nose to nose. Wrap your arms around one another. Who are you now?
11. Take one step back from one another. Is the relationship the same or has it changed?
12. Still maintaining visual contact, make a quarter turn to your right. Who are you now?
13. Make a half turn to your left. Who are you?
14. Another quarter turn to your right. Face one another. Take two steps back. Pause. Who are you?
15. Take three steps back. Who are you now?
16. Still facing one another, move back to your original position. Who are you now?
17. Release.
18. Take a moment and talk with one another. What happened as the space changed? What happened as you changed direction with one another? Did the relationship ever change between you?

Effort: Sustained and light.

Observations. You body never lies. Place your body in a specific spatial relationship with your partner and you will know who you are to one another, and whether the arrangement of shapes in space is appropriate to the facts of the endowments.

Tune yourself to respond to the visual and physical signals your partner is sending to you through shapes in space. Become aware of the signals you are sending your partner through your arrangement of body parts, eye contact, positioning, and direction in space.

Leaving your chest and stomach unguarded and unprotected leaves you open and vulnerable to your partner. One simple way to protect yourself is to cross your arms over your chest, or use one arm to reach across and hold the other. Staying open and unguarded means there is a direct flow of energy between the two of you. Especially from the hips and pelvis.

Direct space leaves you prepared for confrontation. You focus your body on your partner and give her your undivided physical attention. Indirect space splits your focus. What happens when you quarter-turn away from one another? The upper part of your body, still maintaining eye contact with your partner, is ready for one relationship, while the lower part of your body, with pelvis turned away, is preparing for another. You create mixed signals through Body Shape. No matter what you may say, your body is saying you don't really want to be there. Correct this by turning your hips in to face one another.

Your right side is traditionally considered your dominant, active side. It responds directly to commands from the left side of your brain—the logical, analytical, "controlling" side of your mind. Leading with your right means you are withholding and protecting your left.

Your left side is traditionally considered your receptive side. Your left side is closer to your heart and responds to commands from your right brain—the emotive, intuitive side of your mind. Speaking into someone's left ear is much more intimate and emotionally appealing than speaking to their right. Which side do you hold the telephone on when you listen? Do you change sides? When?

We intuitively know where we need to be spatially when we are with one another. We arrange ourselves according to our status within the pecking order of any group. Because status is fluid and constant, the arrangement in space is always transforming. Levels are a prime indicator of who we are to one another; literally, who is on top or who isn't.

The person with the highest status in a group is usually the most secure, relaxed, and open, physically, in space. In a party, the high status person will often stand in the center of the room and let the world come to him. He will always manage to find the power spot in any situation. Stand in a crowded elevator and observe how status shifts and changes at each floor as people enter and exit the space, how we endow one another with status and adjust accordingly.

Cultural and social endowments color and condition how we perceive ourselves in space. People accustomed to large open spaces displace space differently than those who live in overcrowded environments. In the United States, gender influences permit two women to share intimate space, but not two men, although in Italy it is quite natural to see two men walking down the street, arms clasped or entwined. Women also tend to address one another with closed space—hip to hip—whereas men are more comfortable with open space—indirect lower bodies.

"Safe space" in life usually is measured as 18 inches. Closer than that and you imply a situation of intimacy; further than that, and the implication is one of formality or unfamiliarity. Any position in space can unlock emotional as well as psychological associations. During a scene, adjust and adapt in space according to the endowments of your character's relationship as determined by the text and make sure your body language is consonant with the facts.

Kinetic Sculpture

This shape activity exercises your ability to shift and change your body patterns in reach space.

1. Work in teams of three.
2. Move in, around, under, and over your partners, without touching.
3. Try to define the shape of your partners by outlining their silhouette. Use your arms, elbows, knees, or back as the defining instrument.
4. Work as one unit. Move together. The image is of kinetic sculpture, moving and carving its shape into space.
5. When the flow strengthens, merge teams and play in groups of six. Make the merger fluid and part of the playing process.
6. Add endowments to justify the action.

Effort: Sustained and moderately strong.

Observations. If you are being defined, surrender to your partner and do nothing. At the same time, stay active and participate in the activity. You will know intuitively when to move and when to stay still.

Take your time to establish a connection with your partners. Keep the contact strong throughout the activity. The connection will increase and strengthen as the group expands in size. Relationships begin to emerge and the playing will have focus and meaning. Nonverbal scenes will begin to develop. The hurdle of no touch increases the tension in the exercise.

Keep your body shape interesting; your body shape—how you use your arms, legs, spine, head in space—is what you are carving with. You carve shapes in space. Shape triggers image. Image leads to action.

When you become stuck and don't know what to do, do nothing. Wait for someone to trigger your imagination. You don't have to do it all on your own. When you accept your partner's offer, you will know what to do. A direction will emerge. You will automatically endow one another as you play. Scenes transform continuously.

Kinetic Sculpture is especially good for unlocking your imagination. Because your physical involvement is so strong, you have no choice but to surrender to your imagination. Once you connect outside and in, you are in a state of action.

Notice if your partners look connected and in a state of communication with one another. They do not necessarily need words in order to communicate. Action always speaks louder than words.

Blind Offers

This is another shape in space activity.

1. Decide who is A and who B.
2. If you are B begin in the Neutral Stance. Allow yourself to be molded and moved by your partner.
3. If you are A mold, sculpt, and shape your partner actively into a physical position. Your partner must respond to your offer and accept your physical definition of shape.
4. Work without talking.
5. When you have finished molding your partner, step aside.
6. Once you have been molded, take a moment to get the feel of your new body shape. Think of yourself as being suspended in motion. Use your position to trigger your imagination. Use one sentence of dialogue to justify your physical position and then complete your activity.
7. When you have finished the activity, return to a Neutral Stance. Say "thank you" to your partner to acknowledge the shaping offer.
8. If nothing comes to mind and you are unable to complete the frozen motion, return to the Neutral Stance and thank your partner to acknowledge the initial offer.
9. Reverse roles.

Effort: Variable.

Observations.   Work to trigger your partner's imagination through shape. The more extreme and physical the position, the more outlandish and difficult, the more exciting it is to watch your partner respond.

An offer is anything you do to trigger your partner's imagination. A trigger either sparks your imagination or it doesn't. If it doesn't, the next offer will, or the one after that. Be willing to accept every offer as it comes along. Stay open and respond with your first impulse.

There is no right or wrong way to make or accept an offer. There is only the offering and the accepting.

Living Doll

This activity involves surrender, endowment, shaping, and collaborative play. It is an extension of Blind Offers.

1. Player A will be the doll, B and C will be the molders. B and C may not speak to one another, or to the doll.
2. If you are B and C move, mold, and shape the doll. Endow it with lifelike movement. Move the arms, legs, and the pelvis until natural-looking movement develops. Do not travel in space.
3. If you are the doll, allow yourself to be molded. Respond and cooperate. Do not lead or control the shape of the movement. If you feel you are about to lose your balance, lose your balance and let your partners protect you.
4. Move the doll in space. All movement must be fluid and natural.
5. If you are the doll, begin to speak. Do not give instructions or directions. Your speech should be spontaneous and grow out of your physical actions. Let the physical action lead you into speech.
6. Once the doll is moving, bring all the dolls together to play a scene.
7. Repeat the entire sequence twice, reversing roles until everyone has had an opportunity to play the doll.

Effort: Variable.

Observations.   Play slowly at first.

Surrender to one another and work from a shared impulse. The right and left sides of the doll must coordinate and give the doll fluid and natural motion.

Do not impose your own ideas on your partners. It is almost impossible to move the doll fluidly unless you all agree to develop one central shape. Once the shape begins to define itself, the playing becomes easier. Take your time and allow the image to shape on its own.

Don't be afraid to stop if everything becomes too chaotic. Discard and eliminate those elements that are not working. It is important to try everything and then edit your choices to define and clarify the shape.

You will know when the transformation from randomness towards specificity has begun. It is at this stage of the process that you must stay tuned to one another and listen with your eyes. You cannot coordinate your effort if you are not in contact with one another.

Melted Architecture

This activity is a group variation of Blind Offers.

1. Divide into teams of four or five.
2. The first player enters the playing space and freezes in mid-action. The body shape created should be large and strong, dynamic in line and active in space. Bridge or carve away from the center of the body.
3. The second player adds to the first's frozen gesture. The second player's shape should help justify and explain the first's frozen action. Players must touch when adding on. You do not need to use your hands in order to touch.
4. Each member of the team adds on. Circle the expanding sculptural unit, find a point of entry and add on with a shape that helps explain or justify the tableau.
5. Each player adds on until a set sequence has been established. Know your order in the rotation.
6. If you are player 1, when you begin the second rotation, extricate yourself from the architectural grouping and add on to the composition to form a new point of view.
7. All the other players must remain frozen every time one player moves.
8. Continue the rotation in the set numerical sequence.
9. Complete the rotation. Repeat three more rotation cycles.
10. The set sequence must always stay intact.

Effort: Quick and strong.

Observations. This is an excellent activity for strengthening skills in adjusting and adapting, endowing, using an inner voice, and developing flow.

Every time you move you melt the architecture by changing its composition, structure, and shape. All gestures should be large and move away from the center of the body. Every frozen gesture is an offer, an invitation to trigger your teammate's imagination.

A static image transforms into a continuously shifting sequence of images and relationships. Although you remain frozen during the action, stay alive. Keep playing through the freeze. Your inner flow does not stop simply because you are immobile.

The more dynamic the shape, the more interesting the justification. Build your history with members of this particular group. Who are they to you, and you to them? Why are you here with them now? What do you want to do to them, or have them do to you? How do you provoke them, and how do they provoke you?

Endow one another at every moment. Develop strong and dynamic relationships. You are not just moving at random, you are continuously transforming relationships.

Change your point of view often before you add on. Lie on the ground and look up at the group, circle them, change your level, or turn away or into the center of the group.

As you become comfortable with the set sequence, the rotation rhythm will accelerate. Stay alert. You should be ready to move just as the players before you settle in to their new gestures. Work to dovetail moves; start as they freeze. Eliminate physical pauses or hesitations.

Every group has a pecking order. As you move from round to round, change your status in the hierarchy.

Concentrate on reading shapes in space. Every part of your body carries information about your relationship with yourself and your relationship with the other players. Make sure you engage your pelvis with every move. Because your relationships are in a state of constant flux, reading shapes in space is one sure way of determining the effect you are having on your partners.

Variation No. 1.   Add music and play with a new set sequence. Let the music suggest a theme: a family outing, a high school yearbook, paintings in a museum, etc.

Variation No. 2.   Agree on a piece of music and score a scene to the music using Melted Architecture. Repeat the scene three times; once as if within a proscenium, once a thrust stage, and once in the round. Maintain the score and the set sequence; adjust and adapt the playing for the demands of each new space.

FLOW

The third area of focus in the MAP examines the concept of flow. Flow involves directing positive tension, rather than stress, to engage in action. It involves fluidity and flexibility and the physical ability to move evenly or abruptly, or to play with gradual or fluctuating release, at will.

You will develop tools to release your impulse and direct your attention from the inner to the outer by focusing on the other.

By strengthening your use of outward focus you will begin to experience engagement.

You will continue to develop your ability to integrate and coordinate movement between body parts in order to locate new sources of creative energy by triggering.

You will work on creating the sensation of forwardness.

You will strengthen your ability to develop a collaborative relationship with your partners by building communal images involving group owner-ship.

You will also develop your sense of intuitive rightness, integrating left and right brain functions. You will lean how to link your intuitive response with logic in order to create actions that have intent and purpose.

Flow

1. Wholeness Isolation
2. Boats in the Harbor
3. Half Cat
4. Full Cat
5. The Plastique
6. Air Ball
7. Cloud Hands
8. Backwards Mirror
9. Two As One: Talking Partners
10. Talking Hands
11. Group Jump
12. Circus Walks
13. The Wheel
14. The Circle

Wholeness Isolation

This exercise will help you to discover how all the parts of your body fit together to create the sensation of flow.

1. Begin in the Neutral Stance.
2. Imagine your body divided into two surfaces: a front and a back. Move the front of your body, but not the back.
3. Now move the back of your body, but not the front.
4. Imagine your body divided into two surfaces: a right and a left. Move your right side, but not your left.
5. Now move your left side, but not your right.
6. Imagine your body divided into two surfaces: a top and a bottom. Move the top surface, but not your bottom.
7. Now move the bottom, but not your top.
8. Now move your front, back, right, left, top, and bottom at the same time.

Effort: Variable.

Observations. The front is the front of the back, the back is the back of the front; the top is the top of the bottom, and the bottom is the bottom of the top.

You are one entity. You always play with your entire being. You cannot separate, fragment, or isolate yourself. Each part of you is interconnected and interdependent on all of the others in order to function and create a state of flow.

The quality of your flow depends on how you focus your attention. Shifting focus is a way of increasing your engagement in an activity. Did you focus on the part of your body that was mobile or on the part of your body that was stable? How many different points of focus did you use?

Abruptness and evenness are two opposing ways of describing the sensation of flow.

Boats in the Harbor

This exercise uses the outer to trigger the inner.

1. Scatter around the playing space.
2. Stand with your feet touching each other, heels together and toes turned out.
3. Shift your weight from side to side. Create a full body circle by shifting your weight.
4. The image is of boats bobbing on currents of water. Adjust the time and weight of the effort to create different types of boats.

Effort: Variable.

Observations.   Results will be instant. Images develop from the physical activity, and the physical activity, in turn, stimulates the imagination to make the images more specific. Once the image takes hold, look around the room and imagine an entire harbor or marina.

Variation.   Work with a group image—small boats in front, larger boats in the rear. Shift sizes and patterns as a group, without leading or following.

Approach Boats in the Harbor as a musical piece and score it with Silent Music (see Set Sequence for Silent Music).

Half Cat

This activity builds strength, coordination, and a strong sense of evenness in flow. It is a perfect warm-up activity before a rehearsal. Use the outer to connect with the inner.

The Cobra

1. Lie face down on the floor. Cradle your head in your heads.
2. Inhale. As you exhale, lift your eyes up and back. Focus on a point beyond your feet. Move your body in the direction of your eyes.

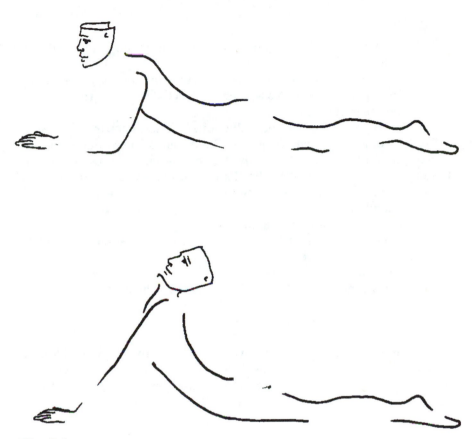

The Cobra

3. Place your hands under your shoulders, as if you were preparing to do a push-up.
4. Continue to move your upper torso upwards and back. Support the weight of your body with your arms. Keep both hips flat on the ground. Lock your elbows. Point your toes.
5. Hold this position and breathe.
6. Reverse the movement.
7. End lying face down, cradling your head in your folded arms.

Effort: Sustained and strong.

Observations. Your pelvis is your center of balance. Keep your pelvis on the ground at all times. If you can lift up only two inches, just lift two inches. Do not place undue stress on your lower back. Greater spinal flexibility will develop over time. Let your eyes initiate and lead the movement.

The Triangle

1. Begin by lying face down on the floor. Move into The Cobra. Curl your toes under you.
2. Lift your pelvis up into the air. Extend your arms and lock your elbows. Straighten your knees. Release your head between your arms. Lift your heels off the ground.
3. Keep your palms in place and pull your shoulders back into your spine. Stretch your heels down to the floor. Your pelvis will form the apex of a triangle. Walk in place, alternately stretching each heel down to the floor.
4. Keep your hips parallel to the floor. Swing them to the right, down through center (without touching the floor), to the left and back into the high triangle.
5. Repeat in the opposite direction.
6. Repeat again to the right. This time, swing your hips in a circle; first to the right, then to the left.
7. Come back into The Triangle.
8. Come down into The Cobra. End lying face down, as you began.

Effort: Sustained and strong.

Observations.   Follow your focus: your eyes lead, the movement follows.

Keep your hips parallel to the floor at all times, especially when you rotate and swing through the circle. Use sound whenever needed to help release into the stretch.

The Triangle

The Coil

1. Begin in the prone position. Move through The Cobra into The Triangle.
2. Turn to your right. Support your weight with your left hand and your left foot.
3. Place your right hand in front of your breastbone.
4. Push your pelvis back towards your feet. The image is of a coil, ready to spring. Slide your body forward until you are fully extended.
5. Bring your right knee up to face the ceiling.
6. Extend your right leg to the ceiling. Flex your foot. Pull your right heel down to join your left foot.
7. Return to the high Triangle.
8. Come down through The Cobra to the prone position on the floor.
9. Repeat, on the left side.

Effort: Sustained and strong.

Observations.   Use your nonsupporting hand to help you balance.

Step One

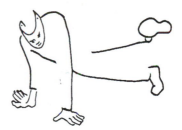

Step Three

Step Two

The Coil

Step Three (front view)

Practice the sliding movement of The Coil a number of times. Your hips must face the direction you move in, either to the right or the left. Don't let them fall back into center. Straighten your knee when you extend your leg. Flex your heel for added stretch. Never allow your hips or pelvis to sag or get too close to the ground.

The Scoop

1. Begin in the prone position. Move through The Cobra to the high Triangle. Stretch your heels to the floor.
2. Touch the floor with your knees. Elongate your toes.
3. Leading with your chin, scoop down between your arms into The Cobra. Your chest should never touch the floor.
4. Return to the prone position. Cradle your head in your hands.

Effort: Sustained and strong.

Observations.   When scooping, lead with your head. Make sure you place the knees down onto the floor—they should not make any sound when touching. Keep your pelvis as low to the ground as possible when scooping and going into The Cobra.

Half Cat Observations.   This is the first sequence in a series of exercises developed by Jerzy Grotowski in the mid-1960s. Once you have practiced each of the individual exercises and feel confident with them, link them together into a sequence, moving from The Cobra to The Triangle to The Coil to The Scoop. Focus on the flow from one movement to the next. When you feel comfortable with the flow pattern, add an animal image to the sequence. Advance the image one more time: make the animal a cat, waking, and stretching. Do not imitate a cat; rather, use the image to trigger and stimulate your imagination and inform the movement pattern.

You may find that you want to hold your breath during the sequence. Use sound to add to the release. Work with the open vowel sounds of "a," "aah," "o," and "ooh."

Shift your weight by shifting the position of your pelvis. You cannot charge through the sequence with sheer brute strength. Work for control and precision.

Vary the dynamics of the activity. Each change in the pattern will trigger a change in effort. The change of effort will trigger a change in the quality of the image of the cat.

Once you start the sequence, work continuously until you reach the end. Do not stop and repeat a step until you feel you've gotten it right. The flow of the sequence is more important than any one of its individual parts. Coordination will develop with time. Continued practice is part of the technique of the activity.

Full Cat

The entire sequence of The Cat involves strong mental focus, endurance, and stamina to create a sense of forwardness and flow.

Shoulder Stand

1. Lie on the floor face down, your head resting on your right ear. Bend your left arm, in preparation for a push-up. Keep your palm under your left shoulder, facing the floor.
2. Bend your right arm. Place your lower arm under your body, palm down. Your hand points towards your left arm.
3. Curl your toes. Walk your feet up towards your pelvis, until your legs begin to bend.
4. Move your feet around to your left hip. Walk your toes towards the palm of your left hand. Support your weight on the triangle you've formed with your left palm, your right shoulder, and your right elbow.
5. Lift your legs off the ground. Balance by placing your knees on your left elbow. Slowly lift your legs by engaging your abdominal muscles: do not kick your legs up into the air.
6. Find your balance and slowly extend your legs until they are straight up in the air.
7. Slowly reverse the process and return to the prone position.

Effort: Sustained and strong.

Observations.   The Shoulder Stand is easier than it sounds. Control your balance by adjusting your pelvis. Because you are working upside down, your legs and knees add weight; work slowly to find and hold your balance. Don't worry if at first you fall over. Always round down onto your spine and start over.

The most difficult stage of the activity is the initial liftoff from the ground to the balance point along the left arm. You may want to overcompensate by kicking (and thereby reduce the possibility of control) or overadjust with the pelvis (you'll fall out of the position).

Work this activity in pairs, one partner working and the other acting as "spotter." The spotter helps you adjust, hold, or balance.

Don't fixate on being able to perform all of the physical activities perfectly the first time through and don't give up if you can't do them. Measure your progress on a daily basis.

Shoulder Stand

Half Bridge

1. Sit on the ground with your knees bent and your legs curled under you. If possible, try and sit with your knees wide apart, your pelvis touching the ground, and your feet on either side of your pelvis.
2. Lift your pelvis forward until your spine is perpendicular to the floor. Lead with your pelvis and let your spine follow.
3. Continue to adjust your pelvis forward. Lift your breastbone towards the ceiling, while you let your head fall back. Let your head touch the

Half Bridge

floor between your feet, while your spine arches up. Rest your arms along the sides of your torso.

4. Lift your head up off the floor and return to the perpendicular position. Use your pelvis to counterbalance your body weight. Do not use your arms for balance or support.

5. Once you are perpendicular to the floor, release your pelvis backward. Sit between your legs.

Effort: Moderately sustained and strong.

Observations. Work within your physical capabilities. Gradually, you will see your limitations dissolve if you practice daily. Bridge only as far as is comfortable for you. Balance and control are the major factors in this activity; flexibility and dexterity develop with time.

Full Bridge

1. Choose a partner. Decide who will be A and who B. A works while B spots and supports.

2. Stand facing one another. If you are B, place your arms around your partner's waist and pelvis, forming a girdle of support.

3. If you are A, reach towards the ceiling with both arms and continue to reach backwards. Lead with your eyes. Your focus moves from the ceil-

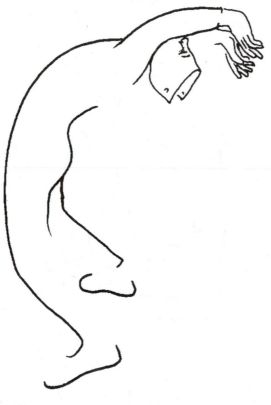

Full Bridge

ing to the back wall to the floor. Continue to reach with your arms until you touch the floor. You are now in the Full Bridge. Support your weight with your hands and feet.

4. Bend your arms. Let your head touch the ground. Roll down the length of your spine, until you have made full contact with the floor.
5. If you are B, hold and support your partner's weight throughout the traveling portion of The Bridge. Once your partner is touching the floor, step aside.
6. Repeat, reversing roles.

Effort: Sustained and strong.

Observations.   There is a moment in this exercise when your weight begins to drop and you will feel as if you have no control. This is the moment in which spotting and partnering is crucial.

Begin with an extremely wide stance. The wider the better. Keep your knees bent, forcing your pelvis to thrust forward. Your balance will be easier if your pelvis is mobile.

Reverse roles often throughout the activity. Become comfortable with supporting and spotting as well as with reaching. Both roles are vital to executing the activity safely.

You may work on your own against a wall if you want to feel more comfortable with the Full Bridge. Stand eighteen inches from the wall, reach with your arms, make contact with the wall, and walk down the wall slowly, using your pelvis throughout for counterbalance. Always reach with your arms and always, always keep your eyes open.

Head Stand 1

1. Rest on your hands and knees. Your partner will spot and help you balance.
2. Adjust your hands so they are under your shoulders. Open your fingers wide.

Head Stand 1

3. Place your head on the ground to form the apex of a triangle with your hands and elbows.
4. Curl your toes under you and walk your legs in towards your torso. Straighten your legs when you can no longer move them toward your chest. Lift your legs off the ground. Bend your knees. Let your knees rest on your elbows.
5. Once you've found your balance, lift your knees towards the ceiling. Keep your legs bent.
6. When your legs are perpendicular to the floor, adjust your pelvis, letting it release and curve forward to counterbalance your spine.
7. Twist and rotate your pelvis from left to right; maintain your balance throughout.
8. Reverse the entire process and return to your starting position.
9. Reverse roles with your partner.

Effort: Sustained and strong.

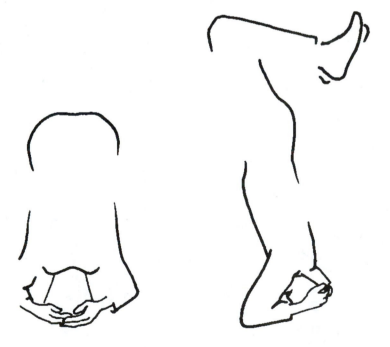

Head Stand 2

Head Stand 2

1. Rest on your hands and knees, your elbows placed on the ground. Cup your hands one inside the other. Do not interlock your fingers. Rest your head against your cupped hands.
2. Repeat Steps 2 through 9 from Head Stand 1.

Effort: Sustained and strong.

Observations. If you overcompensate you will roll out of either position before you begin to lift your legs off the ground. If you do roll over, roll into a somersault and start again.

Avoid overcompensating by working slowly. Find your balance at each phase of the activity. Do not kick or thrust your legs up in the air.

Control of the movement is as important in coming down out of the head stands as it is in lifting up into them

Once you have experienced inverted balance in either head stand you will be able to relate that sensation in any other part of the Full Cat.

The Candle

1. Lie on your back with your legs together, your arms at your sides.
2. Bring your knees in to your chest.
3. Tuck your chin in to your chest. Raise your knees above your head.
4. Extend your legs into the air. Your spine should be perpendicular to the floor. Point your toes. Your legs are straight, your chin presses into your chest.
5. Keep your elbows on the floor. Use your hands to support your waist: do not put your weight on your neck. Rotate and roll your head from side to side to make sure your neck is free and not bearing weight.
6. Place your toes on the ground behind your head. Stretch your heels to the floor.
7. Point your toes. Lift your legs six inches off the ground. Open your legs into a wide V. Then bring them together.
8. Lift your legs another six inches off the ground. Open and close your legs.
9. Return to The Candle. Adjust your spine until it is perpendicular to the floor.
10. Bend your knees. Roll down the length of your spine, onto the floor.

Effort: Sustained and moderately strong.

Observations. To maximize the effects of reverse gravity make sure you work your spine on a perpendicular axis.

The Candle

Support your weight with your shoulders, not your neck. Position your hands at your waist to help catch and control your weight should you want to round forward. You may feel a strong stretch through your hamstrings when you extend your toes onto the ground.

The Bow

1. Lie flat on your back with your legs straight, your arms at your side.
2. Keep your heels and your palms on the ground. Arch your entire body, forming a bow of tension.
3. Place your body back on the floor, rolling down the length of your spine, from your head to your tailbone.
4. Release your weight and the tension into the floor.
5. Breathe deeply for one minute.

The Bow

Effort: Quick and strong.

Observations.   This is the finishing activity for the full cat. Perform it with a burst of quick, dynamic energy and then release.

Full Cat Sequence

1. The Cobra
2. The Triangle
3. Hip Circles, right and left
4. Coils, right and left
5. Scoop into The Cobra
6. Shoulder Stand
7. Half Bridge
8. Full Bridge
9. Head Stand 1
10. Head Stand 2
11. The Candle
12. The Bow

Effort: Variable.

Observations.   Until you have mastered the technique of each phase of The Cat, work slowly, deliberately, and consciously. Once you are comfortable with the physical pattern of the sequence focus on the image of a cat waking up and stretching. Use images of different kinds of cats: different ages, weights, and breeds.

When everyone is confident with the sequence, begin to relate and respond to one another. Adjust and adapt to one another. Play spontaneously. You also may develop a freeform Cat. Use the basic movement vocabulary of the activity, but arrange it into dialogue with your partners, one that has intensity and personal meaning.

Add sound to the sequence. Use natural and open sound. Do not try to filter the sound through a preconceived image of a cat.

The Full Cat is a strenuous activity. You will continually change your direction, balance, dynamic, and focus as you work through the sequence. You will have to master the physical technique before you can play with any degree of spontaneity and inner flow.

The Plastique

This activity links outer and inner to create flow through strong, quick playing.

1. Begin with everyone in a circle in a Neutral Stance. Your legs should be comfortably apart.
2. Isolate your head. Drop it forward. Return to center. Roll it back. Return to center. Repeat.
3. Drop your head to your right. Return to center. Drop your head to your left. Return to center.
4. Make a complete head roll to your right. Repeat to your left.
5. Repeat the entire head sequence.
6. Raise your right shoulder. Drop it and return to center. Pull your shoulder down. Raise it and return to center. Move your shoulder forward to center, then backward to center. Roll your shoulder in a circle. Repeat, reversing directions for the shoulder roll. Repeat the pattern on the left side.
7. Isolate your rib cage. Bring it forward. Return to center. Move your rib cage backwards. Return to center. To the right. Center. To the left. Center. Make a full circle to your right. Now to your left. Repeat.
8. Isolate your pelvis and repeat the pattern: forward, center; backward, center; right, center; left, center; circle, center.
9. Work your feet, shifting your weight forward, back, to your right, and to your left. Work the inside and the outside edges of your feet.
10. Work your fingers, stretching and releasing them.
11. Work your wrists, pulling them into one another and then away from one another. Flex your wrists coming in, and lengthen them going out.
12. Rotate your elbows, stretching through your elbow as you make a large circle.
13. Repeat each isolation until you have absorbed the basic "vocabulary."
14. Use all parts of your body to develop a language using this vocabulary.
15. Engage in a dialogue with a partner. Use this physical language.
16. Change partners frequently.

Effort: Variable.

Observations.   You cannot bluff your way through this activity. You need to practice the vocabulary. Encode it into your muscle memory. Drill the isolations until you don't have to think about them.

The "dialogue" you engage in may not make any rational sense. It is not meant to. Respond immediately: trust your impulse. Respond to whatever is sent to you. Your response will stimulate and trigger your partner's imagination. Do not mirror one another. Once you have established a responsive relationship with your partner, you will know when to end your "dialogue." Shift your focus, and work with a new partner.

Trust your sense of intuitive rightness. Follow your impulse and let it guide you into action. As the impulses link up, you will experience inner flow. The Plastique works best when taken at a quick pace. Work through the fatigue. Once you have broken through that barrier you will begin to work on a deeper, more instinctual level.

Air Ball

This activity uses sustained physical effort to trigger strong inner flow.

1. Begin in a wide Neutral Stance. Keep your elbows alongside your rib cage. Rest your hands just above your waist.
2. Rotate your left hand until your palm faces the ceiling. Turn your right hand so your palm faces the floor. The image is of holding a ball of air between your hands.
3. Slowly turn to the right, holding the air ball between your hands. Do not move the lower half of your body. Keep your hips even and parallel to the floor.
4. While you are turning, rotate the air ball. Your left hand moves to the top and your right hand moves to the bottom.
5. Complete the rotation of the air ball as you turn. Begin to move back through the center to the left.
6. The outside edge of your upper hand cuts through space as you move from side to side.
7. Face a player next to you. Mirror one another as you rotate and turn the air ball from side to side.

Effort: Sustained and light.

Observations.   Resist the temptation to increase the tempo of this activity. Keep the effort sustained and light.

Use the outside edge of your hand as if it were a knife cutting through space. Keep your wrists straight rather than hyperflexed. Keep your pelvis tucked and your knees turned out. The wider your stance and the lower your pelvis to the ground, the easier it will be to maintain your balance over a long period of time.

Keep your focus at eye level. Coordinate your breathing with the rotation of your spine. Only turn as far as you can without engaging or twisting your hips.

Cloud Hands

This activity uses sustained time as a triggering device to connect and coordinate mental and physical efforts.

Cloud Hands

1. Begin in a wide Neutral Stance with feet parallel. Keep your weight balanced in the middle of your feet. Release your pelvis and tuck it forward. Lengthen your spine and let your head float on top of your spinal column.
2. Raise your arms. Bring your hands to the middle of your breastbone. Extend your arms forward to form a circle. Point your thumbs up to the ceiling; keep your fingers long and extended. Your hands should be three inches apart from one another. Release your elbows along the sides of your rib cage.
3. Use the outside edge of your right hand as a cutting surface. Draw an oval shape in space with your right hand. Keep your elbow released and your shoulder down.
4. Continue the cutting motion, scooping down to complete the oval. Finish the shape exactly where you began.
5. Repeat on your left side.
6. Reverse. Repeat on your right, until the shape of the movement feels comfortable.
7. Add movement to your lower arm, from your wrist to your elbow. The outside edge of your right wrist continues to lead the action. Draw a larger oval. Your hands never move higher than your shoulders or lower than your waist.
8. Alternate sides.
9. Add a twist to the movement. Turn your spine in the direction of your moving hand. Keep your elbows low and close to your rib cage.
10. Start to move your left hand as your right hand scoops. Turn your spine in the direction of your top hand.
11. Your hips and lower body should never move. Rotate your spine on a fixed, firm base. Keep your knees bent.
12. Imagine your hands are describing the outline of clouds. Your hands and upper body should appear to float through space, light and fluid, while your lower body is rooted in earth.

Effort: Light and sustained.

Observations.   This is a slow rotation exercise that deals with synchronicity between players. The synchronicity develops coordination between the mind and the body of each individual player.

Do not succumb to the temptation to speed up this exercise. Concentrate on maintaining physical form and mental focus. Do not allow yourself to drift. Maintaining eye contact between players is essential.

Backwards Mirror

This strong flow activity uses physical hurdles to heighten nonverbal communication.

1. Find a partner of the same size and weight.
2. Stand back to back. Move together.
3. There is no leader and no follower.
4. Do not talk.
5. Mirror your arms and hands.

Effort: Variable.

Observations.   This is an offer-and-accept activity. You engage in offering and accepting to create a sense of flow with your partner. Everything you do must work to trigger your partner's imagination.

Surrender to the offer if you are going to move out of inertia. At the same time, be willing to wait for a specific impulse to guide and shape the movement.

Keep your movement spontaneous. Do not develop a cuing system for one another, or rely on rhythm and tempo as a way of communicating. Rely on one another.

Variations.
1. Work with your eyes closed.
2. Work in groups of three, then four.
3. Work side by side rather than back to back.
4. Turn to face one another. Work nose to nose. Move the whole body together, without dancing. Working nose to nose demands greater concentration and greater relaxation.

Two as One: Talking Partners

This activity demands synchronicity of effort and partner flow. Focus, surrender, and release forward into action.

1. Stand side by side with your partner. Wrap your arms around each other's waists.
2. Move together. Do not lead or follow. Work to create the body shape of one character you will play together.
3. As you begin to define the mask, develop the shared shape more specifically. Work in sync with one another to create partner flow.
4. Begin to talk. Form all the words together. Do not lead, do not follow. Talk on the same impulse.
5. Verbalize the mask's inner voice together, speaking the inner thoughts aloud. Create an autobiography. Give an imaginary interview to an imaginary interviewer.

6. As the talking process becomes easier, increase your tempo. Talk in conversational rhythms, with one shared voice.
7. Interact with another mask. Play a scene.

Effort: Variable.

Observations.   Determine the shape of the body and the manner of moving before finding the voice for the mask.

Always speak in the first person. As soon as you can give the mask a name. Speaking in one voice is extraordinarily difficult. However, form the words together. Surrender to one another and, at the same time, work off your first impulse.

At first, your rate of utterance may be extremely slow. As you become more confident and gather information about who you are, your rate of utterance will increase. Try to speak in a tempo natural to the adornments of the mask.

Avoid the temptation to become talking heads. Keep your body active and engaged. Let the physical trigger your imagination. You are working with double trigger action that triggers your body and, with unexpected offers from your partner, also triggers your imagination. Synchronicity of effort is another manifestation of flow.

The overload in this activity is extremely strong. When you overload you deliberately jam your mental control mechanisms with physical stimulation to keep the playing in space, not in your head.

As you become comfortable with the speaking/thinking process, you will begin to discover that halfway through a sentence you know where the sentence will end. You may want to speed up to finish the sentence. This mirrors your natural thinking process in life. Halfway through a thought, you know where the thought is going and you make a straight line to its conclusion.

This is also true of listening. Halfway into hearing a thought you anticipate its conclusion. Beware. This tendency to anticipate is dangerous, especially when you begin to work with a text, because you may want to "jump" to the end of the thought and not listen to your partner.

Flow in this activity is created through an outward focus on your partner and a shared target: talking as one.

Talking Hands

This is another high overload partner flow game.

1. Stand with your partner, front to back. Decide who will be A and who B. Stand in a circle, with A facing into the center of the circle, B behind A.

2. If you are A, reach around and wrap your arms around your partner's waist. If you are B, slip your arms under your partner's armpits. Your arms and hands function as your partner's arms and hands.
3. Work together to create one mask. The mask is an expert in a specific field of knowledge. The mask will deliver a one-minute lecture about his subject.
4. Work together to prepare the lecture. Present the lecture, one team at a time, to the other teams. A verbalizes while B physicalizes.
5. After the lecture, trade roles and repeat.

Effort: Variable.

Observations. In this activity you are forced to work together, and to work off of one another. The flow will strengthen as the activity develops.

Use the mask image as the connective thread between you and your partner. You are both working together to develop and wear the same mask at all times.

Variation. Use the physical action to trigger your speech, rather than using your speech to cue and guide your partner. Use pauses and silence. Let the gesture lead and direct the content of the lecture.

Observations. The level of spontaneity is much higher because you are no longer in control. You truly do discover the action as you go along rather than work off a predetermined plan of attack. You are no longer responsible for making it all happen on your own.

This activity can also be extended into scenes. Try playing a serious scene. Maintain your focus and concentration and see what happens.

The effect of Talking Hands is usually comic. There is an intense release of energy when working with the comic impulse. Laughter becomes a narcotic, and one is tempted to begin playing for the laugh. Forego the temptation to play for laughs and see what happens.

Group Jump

This exercise must be played as an ensemble. Share the impulse and work as one.

1. Begin with everyone in one large circle in the Neutral Stance.
2. Do eight soft low jumps in place.
3. Repeat. Begin together. End together. Repeat until you are all moving at the same time.

4. Advance the pattern. Jump once in place. Make a quarter turn to your right. Jump again. Jump once in place. Add another quarter turn to your right. Jump again. Do a third jump and a third quarter turn. Do a fourth, until you have made one full circle.
5. Repeat without cuing. Begin and end together.
6. Repeat, turning to your left.
7. Jump once in place. Make a half turn to your right. Jump once in place, half turn to your right. Repeat the sequence, making a second circle to your right with half turns.
8. Repeat, making two circles to your left.
9. Jump once in place. Make a full turn to your right. Jump once in place and make a full turn to your left. Jump and turn to your right. Jump and turn to your left.
10. Combine all the parts and play the full sequence: 8 jumps in place, quarter turns to the right and left, half turns to the right and left, full turns to the right and left. You must all begin and end together.
11. Repeat the entire sequence until you are all moving at the same time. End together.

Effort: Quick and strong.

Observations. There are no leaders and no followers in this activity. You must all move together, working off the same impulse.

Listen carefully to the instructions and one another when you are working. It may take some players longer to get it than others. Everyone works at a different tempo. Be patient. Stay with it.

Circus Walks

This activity requires collaboration and concerted, focused effort to sustain group flow.

1. Work in groups of three. Decide who will be A, who will be B, and who C.
2. A: kneel on the floor. Support your weight with your hands and knees.
3. B: stand behind A. C: stand to the side of B. You will work as the spotter.
4. If you are B step onto A's back. Keep your heels together at the base of A's spine, and point your toes outward.
5. Slowly walk up the length of A's spine. C will help you with your balance and guide you when necessary.
6. When you reach A's shoulders, curl your toes over them and balance.
7. Once you are able to balance, jump off A's shoulders onto the floor.

8. Trade roles, until all three of you have walked up the length of your partner's spine.

Effort: Quick and light.

Observations.   Do not move quickly up the spine at first.

When you walk up the length of your partner's spine, keep your focus at eye level. Never look down.

Use the image of a circus tightrope walker. Play this activity with a great deal of flesh, sound, and energy. Make it into a performance.

Variation No. 1.   Walk up the spine with your eyes closed.

Variation No. 2.   Once you've reached A's shoulders, A slowly rises to a standing position.

The Wheel

This slow meditative activity is good for group as well individual flow.

1. Form a circle. Stand equidistant from one another, in the Neutral Stance.
2. Bend your knees. Make sure your weight does not extend forward beyond your toes.
3. Shift your weight from your right leg to your left. Keep your hips even and parallel to the floor.
4. Shift your weight onto your right foot. Keep your left heel in place. Rotate the toes of your left foot to the left, until they form a 45-degree angle away from the center of the circle.
5. Shift your weight onto your left foot. Keep your left foot in place. Step forward with your right foot. Place your heel down on the floor, so that it is directly parallel to, and in front of, your left heel. The distance between your feet is a "channel." Rotate your toes to the right 45 degrees. Bend both knees.
6. Rotate your weight forward from your left leg to your right leg. Reverse. Continue shifting your weight back and forth until the transference from right to left and left to right feels smooth and even. Work with a sustained tempo.
7. Bend your elbows. Rest them alongside your rib cage. Lengthen your fingers, thumbs up, facing the ceiling, palms facing one another.
8. As you shift your weight forward, move your hands out from your waist. As you shift your weight backwards, raise your hands slightly, until your elbows bend and return to the sides of your rib cage.

9. When your elbows rest alongside your ribs, release your wrists down to your waist. The circle begins again.
10. To shift sides, step forward onto the front leg. Form a new channel with your left foot.
11. Complete the activity by bringing your back foot forward. Rest your arms alongside your body and straighten your legs.
12. Keep your focus on a player opposite you and not on the floor. Expand your focus to include the entire group. Breathe and move as one.
13. Repeat on the opposite side.

Effort:　Sustained and light.

Observations.　Once you understand the mechanics and technique of the activity, add the image of a wheel in continuous rotation, moving without beginning or end.

Coordinate your breathing with your physical exertion. Keep it slow, smooth, and steady. Nothing should be rushed or forced. Keep your knees bent and remember to push off from your rear foot. Make the weight transference smooth.

You may carry tension in your arms and hands. Make them "float" during the activity. Keep your spine erect. Do not lean in or lean out. Your head should sit squarely in the middle of your pelvis.

The image of a wheel may include your partner or the entire group. Think of individual wheels inside one collective wheel.

The Circle

This activity is good for tension problems, focusing attention, and strengthening group flow. It is an activity that can be repeated continually as a means of charting growth and progress.

Circle No. 1

1. Form a circle. Throughout the exercise, keep the shape of the circle intact. Turn and face a partner on your right. Stand 18 inches apart.
2. Shift your weight onto your right foot. Bend your right knee. Keep your hips level and parallel to the floor. Your right knee should be directly over your toes.
3. Raise your left leg until your thigh is parallel to the floor. Bend your knee and release your lower leg until it is perpendicular to the floor.
4. Lengthen your spine. Let your head float on top of your spinal column.
5. Relax your arms. Keeping your elbow at the sides of your rib cage, raise both arms until they are parallel to the floor, palms down. Raise your

right palm eight inches from the middle of your breastbone and turn it to your left.

6. Decide who will be A and who B.
7. A: move clockwise in the circle: B: move counterclockwise. Begin moving the circle counterclockwise until you are told to change directions.
8. When you move backwards, step toe first, then heel. When you move forward, move heel first, then toe. Shift your weight with smooth and fluid motion. Always reach forward with your leg, extending from your knee to your toe. Step out in order to move. Keep your supporting knee bent at all times.
9. Shift your hands when you move your legs. Elbows always stay by your rib cage. The outside edge of your right palm swings down in an arc and cuts a path above your waist, until your palm is parallel to the floor. Your left hand moves in with an upward curve. Open palms slide past one another, one curving in, the other curving out.
10. Your hands and legs move in opposition to one another. Keep your spine erect throughout. Maintain your balance without leaning in or leaning back.
11. Change the direction of the circle. Move clockwise.

Effort: Sustained and light.

Observations.   Focus your attention on your balance, posture, coordination, and sense of timing throughout this activity. Do not lean in or lean out. Take large steps. Develop a sense of flow between your body parts.

Swing your arms in a soft, fluid manner. Release the tension in your fingers. Keep your wrists straight. Make one smooth line from your elbows to the tips of your fingers. Your arms should not swing out past your rib cage or move in close to your chest.

You must give up control in this activity, especially when you move backwards. You have to depend totally on your partner for guidance and support. Maintain eye contact throughout. Blink and breathe. Concentrate on moving as one with your partner, without leading or following.

Keep the integrity and shape of the circle intact. Remain equidistant from one another.

Circle No. 2

1. Repeat Circle No. 1, until you are moving together in a smooth, even rhythm.
2. When changing direction, work to maintain the space and spacing within the circle. Each couple must be equidistant from the rest, and the size of the circle should fill most of the playing space.

3. Maintain the group timing. The rhythm and tempo of the moves must not increase during the course of the activity.
4. Focus on moving as one.
5. Change direction frequently.

Effort: Sustained and light.

Observations. Having a specific focus helps you release. When you release, your technical form will improve. Once your focus is off yourself, the entire activity becomes easier.

Be precise in your spatial orientation. The circle may want to close in on itself and become smaller. If you are bunching up, you may want to bypass one another. Don't, even if it means feeling cramped.

Move through space together. Do not mark the activity with baby steps. You will begin to experience "two as one" during this phase of the activity.

Use the outer focus to build a bridge with your partner and create a sense of flow between you.

Circle No. 3

1. Repeat Circle No. 2.
2. Maintain the shape and spacing of the circle. Move together as one group, on the same breath.
3. Use your peripheral vision to stay aware of the couples in front, behind, and opposite you. Maintain and strengthen contact with your partner.

Effort: Sustained and light.

Observations. This phase of the activity brings the greatest release and the greatest sense of flow. Individual technique strengthens through repetition. It also is easier to expand your focus.

Your concentration may be strongest at this phase. The circle will feel its lightest. It is possible, even for just a moment, to experience the circle moving as one. When that happens, you will discover that you alone are not responsible for "making it happen."

As you become comfortable with the activity, regulate and stabilize your breathing.

SECOND TRIAD: PLAYING THE ACTION

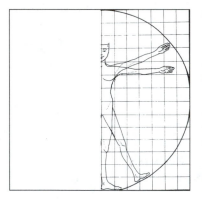

In the second triad of the MAP you will focus on linking the outer with the inner to engage in playing action. You will focus on establishing patterns of action through collaboration, repeating the patterns to establish flow, and intensifying the flow to play with heightened stakes and danger. You will develop skills in transformation, patterns, and endowments.

In Transformation you will focus on creating patterns of action by establishing "points," and then linking the points together; intensifying engagement by using the outer to trigger the inner and "connect up" to play with integrated flow; and building strength in flow patterns by eliminating "jumps."

In Patterns you will focus on collaboration; strengthening the quality of your play by defining and drilling the rules of play, and developing a technique for shaping action to give it consistency and forwardness; and integrating design principles into the flow of your play to create and clarify narrative action.

In Endowments you will focus on defining the boundaries and perimeters of your context by using facts to condition, tone, and color the quality of your play; transforming the facts into physicalized effort factors that give shape and definition to your play; and using these factors to trigger and deepen the quality of your imaginative engagement in the action play.

Combined, these three MAP components focus on the inner movement of action, developing skills in intensifying engagement and building confidence in the processes of playing, collaborating, and shaping scores of action.

TRANSFORMATION

Transformation is a process of physical free association in which one action suggests and leads to the discovery of the next. Transforming involves changing the quality of flow. You will learn how to identify, read, and manipulate the effort factors that create flow. You will exercise your ability to combine and transform these factors in Basic Action Drives. Transforming tests your ability to follow and develop your intuition. When you transform you move from what is known into what is unknown.

The movement forward into the unknown advances the action; you link what has already been discovered with something yet to come.

Continuing the action involves repeating an action to make it more specific. It is the time to pare away excess and hone the action down to its essence. In transformation you will exercise and strengthen your ability to continue and advance action.

You will learn to jiggle an impulse back and forth with a partner until the action defines itself. Jiggling involves risk, surrender, and abandoning control to allow the action to emerge on its own; as you jiggle you will become aware of your control factors at work.

You will also become aware of jumping, which is a safety device for avoiding the unknown. You will develop skills to bypass jumps, skills designed to release your imagination and sustain flow.

You will learn to use physical leads to connect the outer with the inner, eliminating preconceptions and value judgments in the creative process.

You will also focus your attention on the action cycle, initiating, engaging, and completing action. You will learn to close each frame in order to eliminate drift.

In transformations you will develop confidence in your ability to follow an impulse, let it lead you into action, then define, refine, and intensify the action until it is ready to change.

Transformation

1. Basic Action Drives (BADs)
2. Continue and Advance
3. Giants and Elves
4. Space Substance
5. Zig Zags
6. Floor Grid
7. The Corridor
8. Musical Combines

Basic Action Drives (BADs)

Every action involves effort. Effort is the exertion of energy. Effort can be measured in terms of its four factors: time, weight, focus in space and flow.

1. Walk in the playing space. Be aware of your walk and the quality of the effort you use as you walk.
2. Change the quality of the time factor as you walk. Make the time factor quick. Work with quick time.
3. Gradually change the quality of the time to the opposite of quick: sustained. Work with sustained time.
4. Experiment with the time factor in your walk. Move back and forth between quick and sustained time.
5. Shift your attention from the quality of time to the quality of weight. Make the quality of your weight in the effort of walking light. Walk with light weight.
6. Gradually change the quality of your weight to the opposite of light: strong. Work with strong weight.
7. Experiment with the weight factor in your walk. Move back and forth between strong and light weight.
8. Shift your attention between the qualities of time and weight. Walk quick. Walk sustained. Walk strong. Walk light.
9. Combine the factors of time and weight. Walk quick and strong. Walk quick and light. Walk sustained and light. Walk sustained and strong.
10. Shift your attention to the quality of focus in space. Make your focus in space direct. Work with direct space.
11. Gradually change your focus in space from direct to the opposite of direct: indirect. Work with indirect focus in space.
12. Experiment with the quality of your focus in space as you walk. Move back and forth between direct and indirect focus in space.
13. Shift your focus from the quality of space to the quality of flow. Make the quality of your flow bound. Work with bound flow.
14. Gradually change the quality of the flow to the opposite of bound: open. Work with open flow.
15. Experiment with the quality of flow. Move back and forth between open and bound flow.
16. Shift your focus between the qualities of space and flow. Walk direct. Walk indirect. Walk open. Walk bound.
17. Combine the factors of space and flow. Walk direct and open. Walk direct and bound. Walk indirect and bound. Walk indirect and open.
18. Combine three of the factors. Walk direct, strong, and sustained. Make everything you do direct, strong, and sustained.

19. Focus on someone near you. With these combined factors, see if you can **press.** You are a presser. Your action is to press. Pressing is direct, strong, and sustained.
20. Change your focus. Make your time quick, keep your weight strong, and your space direct. **Punch.** You are a puncher. Your action is to punch.
21. Change focus. Keep the space direct and the time quick, but make your weight light. **Dab.** You are a dabber. Your action is to dab.
22. Change focus. Keep your weight light and your time quick, but make your focus in space indirect. **Flick.** You are a flicker. Your action is to flick.
23. Change focus. Keep your time quick and your focus in space indirect, but make your weight strong. **Slash.** You are a slasher. Your action is to slash.
24. Change focus. Keep your focus in space indirect and your weight strong, but make your time sustained. **Wring.** You are a wringer. Your action is to wring.
25. Change focus. Keep your focus in space indirect and your time sustained, but make your weight light. **Float.** You are a floater. Your action is to float.
26. Change focus. Keep your weight light and your time sustained, but make your focus in space direct. **Glide.** You are a glider. Your action is to glide.
27. Repeat these eight basic actions: Press. Punch. Flick. Dab. Slash. Wring. Float. Glide.
28. Return to your own walk. Exaggerate your use of time, weight, and space. Determine whether you personally are a presser, a puncher, a flicker, a dabber, a slasher, a wringer, a floater, or a glider.
29. Exaggerate the action.
30. Exaggerate and play its opposite.
31. Play your basic action one more time. Make it as specific as possible.
32. Minimalize and sustain the external activity.

Effort: Variable.

Observations.   You will have no trouble in responding to each of the "effort factors."

Time, weight, space, and flow are the four primary factors involved with effort. Effort is the tangible, physical, measurable manifestation of intent.

These four factors also have psychological correspondents as well as a physical manifestation. Time is linked with intuition, weight with sense, space with thinking, and flow with feeling.

The BADs: Slash, Wring, and Dab

Each effort factor is experienced as a spectrum of opposites. At one end of the spectrum you have light, at the other, strong. Quick/sustained, direct/ indirect, open/bound—these factors become guidelines for measuring your level of intensity and engagement in action. When you combine two of these factors, you create a "state." When you combine three of these factors, you create a drive.

Time, weight, and flow work together to create a pattern known as a passion drive. A passion drive is where you live when your inner emotional experience is so compelling it takes you entirely out of space. You become sensual, emotional, and intuitive, in a world of your own.

Space, flow, and weight work together to create a pattern known as a spell drive. A spell drive is when time stands still. You are engaged in a trance that commands your sense, feeling, and attention so thoroughly that you relinquish your intuition and lose all interest in decision.

Space, time, and flow work together to create a pattern known as a vision drive. A vision drive is when you lose your weight—you become self- less. Process becomes so important to you that you forget your own ego. You use your intellect, your intuition, and your feelings to guide you in visionary endeavors.

Time, weight, and space work together to create flow patterns known as action drives.

There are eight basic actions: to press, punch, flick, dab, slash, wring, float, and glide. Each of these eight basic actions drives is tied to a psychological center that colors and "frames" how you view the world.

We all tend towards one of these eight basic actions. It is part of our core, an inextricable part of who we are. Never make value judgments when working with the basic action drives. Being a presser or puncher is neither better nor worse than being a floater or glider. The drives simply are. We can work with them from the outside in, or from the inside out. They function either way, and, either way, they always take you into a high intensity experience of action.

When you first work with the basic action drives, you will experience all eight drives. You will feel comfortable with some, uncomfortable with others. Focus on those you feel most uncomfortable with first, to expand your range and develop flexibility. You can always polish and refine those you feel comfortable with later.

Continue and Advance

This activity is an introduction to the basic process of transformation.

1. Close your eyes. Move at random around the playing space.
2. Slowly change levels. Bend. Stand. Stretch. Reach.
3. Exaggerate your movement until it begins to suggest a gesture.
4. Continue, i.e., repeat, the gesture until it suggests an activity. Let the activity suggest an action, an activity charged with purpose, direction, and intent.
5. Advance the action. Make it bigger, smaller, stronger, lighter. Change the direction and visual focus of the activity. Let the change happen gradually. Do not "jump" to a new image. Let the change evolve through your physical effort.
6. Once you have advanced the action continue with it until it is specific and has a sense of purpose.
7. Repeat the entire process.

Effort: Variable.

Observations.   When you engage your imagination in this activity you work from the outside in. You do not have to wait for a "creative idea" in order to begin. You are always in a creative state. Shift your perception to focus on a physical activity—an outer—to trigger and engage your imagination.

Keep your focus on the physical activity. Let it suggest an image. The image itself will trigger an action. When the inner and the outer merge, you'll enter a state of "flow." In "flow," you are guided by your sense of intuitive rightness. You inhibit your analytical response by focusing your attention on the physical activity.

Intuitive rightness is your dominant guide during the early phases of the creative process. Always respond to your first impulse, doing that which feels and seems right. Analytical thinking enters the process at a later point, as you edit and design your choices into repeatable, playable scores of action.

Engage your pelvis in the activity. Do not play with just your arms and hands. You store a great deal of energy in your lower spine. When you release that energy you also will release your imagination. Your sense of flow will be more absorbing and your emotional connection deeper.

By engaging the center of your body in an action you increase your involvement, moving from "gestural" action, using primarily your arms and hands, to "postural" action, involving the trunk of your body.

Sometimes, when you are advancing the action, you may want to "jump" to a new image. "Jumping" is a way of controlling the flow of the action. You impose a disconnected image into the action. You jump from A to C without going through B.

Follow your intuition rather than your mind. One physical image will trigger another. Eventually you will be flooded with mental pictures—images. Use the images to infuse your activity with intent.

When you advance an action the images transform; when you continue an action, you define and clarify its intent by making its physical life more specific.

You will not be aware of "thinking" when you continue and advance. You merely respond to the stimulus of the physical image. You may want to increase the tempo of the activity when you continue an action. Resist that temptation.

Working with your eyes closed deepens your experience when playing. Once you feel comfortable with the gesture, open your eyes.

Giants and Elves

This transformational activity requires quick changes of effort, shape, and flow.

1. Move around the playing space in your own tempo and rhythm.
2. Develop an image of yourself as a sculpture moving in space.
3. Advance the image to that of a giant, with arms and legs ten feet long and a spine twenty feet tall. Develop the physical shape for your giant.

4. Compress the image. Make your arms and legs ten inches long, and your spine twenty inches in length. Develop a shape for an elf.
5. Expand your focus to include the other players as part of your elf world.
6. On a hand clap, return to the giant shape. Add more specifics of your giant's world. Make the context of this world physical.
7. On a hand clap, return to the elf world.
8. Alternate shapes and develop relationships with the other giants in your giant world and the other elves in your elf world.
9. Develop one primary physical image for each character. Let that image form the **key** into each shape.
10. Create two totally separate characters in two totally separate worlds.
11. Select one character and develop it fully. Inhabit a world of both giants and elves.

Effort: Variable.

Observations.   The separate images of giant and elf will, by necessity, begin as stereotypes. The stereotype is merely your starting point, not where you end.

Embrace the starting point, whatever it may be. Don't worry about being original, creative, or unique. Start with your first impulse and, as you continue to work with it, allow it to trigger your imagination so that the image advances and transforms on its own. You will know when you have arrived at the next stage; your sense of intuitive rightness will guide and inform you.

The physical "key" for each character is the central organizing principle of the transformation. This key will always trigger the image of the body/facial shape. It is something you can slip into easily and comfortably, and is highly personal and unique to you. The physical key usually helps unlock the psychological key of the character as well.

Once you have chosen the key, transform from one character to another rapidly. The faster the change, the more fun you can have with the transformations.

Variation No. 1.   Develop a voice for each character. You can play scenes with the other giants and elves once you know how to speak.

Variation No. 2.   Play a scene between your giant and your elf. Play both roles. Keep them separate and make the transformations rapid. Justify the need to speak.

Variation No. 3.   Work with a partner. Develop your giant and your elf. Develop a scene between your giant and your elf and play both roles. Your partner will clone you. From this point on, work with mirror cloning and see how the characters develop between you. Keep the discipline of the scene intact; don't change any of the spoken text, or the physical score of action. Allow the characters to expand and develop by adding details and nuance found in making the physical adjustments while playing.

Space Substance

This transformational activity uses objects and environment as sensory triggers. Focus of attention stays outside of yourself.

1. Walk around the room focusing on the sensory qualities of an imaginary liquid substance. Is it thick, thin, gooey, or creamy?
2. Change the substance into a cream. Move through the substance.
3. Change the cream into oil. Move through it.
4. Change the oil into gelatin. Move through it.
5. Change the gelatin into molasses.
6. As the molasses thickens focus on the sensation of its color. Increase the intensity of the color until it is so dark and rich it becomes impossible to move through.
7. Anchor your feet to the ground and close your eyes. Respond to a breeze that engulfs and surrounds you.
8. Develop a gesture in the breeze. Continue the gesture until it leads you to a specific action.
9. Advance the action. Continue the new action. Condition the quality of your playing by changing your tempos and rhythm.
10. Open your eyes and advance the action until you begin to move in space. Condition the quality of your playing by changing your tempos and rhythm.
11. Change the visual focus of the action. Each transformation changes the substance of the space.
12. Minimalize the size of the action until it is imperceptible. Maintain the internal rhythm of the action while the rest of your body is still.
13. Freeze. Release.

Effort:　　Variable.

Observations.　　The transformational process is always triggered by the external manipulation of the effort factors. These changes stimulate your imagination, enabling the new gesture to develop with more specificity.

Use the effort factors to release and trigger your sensory imagination while playing. The weight of each substance requires a different use of time; time and weight always combine to condition the quality of your playing and influence the flow pattern. When you change these factors you change the way you play. Your effort changes because your parameters change. When you play with very specific physical parameters your action becomes more specific.

Because the effort factors are tangible and sensual its easy to stay focused on your body and out of your mind. Sometimes your effort will be directed towards resisting the substances; sometimes it will be directed towards surrendering to them. Either way, use the physical qualities of the sensory stimulants to condition and tone the quality of your play.

Zig Zags

In this activity you exercise linking up outer and inner to create action/flow.

1. Stand opposite one another, in two lines.
2. If you are at the top of the line, send an imaginary object across the playing space to your partner, opposite.
3. When you receive the imaginary object, receive it with the same weight and tempo with which it was sent. Quickly transform the object and send the new object across the space to the next player in line opposite you.
4. The transformation must be smooth and fluid. Let the object suggest its own advancement. Don't impose or "jump" the transformation. Give yourself enough time to allow the object to tell you how it wants to change. Then transform it quickly and send it to the next player.
5. The object continues to transform from player to player as it zig zags across the playing space.
6. When the object reaches the end of the line, start a new round of playing. Add sound to the object. The sound helps describe the weight and shape of the object. When you receive it, transform the sound as well as the shape of the object.
7. When the object reaches the end of the line, begin again. This time you are the object. Move across the floor playing with the sound and movement dynamics. Establish a pattern (although it doesn't have to be strictly rhythmic). When you reach the center of the space, gradually transform the sound and movement. You will know when you arrive at a new dynamic. Give this dynamic to your partner. Take your time in offering and accepting the dynamic.
8. When you accept the dynamic, imitate it exactly until you have absorbed it. Then move across the floor and transform it.
9. When you have all moved across the floor, divide into smaller teams. Each team transforms the dynamic together.

Effort: Strong, with variable tempo.

Zig Zags

Observations. This is the ultimate continue and advance game. There is no way you can predict the end result. If you are truly playing from moment to moment, each move will be intuitive and spontaneous.

You will probably begin playing with "gestural" action, using your arms and face. Once you are in space, begin bridging and see if you can move into carving, shifting the playing from gestural into "postural" action involving your pelvis and spine.

The stronger your physical involvement the deeper your emotional involvement. Therefore, engage your spine and pelvis and make the body effort total.

Really offer the dynamic. Sustain eye contact with your partner. When you accept the offer match the dynamic exactly. Really accept the offer. Quite often the dynamic goes one step further, becoming more specific at the moment of transferral. As you move into the center of the playing space explore the parameters of the dynamic; see if you can find its dynamic high point, its top, and its dynamic low point, or its bottom, before you reach the center of the space and begin the transformation.

The physical triggers the emotional. When the two are combined, you are in a state of action/flow. You will know it the moment you experience it. You will recognize it the moment someone kicks into it while you are waiting your turn. An action drive is very "present." It is visceral, and you will feel it and respond to it.

Give yourself enough time to allow the transformation to happen. If you "jump," simply return to the original action and allow it to advance in its own time. Do not impose a change out of fear of not being able to create one. Trust that it will happen.

Breathe deeply and fully when you are playing. Breathing is one of your keys in connecting the outside with the inside. Open sound with deep breath and intense physical activity will unlock and trigger a deeper emotional response. Allow your response to emerge.

Quite often you may tap into anger and fear when you first play. The sound may be piercing or extremely violent and frightening. Move through this initial response to develop the next layer of images. At all times, know that nothing dangerous or extreme will happen to you. You can stop the playing whenever you want. You are always in control.

At the same time, don't inhibit your light-hearted or silly responses. The work does not always have to be dramatic or intense. Nor does it have to be consistently light-hearted or comic. Vary the dynamics often for stark contrasts and see what begins to emerge.

When you work with the group transformation, there is no leader and no follower. Work together. Make sure your eye contact with one another is strong. You cannot change the dynamics unless you are looking at your partners. As always, your eyes are another link with the other players.

There is a tremendous release of energy in the Zig Zag, especially when you move into the Action Drive. You may "mark" the passage of another player, imitating their movements, and try to experience it while waiting in line for your turn to play.

When your physical involvement with the activity is complete, quite often you'll push through emotional barriers. Don't be afraid to lose yourself in the playing. The discoveries are worth the risk.

Floor Grid

This exercise explores the power of sensory stimulation to affect, tone and condition your playing. This activity requires at least twelve players and a large playing space.

1. On the playing floor, sketch out a grid pattern, four squares wide by three squares deep. These squares are the individual playing areas.
2. Move into the grid pattern one at a time.
3. Spend one minute in each square. You will play a total of twelve minutes.
4. Endow each square with a strong physical or sensory quality. It can be a smell, a texture, a color, a temperature, or an emotional sensation. You will spend one minute within each environment, responding either to it or against it.
5. You have ten seconds between squares to rest.

Effort: Variable.

Observations.   Initially you may feel you will never be able to sustain yourself throughout the activity. Once you finish you may want to go through the grid a second or even a third time.

Energy creates energy. You will feed off of one another once you begin to play. The energy changes are so rapid that your imagination begins to overload with images in both sound and movement. Without knowing it you will begin to coordinate and fall into sync with one another, so that one one-minute round of playing might be quick and light while another will be strong and sustained.

Since the pattern is additive, there will always be an audience who are either waiting to begin or who have just finished. Use the audience to stimulate your imagination. Do not ignore the performance elements when moving through the transformations.

This activity relies heavily on your ability to work with flow. The exercise also works to increase your awareness of synchronicity—how you automatically and intuitively adapt and adjust to one another when you are all "present."

Variation.   Select a specific theme to be explored in twelve stages. Work within a specific world, either that of a text or of a time and place.

Embrace the abstract in this activity. You can make the abstract specific as long as you establish the parameters you are going to honor, and then play within those parameters.

The Corridor

This activity demands team playing; you must rely on your partners throughout the collaborative process.

1. Work in teams of three.
2. Stand front to back. Imagine a corridor: a long, narrow space moving out in front and behind you, but not extending out to the sides.
3. Move up and down, over and under one another within the corridor. Respond only to the moves of your partners. Move on the same impulse. Move as one.
4. Investigate an image together. The image may be an object, a sensation, a verb, or an action.
5. Create as many varying images within the confines of the corridor as possible in three minutes. Maintain physical contact throughout.

Effort: Variable.

Observations.   Maintain physical contact throughout and respond to one another without talking. Listen with your bodies. Breathing is the connective link that will keep you in sync with one another.

Change the image often. Investigate a variety of ways of touching. Work without hands. Backs only. Or knees only. Always stay in the corridor. Work with your eyes closed. Collaborate. Define each central image together as you work. Then refine it and move on to the next. This is physical free association. Take the offer, respond, offer again.

Keep the contact strong. When you feel you are losing touch with your partners, stop. Wait. Breathe. Begin again.

Musical Combines

This is an additive pattern activity.

1. Work in teams of six to eight players.
2. If you are the first player, enter the playing space and establish a rhythmic sound and movement pattern.
3. Each player enters and adds a new rhythm to the sound and movement pattern. Each additional player transforms the shape of the combine.

4. Continue to play the same pattern until you all are working together to make the musical combine.
5. Each player uses sound and movement to participate in the combine.
6. When adding on, you must touch one another, without using your hands.
7. Use your pelvis as the center for your movement.
8. Keep the rhythms separate and distinct.
9. The sound works in conjunction with the movement and the movement in conjunction with the sound; they describe each other.
10. Transform the combine, so that it is nonmechanical in its essential nature.
11. Develop a specific musical style, i.e., symphonic, pop, jazz, rock, etc.
12. The music you create will shape and determine the physical images. The physical images will shape and determine the music.
13. Continually change the visual and physical focus within the group.
14. Justify all your actions.

Effort: Variable.

Observations.   This activity works best when you use time and weight as your triggers.

The playing style will develop once you begin listening to each other. Work quietly at first to develop a feel for one another. You can expand once you are in sync. If your sound becomes too robust too early the pulse of the

Musical Combines

activity is lost and the process of transformation happens by rote rather than spontaneously. Eventually, if you really listen to one another, it will be possible to develop melody.

Listening is another way of directing your attention. It provides a focus for your imagination. Listen with your eyes, see with your ears. Later, when working with a text, always listen to your partner to hear something specific: nuance of meaning through inflection, pause, accent and stress, use of operative words, phrasing, or pitch variation. Any focus that captures your attention will lead you into a state of absorption and flow.

Variation No. 1.   Work specifically with the music of another time and place. Work to create images that correspond to that era.

Variation No. 2.   Establish a theme and stay within the boundaries of the theme.

PATTERNS

Patterning involves learning the rules of play and developing your skills as one who plays by the rules. Rules of play involve using offers and accepts as tools for bridging with your partner. When you bridge you form a relationship with your partner involving a shared history; this creates synchronicity and flow.

Patterns are the roadmaps charting the transformation of a relationship with your partner. You will learn how to read the progression of the transformation—the score of action—to determine its inner movement. You will transform the inner with focused effort to add direction and intent to the pattern.

In the MAP you will also use patterns to develop skill in narrative action, learning to use yields, blocks, and shelves as tools in story telling.

You will also become proficient in working with creative pattern cycles. You will establish a pattern; deliberately break the pattern by using an opposite to provoke creative movement; and then integrate the new idea into the pattern to transform and advance it.

You will also begin to experiment formally with design elements in patterns. You will: create or observe a pattern; then edit it; then exaggerate or compress the pattern to give it greater clarity, definition, and meaning.

Patterns

1. Think of Nothing
2. In Nine
3. Yes Game

4. The Gift
5. Over Offers
6. Yes, And...
7. Remember When
8. You Never, You Always
9. Yield, Block, and Shelve
10. Nonverbal Scenes
11. All Yield Scenes
12. Leads
13. Balance/Dysbalance

Think of Nothing

This activity exercises the basic precepts in the process of creative thinking.

1. Lie on your back. Close your eyes.
2. Clear your mind. Release all tension in your body.
3. For one minute, think of absolutely nothing.

Effort: Variable.

Observations. Thinking of nothing is impossible. Your mind is like a switchboard, constantly sending and receiving messages, impulses, and images. This process is a constant. You never have to worry about not having a creative thought.

The impulse takes the form of pictures or images in your mind's eye. By focusing on them you engage your imagination. As you start to visualize you will establish an inner voice. The inner voice, connected to your sense of inner flow, chronicles your engagement in transforming the impulse into an image and the image into action.

In Nine

This is a "framing" activity, establishing boundaries and parameters for each pattern within the frame.

1. Lie on the floor on your back, with your eyes closed.
2. Rise to a standing position in nine counts. Use all nine counts.
3. Lie down in nine counts. Use all nine counts.
4. Then repeat, reducing one count at a time, until you rise in one count.

Effort: Variable.

Observations.   The counts are like giant parentheses—they "frame" the action.

Every action exists in its own time and space. It has a beginning, a middle, and an end. The frame ensures that you won't begin the new unit until you have completed the old one. It is a way of giving every action enough time and space to breathe and resonate.

Standing up and lying down are simple physical activities. Eliminating one count in each frame keeps changing the external parameters. Use the outer to trigger the inner—imagine the shape of your move and then transform the image into action.

Anticipation—jumping into the future—is another liability when playing this game. Do not move until you hear the first count. Inhibit your desire to start moving before the counts contract. You may need to repeat threes, twos, and ones until everyone moves at the same time.

Yes Game

The game introduces the basic offer-accept pattern, which is the foundation for all collaborative endeavors.

1. Scatter about the room.
2. Someone makes an offer: "Let's go fishing."
3. You all say "yes" out loud—you "accept" the offer.
4. You then proceed to enact the offer—you fish.
5. Someone else makes a new offer—"Let's ride on a pogo stick"—you all say "yes" out loud, and proceed to ride pogo sticks.
6. You can make an offer whenever you want.
7. You must accept every offer.
8. You can involve and engage the people around you in your activities.
9. All objects are imaginary.
10. Do everything for real.

Effort: Variable.

Observations.   Offering and accepting are the two cornerstone actions in creativity. You cannot invent on a negative impulse. You cannot move forward on "I won't," "I will not," or "It won't work." "No" blocks any creative endeavor.

Yes is the gateway into the unknown. Yes means you are willing to take risks. Yes means you are willing to try, and then, after trying, make a choice. Yes is the positive that allows you to work without preconceived value judgments about what you will discover and what you will make. You surrender to the process of discovery and embrace all possibilities. You acknowledge your fear, and then move through it into action.

An offer is anything that triggers your imagination. It is something you do to trigger your partner's imagination. You make an offer—then you accept the offer your partner makes to you, and then you make a new offer to your partner. Three steps in the process—offer, accept, offer. This is the basic creative pattern. Every game you play, every exercise, every activity, every rehearsal and performance is a variation of this interactive pattern.

Always engage the other players around you—share the task, involve someone else, and see what happens. Accept whatever they offer, and offer in return.

Return to the Yes Game often. It's fun, it's easy to do, and the possibilities are endless.

The Gift

This is a variation of offer and accepts.

Gift No. 1

1. Decide who will be A and who B.
2. A: offer your partner a gift. You must really want to give the gift.
3. B: accept the gift in the spirit in which it was offered. You must really accept the gift.
4. Use the gift in a manner appropriate to its nature.
5. Put the gift aside. Offer your partner a gift. You must really want to give the gift.
6. A: accept the gift in the spirit in which it was given. Use the gift in a manner appropriate to its nature.
7. Put the gift aside. Offer your partner a gift.
8. Continue to offer and accept gifts.
9. All gifts are imaginary.

Effort: Variable.

Observations. Follow your first impulse in using the gift after it has been offered to you.

Genuinely offer and genuinely accept the gift. Respond naturally. Do not assume a role or pretend to respond as you think you should.

Gift No. 2

1. When you make the offer—when you give the gift— trigger your partner's imagination. Offer the gift in such a way to leave the specific nature of the gift in question.

2. When you accept the offer—when you take the gift—respond to your first impulse. Define the gift by the way you use it. There is no right or wrong gift—it is what you say it is. Respond to the physical triggers—the weight, the size, and the dynamic of the gift as it is presented to you and go from there.

3. Once you've used the gift, set it aside and make an offer—present a gift to your partner. Your offer must stimulate and trigger your partner's imagination. Do not feel obligated or responsible for having to name and define the gift. Accept whatever your partner says it is.

4. Continue to offer and accept gifts.

Effort: Variable.

Observations. The playing may change with this variation. Because there is no pressure to be right, there is no need to control the playing. The game is about triggering your imagination, making offers and accepting them.

You may have a specific idea of what it is you are offering. Do not define it verbally or impose your image onto the playing. You must accept whatever it is your partner defines as "the gift." Sometimes you will be in sync with one another, sometimes not. It doesn't matter, as long as you both respond honestly to the trigger. Accept whatever is offered and continue to make offers to trigger your partner's imagination.

The value of this activity is in discovering what "the gift" is. The MAP is about discovering options, using alternatives, spontaneously moving forward from A to B to C to D. You create the As, the Bs, and the Cs, and then find ways to link them all together.

Over Offers

In this offer and accept drill you'll learn to shift and exaggerate your point of view.

1. Agree on a where and play a scene in which you overaccept every offer. You may scream, yell, shout, laugh, cry—whatever you want, as long as you exaggerate your response to the offer.

2. Once you accept the offer, make an offer of your own to your partner, who will overaccept the new offer.

3. Play the scene back and forth, overaccepting each offer.

4. Vary the pattern by "overoffering"—making the offer as dynamic, vibrant, and urgent as you can.

5. Accept the offer simply, and then overoffer to your partner.

6. Play the scene to its conclusion by either overoffering or overaccepting. Vary the pattern.

Effort: Variable.

Observations.   An offer triggers your partner's imagination. Your acceptance of your partner's offer completes the pattern. This pattern game deliberately shifts the focus from one side of the pattern to the other. Use exaggeration to change the dynamics of the playing.

This exercise involves a high release of energy if you are willing to play an entire range of response. If you feel you are getting trapped into responding in one manner, change the pattern dramatically to its opposite and see what happens.

Yes, And . . .

This accept game focuses on endowing to create the parameters of a relationship.

1. Agree on a where. Play an All Yield scene (see All Yield scenes).
2. Every sentence after the initial offer must begin with "yes, and . . .".
3. Accept every offer.

Effort: Variable.

Observations.   Using "and" allows you to accept and build upon the offer. Add to it in some way, amplify and make it more specific. When you make your own offer it must be accepted with "yes, and . . ." and the game continues.

Each offer is an endowment, in which you give your partner some fact or piece of information about the history of your relationship. Because you must accept every offer, the more extreme or outrageous you make the endowment, the more challenging the game becomes.

Once you become familiar with the pattern in the exercise, give vent to your imagination.

Variation: Yes, But . . .
1. Agree on a where. Play an All Yield scene.
2. Every sentence after the initial offer must begin with "yes, but . . .".

Effort: Variable.

Observations.   This is a completely different pattern and changes the direction of the play.

Rather than moving the action and the relationship forward with every offer, as in "yes, and . . .", "yes, but . . ." forces you to stop at each offer and become much more specific. It's as if you are digging a hole and can't quite work your way out of it. You continue to burrow deeper and deeper with every offer rather than advancing further and further into the future.

With "yes, and..." you advance the action. With "yes, but..." you continue the action. Both patterns are active, but each works in a completely different direction.

Play quickly and do not give yourself time for self-censorship. Respond to each offer with your first impulse. Build upon it as you advance the action of the scene.

Once you have played a round of "yes, and..." or "yes, but..." try this simple variation:

add: "and then you..." when you make your offer.

This shifts the focus off of you and back onto your partner. In this way you loop the action forward to deliberately include your partner with every offer.

Remember When

This game exercises another endowment pattern.

1. Sit on the floor.
2. You have an imaginary photo album between you.
3. Thumb through the album. Whenever you want, stop and point to a picture in the album and say "Remember when...".
4. Accept this offer and respond with "Yes, and then you..." and build the memory involved in that photograph together.
5. Whenever you are ready, turn the page and move on to another photo.
6. Repeat "Remember when..." and "Yes, and then you...".

Effort: Moderately sustained and light.

Observations. Name one another immediately, and define who you are to one another. Build the memory with care and precision. Add as many sensory details as you can—sights, sounds, tastes, and smells. The more you can trigger and stimulate your senses, the better.

Take your time with the memories. Work together to create a complete scene. You will know when it's time to move on to another photo. Use the pattern to engage one another in the process of defining the parameters of your past. The memory only emerges when you are in collective agreement.

You Never, You Always

Two more patterns involved in endowing and defining relationships.

You Never

1. Agree on a where and play an All Yield scene.
2. Start each sentence with "You never...".
3. Accept every offer.
4. Be specific. Keep the scene active, physical, and alive.

Effort: Quick and strong.

Observations.   Accept and build upon whatever is offered to you.
Build the history of your relationship together.
Try playing "you never" as a love scene.

You Always

1. Agree on a where. Play an All Yield scene.
2. Begin every sentence with "You always..."
3. Accept every offer.
4. Be specific. Keep the scene active, physical, and alive.

Effort: Quick and strong.

Observations.   When you play quickly you overload your mind with stimuli until there is no time to become intellectual or deliberate, or control the action. You merely have time to accept, respond, offer.

When you overload you usually respond with your first impulse. Your first impulse is your freest, truest, the most spontaneous. You always want to act on your first impulse. Overload games jam the mind to block the desire to censor the impulse.

If you are working together on a scripted scene "you always..." and "you never..." are ways to create a shared past. You accept every offer, amplify it, build upon it with your acceptance, and then make a new offer to further your history together.

Yield, Block, and Shelve

Use these patterns to develop narrative action as well as define the architectural shape or structure of a scene.

1. Divide into teams of two. Each team has a player and a coach. Decide who will be player and who coach.
2. Each coach guides his or her player into yielding, blocking, and shelving an action. You may talk to one another as you are being coached.

To yield, give the other player what he or she wants. Accept the offer and advance the action.

To block, do not give the other player what he or she wants. The action will change direction because you advance a totally different action of your own.

To shelve, block the action initiated by your partner but leave yourself open to the possibility of returning to it at another time.

3. Trade roles and play again.
4. When you are comfortable with these actions, improvise a scene. Coaches call out directions for their players on a line-by-line basis: yield, block, or shelve each offer made by the other player.

Effort: Quick and light.

Observations. This multifaceted activity involves verbal and analytical skills as well as patterning.

Yielding, blocking, and shelving are three ways of looking at narrative action to determine its shape and direction. They are different ways of perceiving patterns of action.

You become dependent on your partner for the moment-to-moment playing of the scene. You surrender your own impulses and respond to those offered by your partner. When you are both hooked into a shared collective image, you will intuit the same direction for the action.

Variation No. 1. Start the scene seated. As you become more familiar and comfortable with the exercise, try moving. Play the scene physically.

Variation No. 2. Approach a scripted scene as a Yield, Block, or Shelve exercise. Continue to play the scene with a player and a coach. Coach each beat in terms of offering and accepting yields, blocks, and shelves.

Nonverbal Scenes

Withholding language is a deliberate provocation used to intensify patterns of action within a scene. When you cannot speak you must focus all of your attention on doing.

1. Agree on a where. Play an all yield scene. Accept every offer. Make as many offers as you can.
2. You may not speak during the scene.

3. You may not use "language substitutes" such as mime or sign language.
4. Play the scene to its conclusion.

Effort: Variable.

Observations. This is a difficult activity. You are dealing exclusively with shape in space, effort patterns, and action cycles; you are exercising your ability to speak in a nonverbal language. The scene must go forward at every moment. You must rely on your partner from moment to moment to understand the nature of the relationship and the nature of the transformation within the scene.

One of the best ways to develop a "feel" for action is to work nonverbally. Your body does not lie. You cannot pretend to do something; you either do it or you don't. Everything you do in a nonverbal scene reveals the pattern of action and the intent of the action as you transform your relationship with your partner.

All Yield Scenes

This activity drills the basic structural patterns you will use in all improvised scenes.

1. Agree with your partner on a where.
2. Play the scene by making an offer. Accept the returned offer. Make another offer.
3. Accept every offer. Offer as many times as possible.
4. Give each other names early in the scene.
5. Find a way to define your relationship with one another early in the scene, by **endowing.**
6. Have a history with one another, so the scene does not become an interview. Assume a past and endow one another with facts from that past. Remember, you must accept every offer, so your partner must accept every endowment you make.
7. Begin with a physical activity that helps establish the where. It will give you something to do and take the pressure off having to talk immediately.
8. Speak only when necessary.
9. Avoid being clever.
10. Always play the scene for real.

Effort: Variable.

Observations. You will know when the scene is over.

All Yield scenes are about moving forward into the unknown future. They are about discovering the scene as you create it.

Always focus and engage yourself physically in what you are doing. Do not feel compelled to talk. You do not have to be clever, funny, or witty. Just play the scene. In an All Yield scene you drill the basic playing pattern: Offer, Accept, Offer.

Be generous with your partners. Take care of them and they will take care of you. Remember that an offer is something that triggers your partner's imagination. Each frame in the scene involves an offer, an acceptance, and a new offer. That is how the scene progresses. Blocks become evident when you are playing all yield.

Rely on your shared past with your partner to provide subject matter for the future. A shared past automatically assumes history. It makes the playing easier, because you have something in common.

Leads

Use these triggering tools to deliberately provoke your imagination when you feel "stuck" or creatively blocked.

1. Play an All Yield scene with your partner. Accept every offer. Make as many offers as possible.
2. React physically to every offer. Do not speak when you physicalize. Let your physical response lead you into speaking. Let your body "lead" you into responding.
3. Do not anticipate what you will say. Let it grow out of the physical lead.
4. Change the pattern. Respond vocally to each offer. Do not physicalize your response. Let your sound lead you into responding.
5. Do not anticipate what you will say. Let it grow out of your sound lead.
6. Alternate between physical and sound leads.
7. Bring the scene to its logical conclusion.

Effort: Quick and strong.

Observations.   Leads usually work in conjunction with thought. When mind and body are in sync, gesturing happens simultaneously with speech. Each re-enforces the other; both clarify and illustrate the thought as it develops.

Leads help break thought patterns. They are unpredictable devices that trigger spontaneous reaction.

Physical and sound leads can be used to trigger spontaneous responses at the beginning of a speech. Or they can be used internally, within a speech, to keep the thoughts active and alive.

Leads take you in unexpected directions. You must give up your preconceived response and go wherever your body takes you.

Balance/Dysbalance

This provocative activity exercises your ability to recognize and analyze synchronicity in patterning.

1. Work in groups of three.
2. Work with music to create a point-to-point set sequence involving relationships in the process of transformation. The set sequence is a fixed
   and repeatable score of action. It may be organized from the outside in,
   i.e., from random spatial relationships or from the inside out, i.e., by psychological relationships defined in space.
3. The group must strive to stay "in balance" pictorially, physically, and
   psychologically.
4. Work within an imaginary proscenium arch.
5. Create a series of "dysbalanced" relationships.
6. One group will perform while the rest of the group watches. Call out
   "balance" or "dysbalance" to identify and name what you see.
7. Tag in, one at a time, to continually change the trio of players.

Effort: Variable.

Observations.   This is a difficult activity.
   Our natural tendency is to move from a state of chaos to a state of order.
To deliberately create a state of chaos—a state of "dysbalance" in relationships—goes against our very nature. We always want to get back to a state
of harmony.
   The first half of the activity—working "in balance"—may be relatively
easy. Spatial relationships are primary. The physical relationship is always
the key to understanding the psychological relationship. Whether it is
approached from the inside out or the outside in, the relationship must be
placed in a tangible, communicable shape in space in order to exist.
   You may disagree when you are watching players work with "dysbalance." This is when the exercise becomes provocative, since you must define
what "dysbalance" means. Is it merely how the bodies are arranged in space,
or is it the balance between three players, or a combination of these factors?
   Dysbalance usually develops the moment one character becomes vulnerable to someone else. When the character takes a risk, he or she throws
off internal equilibrium and tries to find a new balance by disrupting an
established pattern. The other characters immediately adjust in an attempt
to make the relationships work by restoring the old pattern of balance.

Yielding and blocking are useful actions to experiment with in this activity. Effort factors are also crucial, especially weight and tension flow.

ENDOWMENTS

Action does not exist in isolation; every action exists within a context—in relation to every other action.

An endowment is an offer that defines who you are and where you are; it also qualifies and conditions how you play action. When you endow you establish a relationship and invest it with meaning.

Endowing creates the bridge that links you with your world, defining and clarifying your relationship with yourself, your environment, and with others in your environment.

Endowments are physicalized. They are sensory. They are experiential and practical. The endowment always manifests itself in the use of effort factors.

You will learn how to manipulate and transform your outside, through the effort factors, to physicalize the effect of the endowment. You will also use the endowment to trigger and deepen the connection between your outer and your inner.

An endowment may be an inhibiting factor, used to cover and repress an impulse, or it may be liberating, used to release withheld energy and propel you into action.

In the MAP you will use endowments to examine the three areas of relationships: With the self, you will use the endowments to create and define for your "who" a relationship and history with its past; transform that history into a physical form that gives shape and definition to the character; and identify the center, or spine, of the character, from which all choices about its intent are made.

With the environment, you use the endowments to create the sensory stimuli of the outside world that trigger and engage your imagination, rooting you in the here and now of the world you are in; and define and clarify the spoken and unspoken rules of behavior that condition and affect your action, and create a social context in which rewards and penalties for the playing are manifest and operative.

With others you will use the endowments to create a condition in which flow is possible by establishing common bonds and the parameters of a shared past; define and continually re-define the terms and conditions of the relationship as it changes in time; and condition and tone the quality of your play so that you adjust and adapt as you work with your partner.

By focusing on sensory engagement you also will use endowments to forge a link between your analytical and intuitive thinking skills. You will move out of your mind and into your body as you initiate and engage in action.

Endowments

1. As If
2. Blind Rise
3. The Running Game
4. Freeze/Go
5. Changing Tempo
6. Cross Thru
7. Squat Ten
8. Equal Spacing
9. Side Stepping
10. Active Sense Memory

As If

Use this exercise to create a neutral environment and then flood it with physical and sensory endowments.

1. Lie on the floor. Close your eyes.
2. Concentrate on the images floating across your eyelids.
3. Silently, count to ten. On the tenth count, open your eyes. See as if for the first time.
4. Silently, count to ten. On the tenth count, close your eyes. Focus on the images floating across your eyelids.
5. Repeat the sequence twice. Each time, see as if for the first time.
6. Repeat. Listen to the sounds in the room as if for the first time.
7. Repeat twice.
8. Repeat. Smell as if for the first time.
9. Repeat twice.

Effort: Variable.

Observations.   Repetition may seem boring or futile at first until you make very specific choices that guide and focus your attention. General choices lead to generalized playing.

As If is an exercise for isolating your senses through physical endowments and released energy. Tension is a protective device that shuts down and blocks stimulation and sensation. You contract and hold in. When you open your sensorium you unlock your imagination.

Sensory stimulants are always present in the environment. When you endow you deliberately build a bridge to link and use them. You focus your attention outside of yourself to engage and release your imagination.

In freeing your imagination, As If creates a context in which anything and everything is possible. As If leads you forward, into action.

Blind Rise

This is another exercise for creating a neutral environment. Stay open to your sensory impressions.

1. Lie on your back. Close your eyes. Keep your hands at your sides.
2. With your eyes closed, stand up.
3. The entire sequence should take three minutes from start to finish. The time will be called out every fifteen seconds.
4. Do not stop or pause during the rise.
5. Make your focus as simple and direct as possible.

Effort: Very sustained and light.

Observations. Imagine the physical pattern of the move. Transform the image into action. Adjust the pattern of action from moment to moment during its execution. Don't rush through all of the awkward or difficult phases of the activity—those involving weight shifts. You may feel more comfortable once you have shifted from the horizontal to the vertical plane.

Keep the effort of the movement pattern as economical as possible. Do not use more energy than you absolutely need.

Variation No. 1. Increase the amount of time allotted to the activity from three minutes to five minutes, and then from five to ten minutes.

Observations. Each increase demands greater physical and mental concentration. Don't be surprised if you feel exhausted by the intensity of your focus. Focused attention changes your perception of time. When you are absorbed in action, you lose your sense of time.

Variation No. 2. The time allocations are not called out. Estimate the amount of time you use. Adjust your effort accordingly. Justify the change of effort by using a contextual endowment.

The Running Game

This activity uses changing and flexible endowments to condition and affect the quality of your play.

1. Run across the room, one at a time.
2. Run again. Exaggerate an effort factor—time, weight, focus in space or flow—and justify the change in effort by changing a condition of the environment.

3. Run again. Change an effort factor and justify the change as an adjustment to your clothing.
4. Run again. Change an effort factor and justify the change by adding someone or something behind you.
5. Run again. Change an effort factor and justify the change by adding someone or something in front of you.
6. Keep all changes constant.
7. Run again. Change the quality of the flow one quarter of the way across the floor. Justify the change.
8. Run again. Change the quality of the run three quarters of the way across the floor. Justify the change.
9. Run again. Change the quality of the flow four times while running. Justify each change.

Effort: Quick and variable.

Observations. Flow deals with the quality of tension in an activity. Time, weight, and space merge to create flow.

During all the rounds of running, your focus in space and your target—where you are moving to—rarely change. Only the effort changes, and you justify those changes by linking them to the endowments. Endowments always condition and affect the quality of your play.

Endowments "are"—they are the inescapable facts that always exist in time and space. They may transform as relationships change, but they are always present.

You are manipulating the outer—through effort—to stimulate and engage your imagination in creating the "facts" of the context of the frame you are in. Use the "facts" of the endowment to justify the use of the effort.

Once you are familiar with endowments, work the opposite way—start with the "inner" as the endowment and give it physical life to affect and inform the quality of your play.

Select and use endowments that heighten the intensity of the playing. High stakes means high risk. High risk means dangerous playing. Dangerous playing means more intensity in the doing. More intensity means more engagement in the action.

Every action has a past and a future. The past conditions the playing in the present; the potential of the future also conditions the playing in the present. Physicalize these facts to affect your play.

Endowments are also hurdles—they are obstacles built into the context of your relationships.

Overload the hurdles and see what happens to the quality of the play. If the hurdles are sensory and affect you physically, the playing will become more immediate and direct. This means everything you do will have urgency and presence.

Do not get caught up in indicating the endowments. Instead, own them and let them affect your effort differently every time you move across the floor.

Freeze/Go

This game requires quick changes in dynamics.

1. Move around the playing space at your own tempo and rhythm.
2. Freeze.
3. Go. Resume moving.
4. Freeze. Move forward. Freeze. Move backward. Freeze. Move sideways. Freeze. Walk on your toes. Freeze. Walk on your heels. Freeze. Walk on the inside of your feet. Freeze. Walk on the outside.
5. Move on your tip-toes. Justify the action. Freeze.
6. Stay on your toes. Reach up. Reach down. Justify each action. Freeze.
7. Justify every change in rhythm, tempo, or direction.

Effort: Quick and strong.

Observations.   Balance in each freeze. If you are working high, on your tip-toes, don't let your heels come down and touch the floor.

This game involves risk taking. The more dangerous the movement, the more outrageous the gesture, the harder it is to maintain the balance in freeze, the better. Continually challenge yourself in playing. Push through the times when you want to ease up; the discipline will yield rewards. Creation doesn't happen without discipline.

This activity begins with general playing and becomes more and more specific. Use endowments to create forwardness of action for each sequence.

Every action has a target. It is what you want, and it leads you into action.

You can justify any action. Justifying supplies the reason for the doing. Justifying an action answers the basic question: Why did I do that? Motivating an action answers another basic question: Why am I going to do that? Either before or after the action, there has to be a reason for the doing.

Freeze/Go exercises your ability to justify every action by creating interesting endowments to condition, qualify, and affect the target. Because the playing is very physical, and the freezes are random and therefore, unpredictable, you must be present at every moment—you cannot mentally drift. You only have time to respond, do, respond again.

Create a highly charged playing environment by engaging your imagination in creating endowments. Always include the other players as part of the endowments of an environment.

This game is an excellent refresher/charger in the course of any class or rehearsal. Use Freeze/Go to change the dynamics within the room and activate your partners.

Changing Tempo

Use this activity to examine your individual relationship to a group.

1. Move around the room in your own tempo and rhythm. Establish a consistent tempo for your walk.
2. Continually change the direction of your walk. The shape of the movement pattern should be unpredictable.
3. Add environmental endowments to create a where: the time of day, the quality of the light, the temperature, the smells, the textures of the environment.
4. Justify being in the where.
5. Include the people around you as part of the contextual endowments. Endow and create specific relationships with them.
6. Without leading and without following, work together to slow down the walking tempo. Justify the change in the tempo by changing your relationship with the people around you.
7. If the endowments stop feeding your imagination, change them.
8. Walk without making noise. Justify the need for absolute silence.
9. Walk without touching anyone. Justify no touch.
10. Keep your focus at eye level at all times.
11. Once the tempo is extremely sustained, reverse the process and increase the tempo until it is extremely quick.
12. Work without leading or following. Change the tempo together. Justify the change in tempo.

Effort: Variable.

Observations.   Maintain a sense of your individual contribution to the changing tempo. At the same time, remember that this is a group enterprise. You must all collaborate if you are to change the tempo in tandem.

You will feel uncomfortable with the walk until you add endowments to create an environment for yourself to work in. When you invest in the endowments and make them tangible and physical, it is easier to use them as hurdles to strengthen and maintain your interest in the playing.

When you improvise, the endowment is the first offer you make to your partner when playing. You tell your partner who she is, and what the relationship means to you. When you work with a prepared text, the playwright gives you clues about the endowments within the relationship, but you must still fill the clues with your own meaning. Endowing is a way of investing in the action, of creating stakes worth fighting for.

Move from this game directly into Cross Thru.

Cross Thru

This overload game uses built-in endowments to heighten group contact.

1. Move rapidly around the playing space. Always move through the center of the space.
2. Do not touch one another when moving. Justify your tempo. Justify no touch.
3. Gradually shrink the size of the playing area. Let the boundaries close in. Continue to move through the center of the space. Continue to justify no touch.
4. As the playing area contracts, increase your tempo. Continue no touch. Continue to justify the action.
5. Freeze. Release.

Effort: Quick and light.

Observations.   This is a rapid-fire game. There is no time to think, only time to act. The tempo should accelerate throughout the playing.

Once you have established a comfortable rhythm, you will tend to settle into it. In Changing Tempo, you worked to slow the tempo down—that's part of the forward motion of the game. In Cross Thru, you work to accelerate the tempo. There should never be a moment when you are idling, or marking, the action. Action always moves you forward in time and space.

No Touch increases the level of difficulty in the playing, especially as the space contracts. Create a penalty for making physical contact, and see how it affects the quality of your play.

This activity involves both offensive and defensive playing. There is no way you can win. Your focus is on playing, and increasing the quality of your play. You increase the quality of your play by creating challenging endowments that engage your imagination. When your imagination is engaged, you work from the inside out as well as from the outside in.

Squat Ten

This progressively high risk game uses hurdles to trigger endowments.

Squat No. 1

1. Form a circle.
2. Turn around, back to the center of the circle. Play backwards.
3. Move through the center of the circle without touching one another.

4. If someone touches you, or if you touch someone, squat down to the floor, silently count to ten and then resume moving to the other side of the circle.
5. Once you are safely through the circle, turn around and repeat the activity. The playing is continuous.
6. Do not look behind you while moving.

Squat No. 2

1. Repeat Squat No. 1.
2. You may not touch anyone while moving.
3. You have a secret. The secret explains why no touch is imperative.
4. Change your secret whenever it diminishes the intensity of your playing.

Squat No. 3

1. Repeat Squat No. 2.
2. Increase the intensity of the secret.
3. Close your eyes. Play blinded.

Effort: Variable.

Observations.   The quality of the play changes dramatically between rounds one, two, and three.

In round no. 1 there isn't a reason for doing anything. Your focus is random and scattered, and you don't have any relationships or endowments to charge the playing or make it vital.

Endowments take you forward. Once you add your secret and create boundaries and conditions for the game, the quality of your playing improves. No Touch gives you a purpose, a reason, an intent to inform your playing—to make it to the other side of the circle intact. You automatically endow everyone around you—they are potential threats to your safety. Because there are consequences to your action—stakes—playing carefully becomes mandatory, as a matter of survival. You can feel the tension in the circle. It's dangerous. And it's more interesting.

Blindness, in round no. 3, increases the danger quotient. By removing two senses, sight and touch, you compensate by using the other three. The atmosphere feels more electric and you play much more slowly, more carefully, with greater focus and deliberation. Your engagement is total. There is excitement to your playing.

Playing is both offensive and defensive. There is no way you can win. Winning has no value or meaning in the game. The value of the game is in the playing of it, and playing well.

Accept the unpredictable. There is no way you can control the behavior of any other player. Stay responsible for the quality of your own playing, and adjust/adapt to the unpredictable.

Remember to breathe when you play. Do not cue one another with sound. You must play in silence. Justify the silence.

Equal Spacing

This activity strengthens adjusting and adapting skills.

1. Scatter around the playing space.
2. Adjust so that you are equidistant from the person on your right, on your left, in front, and behind you.
3. Move one step at a time in any direction. You must remain equidistant from your partners at all times.
4. Play with freezes and stop-starts.
5. Endow your partners. Justify the need for maintaining equidistance through the quality of the endowment.
6. Keep your focus at eye level. If you are caught with your focus on the floor, you will be "snapped" out of the game.

Effort: Moderately sustained and light.

Observations.   You will want to play quickly at first, moving rapidly into any open space around you. Slow down and take your focus off yourself and onto your partners.

When you are your primary focus, you exist in a void. There is nothing to trigger your imagination, no one to make you move forward into action. There is only self-consciousness and a sense of idling in time and space.

When you shift your focus onto another player you build a bridge to the world. When you begin to endow your partner you engage yourself in a world of action. Endowing forces you to lose your self-awareness; your focus is on your relationships with others and not on yourself. You will lose all sense of awkwardness when you give yourself over to action.

Acting involves interacting, absorbing energy, and responding to it. You respond to energy by adjusting and adapting. Adjust and adapt are reactive actions, but they are perceived as active, because they involve changing the focus of the energy in a spontaneous way.

Take the time you need to react to each adjustment your partners make. Adjust to their moves. Adapt your playing to respond to them. They will be doing the same with you. You are constantly triggering one another, working with the same endowments, but adapting them to suit the needs of your own particular imagination.

Side Stepping

In this activity you use endowments to bridge with your partners and create a context for the action.

1. Stand in a circle with your legs wide apart.
2. Shift your weight to your left.
3. Step to your left and lift your right foot off the floor, heel-to-toe.
4. Place your foot down, toe-to-heel.
5. Continue side stepping to the left.
6. Change direction. Side step to the right.
7. Expand the size of the circle by continuing to side step to the right.
8. Justify the expansion by endowing your partners—give yourself a reason for moving apart.
9. Develop relationships with the person on your right, on your left, and opposite you.
10. Arrive at a communal sense of time and place.
11. Freeze.
12. Repeat the entire activity using As If.

Effort: Variable.

Observations. Although you are all engaged in the same activity, you play in different ways, with different rules and different endowments. Ultimately, however, you all want to play together in the same world.

You create a world by agreeing with one another. Agreement is your collective contract. It is another form of the Yes Game. You make a contract with one another to agree. You may even agree to disagree. Define your rules and know your boundaries. Honor them. If you violate your contract, you break a trust, and you can no longer work together.

In Side Stepping you must find a way to come together. You need a communal impulse to set your world in motion. When you endow one another and form relationships with your partners your energy has an outward focus and flow.

Read the body language of your partners. Adjust and adapt to one another. Let the images "jiggle" back and forth between you. "Jiggling" is an extremely important part of the creative process. It is a collaborative effort; you move images back and forth between you, advancing them by challenging one another until the image roots itself in your body, triggers an impulse and moves you forward into action.

"Jiggling" is also a way of free associating with one another without performance pressure. Pressure is a positive factor when you want to make choices and shape your work and need strong boundaries. But it can be an inhibiting element in the early phases of work, when you want to come together in a leisurely, playful way. "Jiggling" the endowments to affect the quality of your play is one way of building spontaneity into your work process.

Active Sense Memory

In this activity experiment with environmental and sensory endowments to trigger your inner flow and deepen your engagement in playing.

1. Begin in the Neutral Stance with your eyes closed.
2. Image a specific character from a specific play. Keep your focus of the character sharp and clear. Fill the image with physical details of what the character looks like and is wearing.
3. Open your eyes and stay with the character image.
4. Walk with the image until the character mask begins to form.
5. Imagine and then walk in an environment suitable for the character.
6. Find a chair and sit in it. The chair has a memory connected with it. Recall the memory.
7. Stand. Find another way of sitting in the chair, and another memory associated with the chair.
8. Find an object in the room. Pick it up and examine it. Let the object trigger a memory. Find four different objects in the room and recall four different memories, each triggered by the objects.
9. Look around and recognize an old friend. Greet one another.
10. Maintain physical contact with one another.
11. Find a place to sit and recall a shared experience. Use Remember When.
12. Separate and return to your starting position.
13. Close your eyes and remove the mask.
14. Open your eyes and walk about the playing space.

Effort: Variable.

Observations.   The emphasis throughout is on touch, sight, sound, taste, and smell. Use anything connected with your senses to trigger an image or a memory. Let any memory trigger your senses.

You will not be inhabiting your own memories but those of your character. Use objects found in the present, throughout the playing space, to trigger your sensory imagination of the past. Endow those objects with personal meaning for your character. When creating a collaborative memory with your partner, accept each new sensual image as if it really happened.

Continually endow the objects you work with as well as the environment you are in. You do not exist in a void. You are always in a specific place, and you always have a specific relationship with your environment.

THIRD TRIAD: STRUCTURING THE ACTION

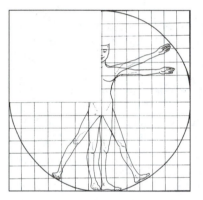

In the third triad of the MAP you will focus on structuring action. You will work with three specific areas of attention to examine the dynamics of action in relationships: status, targets, and hurdles. To study the structure and dynamics of relationships you will improvise and play scenes created from your imagination.

You will initiate, engage, and complete frames—or units—of action. You will link the frames together to form a sequence—or score—of action. Every action within the score has a structural purpose. It moves the story forward. The score is the architecture of the scene.

Every action involves making a move to change the balance within a relationship. You will examine your relationships with yourself, with your environment, and with others in your environment.

In Status you will examine the moment-to-moment balance which affects all relationships. You will learn to raise and lower as well as widen and narrow the gap.

By using Targets you will develop a technique for directing your focus forward and out, so that your playing has intent and purpose.

In Hurdles you will focus on overloading to develop skills in blocking over-intellectualization. You will integrate internal and external endowments to intensify the quality of your play and you will continue to use provocation as a deliberate tool to stimulate your imagination.

In this triad you also will begin to develop a formal technique for moving from your intuitive right brain to your analytical left brain, and then merge and synthesize these two ways of perceiving through focused play.

The dynamics of your play will transform as you become bolder and more confident in making choices for action.

You will strengthen your skills by exercising them with progressively more complex problems in creativity, requiring the integration of the outer and inner in order to solve problems with increasing dexterity, agility, and imagination.

Combined, these three factors focus on intensifying engagement through forward motion, clarity of relationships, and increased awareness of skills involved in the creative process.

STATUS

Status tells you who you are and who you are with. Status creates the structural architecture of every scene and is the balancing act between you and your partner. Every move you make, either physically or psychologically, defines your position in relationship to your partner.

A status gap identifies the degree of tension that exists between you and your partner at any given moment in a scene. Status and the gap are transformational; they are always relative to the endowments of time, place and context. When you focus on status you focus on the movement in your relationship between your inner and outer selves; yourself and your environment; and your self and the objects and people in your environment.

In this module, when you focus on status with your self you will learn to define the difference between the inner and the outer selves, separating who you, as the character, think you are from who you want the world to see; and use status to establish your cover, which hides and protects the inner from the world, and create your history and biography to give definition and shape to your patterns of action.

When you focus on status with your environment you will learn to use outward focus to bridge with the world around you; define your gap with the world in order to position yourself in your context; and create a clear and specific context for yourself so your actions will be appropriate and in sync with your world.

When you focus on status with others you will learn to establish balance from moment to moment through positioning, adjusting, and adapting to your partner; define and use a target to affect and change the balance in your relationship through forward motion with intent and purpose; and raise and lower your partner in order to widen or narrow the gap.

You also will focus on status within groups to study hierarchies and pecking orders. You will learn to define the social boundaries and cultural perimeters that govern and inform interaction.

Status roots you in your world, providing a base of security about who and where you are. When you know who you are to one another you will know how to affect one another.

Status provides a structural context for making moves to affect and change your partner. Playing by the rules creates an environment for spontaneity and forwardness in action.

Status

1. Status Bodies
2. The Peel
3. Triangles
4. Seesaws
5. Raising and Lowering/Compliments and Insults
6. Status Transformations
7. Maxi and Mini Gaps
8. Pyramids

Status Bodies

Use this activity to investigate the physicalized shape of status.

1. Stand in a Neutral Stance.
2. Keep your focus at eye level at all times.
3. Lift your spine and chest.
4. Work with strong gestures. Everything is specific, firm, direct.
5. Use a wide stance. Cover a lot of space when you walk and move.
6. Walk around the room, meeting and greeting people. You are at a high school reunion. Endow one another with names and a history.
7. Return to neutral.
8. Shift your focus to the floor. Let it dart or flick up and down rapidly.
9. Sink through the chest and spine. Everything in your body wants to sink or turn in on itself.
10. Move with small, quick steps. Everything you do is indirect and quick.
11. Move around the room, meeting and greeting at your high school reunion.
12. Freeze. Standing with a partner, decide who is A and who B.
13. A: work with strong body and direct gaze. B: work with quick body and indirect gaze.
14. Reverse roles.
15. Freeze. Release.

Effort: Variable.

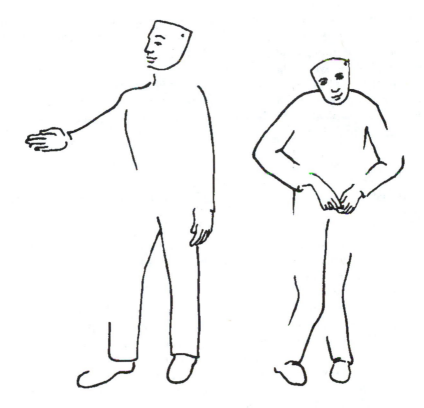

Status Bodies

Observations.   Your eyes are the key to the Status Body.

Working with strong body and steady gaze, you wear the high status body. High status bodies tend to radiate strength and energy. They are comfortable in space and appear to be comfortable with themselves. The direction and focus of the body is outward.

Working with quick body and indirect gaze, you wear the low status body. Low status bodies tend to apologize. They appear uncomfortable with themselves in space. Every body part turns in and implodes.

Your status is always relative to your context and to the endowments of your time and place. One of these bodies will feel more comfortable than the other. Whichever body feels least comfortable is the body you need to focus on most. Develop flexibility in moving between the two. There will be time to specialize later.

Use your eyes as your key into the Status Body. Investigate the use of direct and indirect focus to establish patterns of contact.

Eye contact is an important tool in developing the score of action of a scene. Sometimes it is impossible to play a scene with your partner if you do not look at one another. Or it is equally impossible to play a scene if you never break your eye contact with one another. "Eye lock" may be useful as a rehearsal tool at one stage in a scene's development, but once you have established contact, realize you don't always have to look at one another in order to communicate. Use the eye focus as a key in charting your character's status.

The Peel

This transformational activity examines the complexities of self-endowed status.

1. Use putty masks (see Masks) to create a face and body for a character.
2. Once you mold the character, find its walk. Define your status through your walk and body shape.
3. Find your voice.
4. Greet one another, engage in conversation.
5. In the middle of the conversation, begin to peel: strip away the outer shell of your character in order to reveal another character just below the surface. This new character has either a slightly higher or slightly lower status. Let your new status trigger your physical transformation.
6. Resume playing. Establish relationships based on the new characters and their status with one another.
7. Peel this character away to reveal another character just below the surface.
8. Liberate this character. Strip it off.
9. Freeze.
10. Move quick and light. Balloon breathe.

Effort: Variable, usually strong.

Observations.   Inside every outer there is an inner waiting to become an outer.

Let the face determine the emotional life of the character and its status as you peel. Keep the face fixed and frozen in the emotional expression of each character. Sink into each character; surrender to it and allow it to take over. The experience will be intense, but you can peel down to the next layer whenever you want.

Variation No. 1.   Play using animal images for The Peel. Each layer reveals another animal aspect of the character. The animals should be imaginary.

Variation No. 2. Do an age transformation. Each layer of The Peel exposes the character at an earlier/older age. Status develops and changes as the transformation progresses.

Triangles

This exercise physicalizes the process of moment-to-moment balance in relationships.

Triangle No. 1

1. Select a partner, same size and weight. Decide who will be A, who B. Stand face to face.
2. If you are A, walk forward until you step lightly onto your partner's feet.
3. Hold on to each other's wrists and touch noses.
4. Keep your heels in place. Slowly lean apart from one another until your arms are fully extended. Lock your elbows. Pull your shoulders down into your back.
5. Reverse direction. Pull in towards one another. Stand nose to nose. Step off your partner's feet.
6. Repeat the entire sequence, reversing top arms and feet.

Effort: Moderately sustained and moderately light.

Triangle No. 2

1. Repeat Triangle No. 1.
2. Once you have extended out into the triangle, bend your knees. Slowly work your way down to the floor. Continue to hold on to one another's wrists.
3. Sit on the floor. Both hips must touch the ground. Extend your arms fully.
4. Reverse directions. Return to the triangle.
5. Return to your beginning position.
6. Repeat the entire sequence, reversing top arms and legs.

Effort: Moderately sustained and moderately light.

Triangle No. 3

1. Repeat Triangle No. 1.
2. Once you are in the extended Triangle, begin to seesaw. Shift your pelvis forward and back to vary your weight; move up and down to counterbalance one another.

Triangles

3. Continue to seesaw up and down while pushing and pulling back and forth. Vary the height and weight as you go from standing to sitting and from sitting to standing.

Effort: Variable.

Observations. Don't be afraid to go off balance. Once that happens you can continue to play without fear. The worst that can happen is that you will land somewhat abruptly. Your partner is there to help you at all times.

You must surrender at the beginning of the game to the danger involved in balancing and trust your partner to help you. There is no way to win. Both of you are in the game together. In order for the game to continue, you must work together at every moment, including those moments when you go off balance. Rely on your partner to join with you in arriving at a state of balance. Relinquish control. Counterbalance your partner.

Keep your pelvis engaged and forward. Drop your shoulders; they should form a straight line with your pelvis. You will go off balance the moment you pull back with your pelvis.

Look at each other. When you break eye contact, you break the connection between you. Remember to breathe. Release the breath with sound. Always hold each other's wrists; palms get sweaty, and you could pull apart and injure yourself.

Variations. When you seesaw, play a nonverbal scene. Engage in a silent dialogue with one another. Justify the moment-to-moment shifts and changes in the balance by changing the dynamics of the relationship through the endowments.

Seesaws

This activity extends the Seesaw principle of balance and moving into direct interaction with a shared activity.

Seesaw No. 1

1. Sit opposite your partner.
2. There is an imaginary substance on the floor. Without talking, define the substance and create an object with it.
3. While the object is under construction, define your status.
4. Do something to change it.
5. Freeze.

Effort: Quick and light.

Observations.   While you may readily agree on the imaginary substance and set about building an imaginary object with it, defining your status may be more difficult.

Status does not necessarily involve power, although power may be one of the elements involved in your relationship.

Seesaw No. 2

1. Return to the construction of the imaginary object with the imaginary substance.
2. Continue to create the object. Do something to define the status of your partner.
3. When ready, do something simultaneously to change your partner's status.
4. Once you have changed the status, redefine your relationship. Make it more specific.
5. Continue and advance the status reversals.
6. Freeze.

Effort: Quick and usually strong.

Observations.   You may initially move into role playing with broad or stereotypical attitudes. The action becomes more interesting when the relationships and the endowments become more specific.

Seesaw No. 3

1. Finish creating the imaginary object with the imaginary substance.
2. Change status as quickly as possible.

Effort: Quick and light.

Variation.   Play within a set time limit; play for one minute and change status six times.

Observations.   Your focus will shift from building the object to affecting your partner. Continue to focus on completing the construction.

By Seesaw No. 3 you will have a strong feel for status shifts and status action, even if the moves themselves are not entirely clear. Focus on the sensation of relationships transforming. Keep your focus on your partner.

Scenes are about relationships changing. The more comfortable you are experiencing the moment-to-moment shifts, changes, adaptations, and adjustments, the more lively, spontaneous, and active your playing will become.

Do not confuse your own status with that of the character you are playing.

Status involves physical relationships and mental attitude. Status is a tool for creating and defining structure in a scene. When your relationships are specific, your moves are specific. When your moves are specific your playing has clarity, intent, and focus.

Raising and Lowering/Compliments and Insults

These are specific status moves.

Compliments

1. Agree on a where and play an All Yield scene with your partner (see All Yield Scenes, Endowments). Name each other and define your relationship as soon as you can. Accept every offer. Make as many offers as possible.
2. Gradually compliment one another. Let the compliments develop naturally in the course of the action. Compliment one another as much as possible.

Effort: Variable.

Observations.   When you compliment your partner, you raise your partner's status.

Insults

1. Agree on a where and play an All Yield scene with your partner. Name each other and define your relationship as soon as you can. Accept every offer. Make as many offers as possible.
2. Gradually, in the course of the scene, begin to insult one another. Continue to insult each other throughout the scene.

Effort: Variable.

Observations.   When you insult your partner you lower your partner's status.

Status is a seesaw. You always counterbalance one another, continually adjusting and adapting as the relationship changes.

These status shifts—these adjustments—are what playing is about. It is impossible to play a status transformation alone. Your focus is always on your partner and the effect you are having on him.

Playing an all compliments or an all insults scene becomes static because the relationships never vary. You may start to feel you are treading water—you want something more to happen. More forward movement. More conflict. More action.

Compliments and Insults

1. Agree on a where. Play an All Yield scene with your partner. Name each other and define the relationship as soon as you can. Accept every offer and make as many offers as you can.
2. Raise and lower your partner's status throughout the course of the scene. Do not predetermine who you are or what you will do in the course of the scene. See how the relationship shifts and changes.

Effort: Variable.

Observations.   With Compliments and Insults, the relationship is unpredictable and the playing is more dynamic and interesting. You have control over the elements within the scene, yet you cannot direct the course of the action.

When you raise or lower your partner, you create a status gap, defining the distance that exists between you in the relationship. When the gap is large, the raising and lowering is easier to see. When the gap is small, the adjustments are more minimal and subtle.

Status action involves widening or narrowing the gap between you and your partner. You may work on changing the gap in psychological, social, emotional, political, or physical terms. The gap is concrete, tangible, and a definite presence in every relationship. It gives you something to focus on at all times.

Raising and lowering as well as widening and shrinking the gap are generic structural moves that become more specific in their context. These moves determine the structure of the score of action within a set score by the playwright. By engaging in them you move out of inertia and into change by adding forwardness to your play.

Status Transformations

Advanced seesawing, this activity defines another structural pattern inherent in scenes.

1. Agree on a where and play an All Yield scene. Accept every offer. Make as many offers as you can.
2. One of you begins the scene with high status, the other, low status.
3. In the course of the scene, exchange status positions.
4. Make the transformation as smooth, seamless and even as possible.

Effort: Variable.

Observations. As with any transformation, play without "jumps" (see Zig Zags, Transformation). The transformation happens through a series of offers and accepts; the process is gradual and in continual motion.

In the first few frames of the scene you usually endow one another to establish the context and history of your relationship. Do not predetermine who is high and who low; discover that as you play.

Once you begin the transformation, continue and advance. Do not idle or stall. Keep the action and the thought moving forward. You will know when you are idling—nothing new will be happening; the relationship will feel static. Return to offering and accepting to keep the sequence alive and in motion.

You may discover that you feel more comfortable in one position than the other. High may be easy, low difficult, or vice versa. Whichever position is most difficult for you is the one you should focus on. You want to develop as much flexibility and mobility as possible. You cannot do that if you become a specialist, locked into playing one position all the time.

Do not confuse your status with the status of the character you are playing.

A status transformation is a structural pattern. There are five status moves: raising your partner, lowering your partner, widening the gap, narrowing the gap, or maintaining the gap.

Maxi and Mini Gaps

This is a tool for defining status in roles and positions.

1. Play an All Yield scene. Accept every offer. Make as many offers as possible.
2. One of you will be the master, the other the servant.
3. Master is getting dressed for the day.
4. The master calls the servant by the servant's first name as often as possible in the course of the scene.
5. The servant calls the master Sir, or Madame, as often as possible in the course of the scene.
6. Focus on completing the tasks of preparation and dressing.

Effort: Variable.

Observations. Master/servant scenes use exaggerated positioning to create maxi gaps—the largest gap possible between people. Often gaps are unpredictable; sometimes the servant is high and the master low. Positioning is always relative to the endowments of its context.

Master/servant allows you to see the gap with clarity because it is extreme. Substitute different names for master/servant and see what happens: mother/father, husband/wife, employer/employee, parent/child. You will discover how status works in all these contexts and situations.

Variation. Work with a mini gap. A mini gap relationship is closer, more balanced, and less extreme. Mirror one another physically. Keep the shifts small and extremely tight—nothing major, just small moves up and down the status ladder.

Pyramids

This activity investigates status as it affects a group.

1. Agree on a where.
2. Enter the where and begin performing a task.
3. The second person to enter will be either one step above you on the status ladder, or one step below you. She behaves accordingly.
4. The third person to enter will either be a step above or one step below the second player.
5. The Pyramid should build in only one direction: either high or low. Do not change direction once it has begun. The first player is always neutral until his position is defined by the second player.
6. Do not play with more than four players.

Effort: Variable.

Observations.   Pyramids are fixed hierarchies. They do not shift, change, or move. The task is to come in exactly one step above or one step below the previous player. Maintain your position throughout the course of the scene.

Every group has its own pecking order and hierarchy. Your task is to know where in the pyramid your character falls, and whether your target involves raising, lowering, or maintaining your position.

Pyramids deal with social order and your relationship within a group. While the positioning may be static and rigid, it is vital to know where your character fits in, and what you must do in order to define your status within the group.

TARGETS

Every action has an intent, a meaning, a point of focus. The intent, or point of focus, defines the target of your action. It is what you aim for; it is where you want your status with your partner to be by the end of each frame. Using a target makes you define what you want and it leads you into doing something to get it.

To hit your target you need to know who you are, where you are, who you are with, what you want, what you will do to get what you want, and why you want it. Targets are always expressed as verbs: "to win, to pursue, to arouse." They are always active, specific, and physical.

Targets are influenced by the endowments—the rules of play that govern the world you are in—and by your status and relationship with the other players in your world. Targets become more specific as your perception of your context and world becomes more specific; they change from frame to frame, scene to scene, act to act. The targets are the structure that makes logical sense out of your patterns of action. Targets are always pulled forward by a magnet—something you want for yourself that exists at the end of the scene.

The only way to get something you want for yourself is to affect and change the people around you. The target is always something you want rather than something you feel. Working with targets requires flexibility and dexterity. By working with targets you will strengthen your ability to start with your body to unlock your mind.

You will begin by initiating physical action and then engage your mind to give it intent and meaning. By repeating the action you will define and clarify its intent. As the intent becomes specific you will adjust and adapt the endowments to hit your target with power, precision, and directness.

In Targets you exercise your skill in moving from your intuitive right brain to your analytical left brain and then synthesize the two processes through focused play. You will learn to consciously work from the outer to the inner to the outer.

Targets

1. Hit the Mark
2. Felt Tip Pens
3. Changing Places
4. Cock Fight
5. The Hunter and the Hunted
6. Unnoticed Gesture
7. I Love You
8. Changing Focus
9. The Squeeze

Hit the Mark

This activity deals with the forward motion of a target.

1. Imagine the floor is divided into a series of parallel lines. Stand with your feet as wide as your shoulders. Line up the outside edges of your feet so they touch two of the parallel lines.
2. Shift your weight forward. Try and define "the mark," i.e., the single point of balance before you fall forward. Once you have established that point, hit the mark and hold it.
3. Repeat, finding your backward "mark."
4. Repeat, finding the mark to your right.
5. Repeat, finding the mark to your left.
6. Return to center. Find your forward mark. Hit it. Hold it. Get up on your toes and continue to hold the mark. Imagine you are on the edge of a snake pit. Continue to hold the mark.
7. Return to center.
8. Release.

Effort: Moderately quick and strong.

Observations. You will want to play it safe. However, you will never be able to define or hit the mark unless you are willing to go beyond it. Falling in any direction means confronting the unknown. It requires courage, curiosity, and a sense of adventure. When you are willing to go "over the top" you confront your own fear of the unknown. Through that confrontation you have defined a new boundary, learning how far you can go in any one direction, and what the consequences are if you exceed the boundary.

When you fall forward, use your hands to help break the fall. Remember to breathe. When you are afraid, release the fear by adding sound to your breath.

Falling backwards is more threatening than falling forwards. You don't need to crash to the floor, although that may happen. Use your hands to help take the fall.

Once you hit the mark, come as far forward as you can. Come right to the edge and flirt with danger. Danger is a positive element. It exists as a result of the power of your belief in your imagination. It forces you to increase the intensity of your effort in avoiding or overcoming it, and therefore moves you forward.

Hit the Mark is about aiming for a target and then hitting it.

Felt Tip Pens

This targeting activity exercises forwardness in action by playing to the end of the frame.

Pen No. 1

1. Begin in a circle in the Neutral Stance. Place your heels together and turn your toes out.
2. Imagine a large sheet of beautiful, handmade paper, suspended from the ceiling, resting six inches above your head.
3. Imagine a felt tip pen, balanced in the center of your head. The tip of the pen touches the center of the sheet of paper.
4. Anchoring your weight, rotate your body and draw an expanding spiral. Begin in the center of the paper; the spiral starts small and grows larger and larger, until it can no longer fit on the sheet of paper.
5. The pen must stay in contact with the paper at all times. If you lean forward or backward you will break contact with the paper and must start over again.
6. Draw with a smooth, unbroken line.
7. Reverse the process and draw a decreasingly concentric spiral. Move from large to small, with one fluid, unbroken line.

Effort: Variable.

Pen No. 2

1. Divide into two groups. Stand at opposite ends of the playing space. The more space between you, the better. Decide which team will be team A

and which B. Team A will move first, while team B watches. When team A finishes, team B will work.

2. Imagine two sheets of paper, each sheet no higher than your shoulders. The sheets extend the length of the room, to the wall opposite, forming a corridor. You are in the center of the corridor.

3. You now have two felt tip pens, one in each ear. The tip of each pen extends out of your ears and touches the sheets of paper.

4. Move across the playing space. Draw a single, unbroken diagonal line on the paper. The line begins at ear height and ends on the floor at the opposite end of the room. The descending line must be smooth and unbroken.

Effort: Variable, but usually quick.

Pen No. 3

1. Repeat Felt Tip Pen No. 2.
2. The entire activity, from start to finish, must last three minutes. Use all 180 seconds to draw the line. The time will be called out every fifteen seconds.

Effort: Sustained and light.

Observations. All of the Felt Tip activities should be done in sequence, without interruption. The impact of the activity is cumulative.

Focus on your target—where you want to be at the end of the activity. When you have something specific to do, it is easy to become absorbed in action. Focused attention directs your energy forward and out. If you have a target—a goal, something you want that has meaning for you—you can move towards it in a straight line. That movement forward is action.

You may want to look down to the floor when you are working on Felt Tip Pen No. 1. Downward focus is an indication of deep inward concentration. Sometimes you will work with downward focus, sometimes with focus at eye level. Always use your eyes to trigger and direct your attention.

Action becomes more difficult, and more interesting, when you define its context and use dynamic endowments as hurdles. The endowment conditions and affects the quality of your playing because it gives you something to resist or overcome. It adds urgency and intensity to the situation.

Time is the hurdle in Felt Tip Pens.

Changing Places

This fast-paced, highly energized activity exercises design skills with endowments, physical targets, and pattern making within an additive format.

No. 1

1. Form a large circle.
2. Choose one player to be "it."
3. If you are "it" stand in the center of the circle.
4. When the "it" calls "go," look around the circle. The moment you make eye contact with another player start to change places with them. Move through the center of the circle to reach your partner's vacated spot.
5. If you are "it", try to reach that vacated spot before the moving player. If you do, the moving player becomes the new "it" in the center of the circle.
6. Walk through a practice round until you all understand how the game works. Once everyone is comfortable with the game, play at a brisk tempo.

Effort: Quick and strong.

Observations. The player in the center is looking to rejoin the circle. Players in the circle are looking to relocate. Everyone has a simple, tangible target.

Targets must be doable and within the realm of probability for the player or character. They must be specific, and are always expressed as a verb. They are always positive and always involve another player. They are what you want: "I want to ..." or "I want you to ...". A target leads you into action.

Because this activity is highly physical and involves a great deal of running, assume responsibility for physical control. When you lose physical control, you lose your sense of awareness. Accidents happen when you aren't aware. Prevent an accident by staying alert and in control of yourself.

This game demands eye contact and agreement. You may not move across the playing space unless you and your partner agree to move. If you begin to move without agreement, you will be stranded.

Move only to a targeted spot in the circle. You may not create your own spot simply to get into the circle. Although a spot in the circle represents safety and security, the excitement of the playing is in getting out into no-man's land and seeing what happens.

The circle may seem chaotic at times because everyone is moving at once. If you lose the "it" or if you have more than one "it," stop and select a new "it" and then begin again.

Once the "it" calls the first "go," the playing is continuous.

No. 2

1. Resume playing.

2. Every time you arrive at a new spot in the circle, say the word "frame" out loud.

Observations. Think of the space within the circle as a playing field. A field of action, in which anything and everything can happen.

A "frame" is a unit of action. Each frame has a beginning, a middle, and an end. When the action changes, the frame changes.

No. 3

1. Resume playing.
2. Continue calling out the "frames."
3. Find a way to accent the beginning of each frame. Place all of the dramatic stress and focus on the "trigger."

Observations. The central organizing principle of the activity is agreement—how you make eye contact with your partner and say "yes" to one another. Make a quick, nonverbal contract to engage with one another for each frame with your eyes.

Find a way to highlight and accentuate this action. Endow one another, create a dramatic context for your move. Make this initiating gesture the most important element within the frame.

To help accent the trigger, create contrast. Make the rest of the frame less meaningful. Don't throw it away or abandon it, but place the stress where you want it to be.

The "trigger" moves you forward. It stimulates your imagination and propels you into action.

No. 4

1. Resume playing.
2. Move the accent to the middle of the frame. Continue to use a trigger, but accent the "hook," when the two of you come together as you cross through the center of the circle.
3. Something must happen between the two of you when you "hook."
4. Finish the frame after you have accented the hook.

Observations. The hook moves the highlight off the impulse forward and directs it into your transaction with your partner by adding a target.

When you meet, respond to your impulse with each other. The action is an interaction that involves your partner—it is something that can happen only in a specific manner because of who you are to one another.

Use contrast to help set off the hook. The beginning and the ending of the frame are not as important as its middle.

No. 5

1. Resume playing.
2. Move the accent off the trigger and the hook and onto the "transformation" at the end of the beat.
3. Continue playing.

Observations.   The focus shifts to the end of the frame and how you complete the action and transform.

You used the trigger to move forward into a state of action.

You used the hook to define your target with your partner so that something could happen. Now accent how you finish the action and how it affects your relationship with your partner.

The change can be arbitrary. It doesn't matter how you choose to play it. You are drilling using a target to trigger and focus your action. You'll want to become familiar and comfortable with each component in the frame. The best way to do this is to exaggerate—expand the size of the action, blow it up out of proportion, examine every aspect of it in detail, de-mystify it, and then reduce it in size and place it back into its context.

You now have a unit of action—a frame—that has a clear and specific beginning, middle, and end, with a target leading you forward. Shift the focus from the frame itself to how the frame links up to form a sequence.

No. 6

1. Resume playing. Use the target to take you into the transformation.
2. Do not let the energy drop at the end of the transformation.
3. Begin the new frame with the same dynamic you used to end the previous frame.
4. The energy and dynamic should change within each frame. This will depend on the intensity of the target.

Observations.   You are now working with a magnet to pull the action forward.

When the energy drops at the end of the unit, you close the frame. This "down ending" is like the period at the end of a sentence. It marks the completion of a unit of thought and action.

But sometimes you want the thought to continue in a direct manner. "Sustained" endings link the end of one thought with another in an active, driving manner. They keep the energy moving forward and demand attention from the listener. You do not let your partner off the hook with a sustained ending. You send a signal that you have more to say and you mean to have your say.

The frames link in a direct, even way. Each frame is given equal weight. You connect frame A with frame B by drawing a straight line between them with a magnet. When you work with a "down ending" the line arcs in the middle of the unit and literally ends down. Each new unit involves lifting the energy at the trigger and starting all over again. Sustaining takes you into a more continuous and economical use of energy. It is constantly flowing rather than stopping and starting. Down endings are exhausting to listen to, whereas sustained endings pull you forward.

No. 7

1. Resume playing.
2. Make the beginning of each frame a half step stronger and more dynamic than the ending of the previous frame.
3. Continue to build the frames until you reach a climax, and then start all over again.

Observations.   You are now working with an "up ending." The focus links the end of one thought to the beginning of the next with an ascending line. The thought grows and develops in intensity as it progresses. You are drawn forward and upward until the thought reaches its climax.

Throughout this activity you have been drilling ways of perceiving. The action has moved from the general to the very specific. You've progressed from the first round of Changing Places, which focused on learning the rules of the game, to examining each of the components in the game—the trigger, the hook, the transformation—to linking the elements together and giving them design and shape through triggers, targets, and magnets.

Play one more round of Changing Places, and play it in slow motion. Justify slow motion with an endowment. Does the quality of your playing change?

Cock Fight

This activity exercises targeting as well as balance and forward focus.

1. Select a partner of the same size and weight. Face one another.
2. Balance on the balls of your feet. Bend your knees and squat on the floor.
3. Bounce and move around the playing space in this squatting position.
4. Hold your hands close to your chest. Your palms should face away from your body.

5. Practice pushing your palms forward, as if you are pushing something, or someone, away.
6. Face your partner. Squat and move around the playing space. Try to throw your partner off balance while maintaining your own balance.
7. When you have knocked your partner off balance, or when you have been knocked off balance, stand, straighten your legs, touch your palms to the floor, and hang over for a count of ten. Resume playing.

Effort: Quick and strong.

Observations. This is a high-intensity, high-stress game. Your aim is to change your partner by throwing him off balance. If your attention wanders, you will be thrown off balance.

Play in short rounds and change partners frequently. Begin playing with a partner who is your size and weight, but progress to partners who are different sizes and weights. See how you balance one another. Or not. You may be surprised to discover the amount of reactive energy you can release in this game.

The target gives direction to the activity. Add a reason—an endowment—to give the action a context and an intent. Stay on target at all times.

The Hunter and the Hunted

This high-intensity game investigates tunnel-vision targeting.

1. Stand in a large circle. Extend your arms out to your sides.
2. Two players are selected, one as the hunter, the other as the hunted.
3. If you are the hunter, you must capture the hunted. A capture involves touching the hunted with both hands.
4. If you are the hunted, you must try to evade the touch of the hunter.
5. If you are standing in the circle, you use your arms to form the boundary, keeping the players inside the playing space.
6. You may help the hunted by offering whatever assistance you feel is appropriate. You may guide or direct the hunted. You may not help the hunter.
7. Allow the hunter and the hunted to play as much as possible on their own.
8. The hunter and the hunted play with their eyes closed.
9. The hunt needs to be played in absolute silence.
10. Play with a ninety-second time limit.

Effort: Quick and strong.

Observations. When you work "blind" your other senses compensate and heighten your awareness. A "blind" hurdle heightens the risk and danger involved for all the players.

You may want to stay close to the sides of the circle and let the circle/ other players control your moves. Take the initiative and play on your own in the center of the circle. Playing in the center of the circle is extremely dangerous. There are no immediate safeguards and you have to rely on yourself and your own instincts. See if the quality of your playing changes.

You will immediately expose your "risk response"—how you adapt and respond to danger—when you play The Hunter and the Hunted. Whatever your playing style, there is no hiding when you play this game.

It is essential that you play in absolute silence. There can be no sound or cuing from the sides; the hunter and the hunted must play on their own, without interference. They must stay inside the circle.

Feed the drama of the hunt. Give it all your focus and attention. As part of the circle, you are a vital part of the action. The game could not be played without you. When you play, you will want support from the group. Be willing to offer it to the other players.

In The Hunter and the Hunted, the structure of the game—the chase— can only work if the targets are constant. The moment focus wanders, a capture can happen.

Because you are working "blind" you will engage your senses in the hunt. The deeper your engagement, the more you can release and surrender to the playing of the game.

Unnoticed Gesture

Use this overload activity to drill staying on target.

1. Three players sit in three chairs, side by side. Play an All Yield scene. Accept every offer. Make as many offers as you can.
2. Play the scene as a job interview. The player in the middle interviews applicants for the open position. Each player is an expert applying for the job.
3. If you are are sitting in one of the outside chairs when the "boss" turns away, make as many faces and rude gestures as you can to your partner seated in the center chair.
4. If you are sitting in the center, play the scene seriously. If, in the course of the scene, you happen to catch either partner making a face, snap your fingers to "snap" the player out of the game.
5. If you are caught mid-gesture or mid-face, try to justify your action and stay in the scene.

6. The target is on maintaining and playing the scene as accurately as possible.

Effort: Quick and light.

Observations.   This activity involves strong moment-to-moment playing since no one knows what will happen next.

If you are the interviewee, remember that you want the job. If you are the interviewer, remember that you want to hire someone. Positive targets lead to positive actions.

Make the faces and gestures dangerous. Lean in close to the interviewer. Play with large gestures. See how you can justify them and talk your way into staying in the game. The first time you play you are always learning the rules of the game. The second time you play you are finding your way through the game with the benefit of hindsight. The third time through is the charm.

The overload in this game involves a great release of censored energy.

It is best to play this activity within a strict time limit—ninety seconds per round. The tight time boundary keeps the playing focused and direct. Every moment counts. If the interviewer cannot make a catch in ninety seconds the interviewer is snapped out of the game.

Variation.   Play Unnoticed Gesture with a scripted scene from a play. See what happens when one character's back is turned—what can you release, and what can you define in the release that clarifies your relationship with that character? How do you stay on target throughout?

I Love You

Use this target drill to develop skills for staying in focus during a scene.

1. Play an All Yield scene. Accept every offer. Make as many offers as possible.
2. Name each other early in the scene. Endow one another; have a history together.
3. In the course of the scene, try to say "I love you" to the other character.

Effort: Variable.

Observations.   You may never reach an actual point of saying "I love you." If it becomes evident that that point cannot be reached, stop the scene. It is important to stop while you still feel comfortable with the quality of the play.

Because you have a fixed target in the scene, the quality of each offer is crucial if you are to successfully reach your goal. You have to help each other in the playing. You must create a climate together in which it is possible to say "I love you."

This means you must both be in agreement about the tone and tenor of the scene, and what you are trying to accomplish. Whether you succeed is immaterial to the pursuit of the target. The target gives you direction and sets you in motion.

Adjust and adapt the endowments to make the playing more dynamic and interesting.

Changing Focus

This activity investigates ways of using targets to move from the outer to the inner.

1. Work in groups of four.
2. Respond physically to a rhythm clapped out by hand.
3. Change your visual focus on each clap. Your eyes lead, your body follows. Movement may be large or small and must include a change of level.
4. Develop a group focus. Give and take the focus within the group.
5. As a group, give the focus to another group.
6. As a group, take the focus from another group.
7. Develop a scene that justifies a shift and change in focus.
8. The hand clapping stops. As a group, develop your own internal rhythmic pattern in silence. Play as Silent Music.

Effort: Quick and variable.

Observations.   At first, you will want to cue one another heavily in order to stay connected.

When you move away from the comfort zone of the expected and known, you will develop more interesting rhythmic patterns. The playing will begin to feel more alive, dangerous, and spontaneous.

Your initial temptation may be to make everything abrupt. As the flow gets stronger you can venture into more interesting patterns and shapes. Use silence as integral elements of the pattern.

Your focus will become extremely concentrated in the course of the action. The connection with your partners strengthens as you know who you are to one another through level and direction in space. Using an external focus also releases the pressure of self-consciousness. You no longer have to think and focus solely on yourself. Your outer focus—on your partner—

releases your creative energy. You are freer to respond spontaneously. As you add a target to the playing—changing your partner's status and relationship in space—your playing will have more intent, clarity, and personal engagement.

Note the progression within the activity: you begin by moving just your eyes. Then you add your head and then your full body. Repeating the pattern leads to a frame of action. You link the frames together to form a score of action. You then can add different stresses within the score to vary the pattern. Varying the stresses creates shape within the individual frames.

The Squeeze

This activity develops dexterity and focus in switching targets from moment to moment.

1. Four players. Agree on a where. Play an All Yield scene. Accept every offer. Make as many offers as possible.
2. Play seated, with the chairs lined up next to each other. You may face into one another. Give each other names as soon as possible.
3. Try to squeeze—or eliminate—one player out of the group. Do not talk about who you will squeeze out. See if it is possible to agree silently and eliminate one player from the group.
4. If you feel you are being squeezed out, do whatever is necessary to stay in the scene.
5. You may move out of your chair at any time in the course of the scene as you fight to stay in the game.
6. Play with a set time limit.

Effort: Variable.

Observations. This exercise uses status to seek and define a target.

You will continually jockey for position. It will become obvious fairly quickly who is high and who is low within the group, although that may change during the course of the scene.

When appropriate, freeze the action while playing and observe the body language of the players. Who is turned in to whom, who is turned away, who is standing, who seated, who is linked physically through touch? How does this body language match the status of each player at any given moment in the scene? How does body language automatically work to mirror the moment-to-moment balance within a relationship? How does body language reflect the use and engagement in the target?

What tactics do the players use to stay in the game and on target? How does the pecking order establish itself, and how is it maintained?

Remember, the target is to squeeze another player out of the group while you stay in it. Pursue that target and see if the quality of the play transforms. Don't worry about being nice; play the scene and see what happens.

The Squeeze involves a tremendous release of energy through highly engaged playing. It is also easy to monitor and observe, because the body language is direct and obvious. This activity provides tremendous insight into the connection between the physical and the psychological. The body never lies. Your body always tells you who you are in relationship to your context.

One way of changing your dynamic in a relationship is to change your physical position in the relationship. Move in, move out, turn into or away from your partner. Stand above them or below them and see what happens. Physical positioning in space is a powerful tool in defining and clarifying how you aim and pursue your target.

HURDLES

Hurdles break patterns. They create blocks that change your use of effort. You cannot drift when you confront a hurdle; you must move over, under, or around it. You do not always return to the same path once you've confronted a hurdle.

Hurdles can be either inner or outer endowments that define your effort and shape your action. Inner hurdles are the personal roadblocks built into the character's center that inhibit or prevent the free flow of energy. Outer hurdles create pressure and stress to color and condition the quality of your play.

By creating rewards and penalties, hurdles define the rules and intensify the stakes inherent in the dramatic context. Hurdles clarify and define targets.

You will learn to use hurdles as overloads to provoke, stimulate, and challenge your imagination when you are creatively stuck. You will use hurdles to jam your circuits and trigger spontaneity. You will develop skill in using hurdles to intensify effort and transform the physical quality of your play.

Hurdles

1. 2/3 and 3/4
2. Six-Count Circle
3. Energy Ball
4. Electricity

5. Obstacle Course
6. Touch and Talk
7. One-Minute Scene

2/3 and 3/4

These high overload activities test coordination as well as patience.

2/3

1. Begin in a Neutral Stance.
2. On your left side, develop a two pattern: on the first beat, punch your left arm down. On the second beat, punch your arm straight up towards the ceiling.
3. Repeat the two pattern with a steady, even beat.
4. On your right side, develop a three pattern: on the first beat, punch your right arm down. On the second beat, punch your arm straight out to your right, parallel to the floor. On the third beat, punch your arm up towards the ceiling.
5. Repeat the three pattern with a steady, even beat.
6. Simultaneously, play the two pattern on your left and the three on your right. Repeat the pattern twice. The pattern ends when both arms face the ceiling.
7. Repeat the 2/3 pattern until the rhythm is smooth and consistent.
8. Keep your focus at eye level throughout.

Effort: Quick and light.

Observations. Don't overattack the problem. It is an exercise to jam your analytical faculties and focus your attention on your body.

In order to make the 2/3, and the next pattern, the 3/4, work, you must relinquish any sense of mental control and let your body take over.

3/4

1. Begin in the Neutral Stance.
2. On your left side, develop a three pattern: on the first beat, punch your left arm down towards the floor. On the second beat, punch your arm straight out to your left, parallel to the floor. On the third beat, punch your arm up towards the ceiling.
3. Repeat the three pattern with a steady, even beat.
4. On your right side, develop a four pattern: on the first beat, punch your right arm down towards the floor. On the second beat, cross your right arm to touch the left side of your chest. On the third beat, extend your

arm straight out to your right, parallel to the floor. On the fourth beat, punch your arm up towards the ceiling.

5. Repeat the four pattern with a steady, even beat.
6. Simultaneously, play the three pattern on your left and the four pattern on your right. The pattern ends when both arms face the ceiling.
7. Repeat the 3/4 until the rhythm is steady and consistent.

Effort: Quick and light.

Observations.   You may become extremely frustrated when you can't put both parts of the pattern together. There is a right side pattern and a left side pattern. They are distinct and separate. You play them simultaneously.

Shift your focus from your right to your left and from your left to your right. Choose which part of the pattern you wish to focus on at any given moment. Change your focus whenever you want.

Don't give up. You may want to take your visual focus down to the floor to concentrate more deeply. Don't. Keep your focus at eye level.

When the coordination of the pattern becomes easier, hum, sing, or recite a Shakespearean sonnet. Keep increasing the overload.

Variation.   Reverse patterns and work them on opposite sides of your body.

Six-Count Circle

This is another overload activity to jam your analytical circuits and intensify your focus on your target.

1. Form into a circle.
2. Imagine the circle is a clock. Decide where the twelve is.
3. You will move counter-clockwise.
4. Walk in a set pattern:

   Six steps forward;
   Five steps forward, one step back;
   Four steps forward, two steps back;
   Three steps forward, three steps back;
   Two steps forward, four steps back;
   One step forward, five steps back.

5. Return to the beginning of the pattern and repeat.
6. Move continuously.
7. Keep the spacing within the circle equidistant at all times.
8. Keep your focus at eye level.
9. Sing, hum, or voice your inner thoughts.

Effort: Quick and strong.

Observations. This exercise requires tremendous focus of attention. At the same time it requires surrender and letting go. The pattern is easier once you find the flow of it.

Don't try too hard. You will only get in your own way.

You may walk into another pattern, especially when working backward. Work to keep the spacing equidistant and the shape of the circle intact. Keep the structure of the game intact. Maintain the discipline of your playing.

You may become angry or frustrated if you are unable to master this activity the first time through. Stay with it and remember to breathe.

A group identity will emerge as you concentrate less and less on the perfection of your own performance and focus more and more on being a part of the collective effort of working together to play as one.

Energy Ball

This overload game is useful for expanding awareness and jamming over-analytical thinking.

1. Divide into two circles.
2. Pass an imaginary ball around the circle. Toss it back and forth and around the circle.
3. Concentrate on keeping the ball intact as it travels through space. Receive it exactly as it was sent. Do not transform its shape or energy.
4. Add sound to the ball. One that helps describe its energy.
5. Stop using your hands. Send and receive the energy ball with your entire body.
6. Add a second ball, and then a third. Keep all three balls moving at the same time.

Effort: Variable.

Observations. Concentrate on maintaining the exact energy of the ball every time it is sent. You may not change the size or weight of the ball or its rhythm and dynamic.

Eliminating hands is a deliberate hurdle used to provoke your imagination. It forces you to vary your physical response and increase the intensity of your playing.

Using sound and multiple focus forces you into sensory overload. It heightens your involvement in the playing and helps get you out of your mind and into your body-in-space.

Energy Ball works best when played quickly, in short bursts.

Electricity

Use the overload hurdles in this game to jam your mental circuits.

1. Sit in a circle on the floor. Cross your legs.
2. Cross your arms over your chest. Hold hands with your partners on each side. Place your left hand into their right, your right hand into their left.
3. Whoever starts squeezes a pattern into the hands of the player on their right and another pattern into the hands of the player on their left. The pattern may be two long squeezes and a short, for instance.
4. Each player passes the pattern on to the next player. If you receive from your left, pass to your right. If you receive from your right, pass to your left.
5. Close your eyes.
6. The sender may send more than one pattern at a time.
7. Send exactly what you receive. Keep the currents moving as quickly as possible.

Effort: Quick and light.

Observations.   You will be receiving currents from both your right and left sides at the same time. Working with your arms crossed helps complete and intensify the overload.

As you get used to the sensation, you will settle into the game. Your attention will deepen and become stronger.

You have to make choices throughout the playing of the game. You cannot respond to everything all at once. You must focus specifically on either your right or your left side. You may shift the focus back and forth rapidly. If you freeze, the game stops. You jam up the works for everyone else.

When you are in overload, your analytical mind receives too many messages to process at once. You begin to bypass the analyst and respond with instinct. You want to bypass judgment and sidestep over-intellectualization. You want to get out of your head and into your body. Overloading is a technique for doing just that.

In overload, the emphasis is always physical. You engage all of your senses with as much stimulation as you can stand. Sight, sound, and touch are your primary targets.

Make sure, as you overload, that you always have a sense of forward motion in the game—that the overload leads you somewhere. You will know the where when you arrive at it.

Obstacle Course

This activity deals with hurdles and their use in strengthening targets and endowments.

1. Divide into two teams, A and B. Select a partner in the opposite team.
2. Stand opposite your partner at either end of the playing space. If you are on Team A, turn your back to Team B and close your eyes.
3. Everyone on Team B silently litters the playing space with any objects you find in the room, i.e., chairs, shoes, bags, books, etc. Return to your position opposite your partner.
4. A: Keep your eyes closed throughout the entire activity.
5. Move across the room to your partner. If you touch any other players, or if any other player touches you, open your eyes and return to your starting position and begin again.
6. B: Help your partner across the room by calling out directions to him or her. Never refer to your partner by name. All directions must be communicated strictly by tone of voice.
7. A: Move through the center of the playing space.
8. B: Coach your partner to avoid contact with any other players or objects. Coach your partner through the center of the playing space.
9. Play within a fixed time period.
10. Once you make it across the room, open your eyes and watch the other players.
11. At the end of the time period, repeat the activity. Reverse roles. Change the positions of the objects within the obstacle course.

Effort: Variable.

Observations.   This is a high overload game.

Because you are talking simultaneously, speak in a normal tone and with normal volume. Do not yell. Take your time and don't become frustrated. As long as you are in contact with your partner, the game will proceed. If, for any reason, you lose contact with your partner, or if your partner can't hear you, stop and wait until you've re-established your connective thread.

You will be utterly dependent on your partner. You cannot play this game unless you are both in contact with one another.

The hurdles heighten and increase the amount of risk and danger involved in the playing. They serve to make an activity more interesting and engaging. The greater the danger, the more interesting and dynamic the playing. Hurdles exist to define the target; they force you into clarity and specificity because you must change your effort to overcome them.

Touch and Talk

The rules of the game define the rules of behavior. Integrate and justify the rules of the game in your playing and make them your hurdles.

1. Decide on the givens of the situation, including a where and a when.
2. You can talk only when you touch your partner.
3. Justify touching.

Effort: Variable.

Observations. You must touch in order to talk. At the same time, you must integrate the touch into the natural fabric of the scene. It cannot stand out as a gimmick or a device. It is best when the touch goes unnoticed.

Resist the temptation to play a comic scene. Use silence as a prime factor in the relationship. Speak only when necessary. Touch only when necessary. Justify the touch by the rules and endowments to create a context for the relationship.

Variation No. 1. You can talk only when your partner touches you. This variation changes the quality of the play. You are no longer in control of the action. You truly need your partner in order to speak. You must play the scene together, frame by frame, moment to moment. There is absolutely no way to predict what will happen. Give up and surrender into the unknown of the scene. Allow the unspoken tension of the scene to emerge. Make the changes work for you rather than against you. Make spontaneity a positive element in your playing.

Variation No. 2. Work from a scripted text. You can talk only when your partner touches you.

Variation No. 3. Three or more players work at once.

Variation No. 4. Play using eye contact as your form of touching/not touching.

Use the rules of the game—the context—as the hurdle to intensify, color, and condition the quality of your play.

One-Minute Scene

This exercise uses time as a positive hurdle to help define and shape the structure of a scene.

1. You have one minute to play a scene with your partner.
2. Use the first thirty seconds to establish the relationship through the endowments.
3. Use the last thirty seconds to resolve the scene and bring it to its natural conclusion.

Effort: Quick and strong.

Observations.   Everything within the scene must appear to be natural, planned, motivated, and fully justified.

If you rely on the relationship endowments from the onset of the scene you will find a satisfactory ending. The endowments contain all the clues you will ever need in order to determine your relationship with your partner. They are there before the scene begins, and will be there after the scene ends. The narrative action of the scene charts the transformation of your relationship with your partner.

The time pressure of playing the scene in one minute will trigger your imagination and take you into unexpected areas of action. When you "get stuck" creating, add time pressure as a provocative tool to unlock your imagination and get you moving. Hurdles can be positive pressure points.

FOURTH TRIAD: PERFORMING THE ACTION

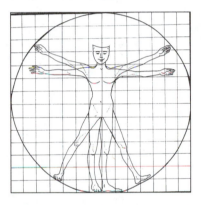

In the fourth triad of the MAP you will develop skills leading to performing action. You will extend and expand action by moving from expression to interpretation and communication. You will develop skills in using masks, language, and set sequences.

In Masks you will focus on the transformation of the self, surrendering to the impulse, and linking the outer and the inner to create character.

In Language you will focus on transforming thought into action, anchoring the impulse to speak in action, and using words to reveal or conceal intent.

In Set Sequences you will focus on reading a score of action, collaborating with partners to rehearse the score, and collaborating with an audience to complete the playing process.

In the MAP these three factors combine skills in analysis, transformation of intent into action, and collaboration to create the communal process of ensemble, which lies at the heart of every theatrical event.

MASKS

Masking involves synchronicity between the outer and the inner. The mask is determined by the targets; the endowments of time, place, and context; and the effort expended through patterns of action.

The mask may be a physicalization used to reveal the character's relationship with itself, or it may be a cover to conceal and hide its true nature and identity from the world.

In Mask you will focus on surrendering and releasing the impulse into action, transforming the impulse into shape, and using physical keys to trigger inner flow within the shape.

When you wear the mask your inner merges with your outer to carry you along in a strong state of flow. Once you are in this flow, your sense of intuitive rightness will take over and guide you.

In Mask you will strengthen your ability to "know" when you are right and when you are wrong, when you are on and when you are off the mark.

The outer form—the physical life of the mask—will release your imagination to create an intuitive sense of who you are. Once triggered, the inner image defines and conditions the external physical form.

Masking integrates the process of working from the outside in and from the inside out. In Mask you will exercise your ability to move from idea to shape and from shape into patterned action.

Masks

1. Invisible Envelope
2. Walking in Space
3. Half Masks
4. Grab-Bag Characters
5. Putty Masks
6. Instant Characters
7. Cloning
8. Mirror Cloning

Invisible Envelope

This mask technique is useful for triggering keys to create outers and inners.

1. Observe one another in daily activities.
2. Collect mental photographs of specific body parts, i.e., lips, eyes, noses, shoulders, fingers, etc. of one another.
3. When you play a scene, select one of these body parts and wear it as part of the face or body of the character you are developing. It is an Invisible Envelope.
4. Wear the Invisible Envelope, as a secret, throughout the scene.
5. Let the envelope trigger images of behavior, gesture, or psychological motivation for the character.
6. Use the envelope as a physical key to create the mask. The key is connected to and helps unlock the inner of the mask.

Effort: Variable.

Observations. The Invisible Envelope must be based on actual observation, not imagination. It should be molded accurately and specifically onto your face or body. It is always worn as a secret.

The envelope is something you slip into when you need it. It is linked to one specific part of the body. As a key, it can trigger images of many different facets of the character.

Because it is secret, it should always remain hidden from the other characters. It is an image that is personal to you, and is yours alone.

Walking in Space

This high sensory overload activity integrates body and facial masks.

1. Move around the room at your normal walking tempo.
2. Slow the walking tempo down and justify the new tempo by changing the substance of the space. Make it thicker, thinner, more liquid, etc.
3. Change the tempo again. Justify the change. Add color and texture to the new space substance.
4. Change your level while you walk. Justify the change. Add sound and smell to the substance environment.
5. End the walk near an imaginary waterfall. Shower in the waterfall.
6. Dry in the sun. Dress in imaginary new clothes.
7. Move with the new clothes until the image of the clothes triggers a new body shape. The new body shape triggers a walk, which triggers a mask.
8. Mold the facial mask.
9. Change the tempo of your walk until you establish the new walking tempo of the mask.
10. Discard the body and facial mask.
11. Continue to walk and return to your own shape and tempo.

Effort: Variable.

Observations. The strong sense of flow in this activity is a result of your response to the the dynamics of the sensory endowments.

You work from the outside in throughout the activity. All changes are triggered by physical suggestions that you accept and respond to. You work in a highly charged sensory environment and respond to that environment. What you feel is a result of the doing; the "doing" is conditioned by the endowments in the environment.

Justify each change by altering your environment. You must adjust to each new where. Always include the other players in the room as part of the environment.

Each new environment will require a shift in body shape. Body shape will trigger the image of the body mask. Body mask will, in turn, trigger facial mask. The physical response triggers the internal, which in turn triggers the physical/external. Make sure you engage your spine and pelvis in each body shape and in every transformation.

Variation: Move through the space and its various substances trying to indent, or press into, the space. Continue moving forward and leave a trace pattern, similar to a path cut through fog. Make the trace pattern as sculpturally interesting and complex as possible, by changing levels, shape, tempo, and action dynamic.

The body shape and trace pattern will trigger the body mask. The body mask triggers the face mask. The outer triggers the inner which redefines the outer.

Half Masks

This activity involves a high release of energy and requires strong endowment.

Note: You will need plastic masks and a hand mirror large enough to see your entire face. The masks should be cut into small pieces; use either the lower or the upper half of the mask. You also may use just the nose and cheeks. The mask sections will transform your face yet allow you to work with mobility and flexibility.

Half Mask No. 1

1. Select a mask and study it for one minute.
2. Put the mask on. Do nothing.
3. When you are ready, look into the hand mirror for no more than five seconds.
4. Retain the image of the mask and start to move. Find the body of the mask.
5. Find the walk of the mask.
6. Freeze.
7. Remove the mask.

Effort: Variable.

Half Mask No. 2

1. Select a partner. Decide who will be A and who B. If you are A, study your mask.

2. Put on your mask and wait.
3. If you are B, begin to mold, sculpt, and create a mask body for your partner. The shape you sculpt will be the endowment you offer your partner.
4. If you are A, allow yourself to be molded. Accept the endowments. Walk around the room until you have found the mask's walk and are comfortable with it.
5. Freeze.
6. Remove the mask. Reverse roles, with either the same mask or a new one.

Effort: Variable.

Half Mask No. 3

1. Repeat Half Mask No. 2.
2. Once the mask has been endowed, begin to perform physical tasks. Concentrate on the development of a strong inner voice. Retain the mental image of the mask throughout.
3. Freeze.
4. Remove the mask. Reverse roles.

Effort: Variable.

Observations.   Enter this activity without preconceptions or expectations. When you see yourself in the mask, you will intuitively understand the nature of the mask's character. Hold on to that image while you work. It allows the character to grow.

The energy level of a mask is extremely high. You may experience an enormous surge of power when you wear it. You will immediately come out of the mask when you remove it.

Allow your physical impulses to guide you in the creation of the mask persona. Let the endowments trigger your imagination. Add physical detail as you move. Fill in the gaps. Refine the image. A mask is physically fearless.

As the mask becomes specific, the inner voice will come into focus. Your inner voice is the conversation you have with yourself inside your head. It is how you perceive and process information. It is either analytical or emotional. It is triggered by action.

Conduct an interview with yourself. Ask yourself questions. Let the mask answer.

Allow yourself to transform both physically and mentally. The more comfortable you are with the transformational process, the smoother your transition from improvisation and games to a prepared text.

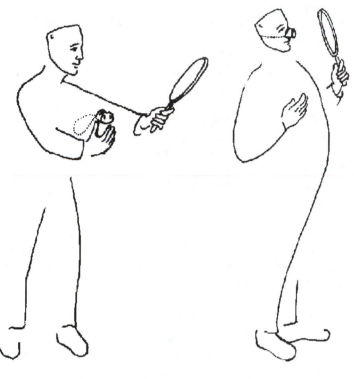

Half Masks

Grab-Bag Characters

This activity tests skills in keying into a mask.

Note: You will need to use five pieces of clothing per person as preparation for the activity. All clothing should be displayed on the floor. Everyone must have access to all the garments.

1. Select three to five pieces of clothing, at random, and put them on.
2. Once you are dressed, begin to walk. Use the clothing as your trigger in forming the character mask.
3. Start with the body mask. Once you have clearly established the image for the body, move on to the facial mask.
4. After you have formed the facial mask, find the voice for the mask.
5. Use your inner voice to whisper aloud. Give an autobiographical interview to an imaginary interviewer. Clarify your history. Be sure to name the mask.

6. All masks are in a public space—a waiting room. Develop relationships with each other.
7. Make an entrance into the waiting room. Make an exit from the waiting room. Know where you are coming from and where you are going to.
8. Freeze.
9. Take off the clothing.
10. Play a quick round of Freeze/Go.

Effort: Quick and strong.

Observations. The mask will develop in response to how you move in the clothing. The mask may not be imposed or manipulated to conform to a pre-determined concept. It must arise spontaneously from your movements in the garments.

Look to create a physical center for the character, a key, that will unlock the inner life of the mask. Use the physical as the trigger to stimulate your imagination.

Work with clothing from the opposite sex. Create a character of the opposite sex. Play the character for real. Make as many physical adjustments

Grab Bag Characters

as you need until you find your key to the mask. The voice will be difficult, but justify the quality of the voice by autobiographical circumstances, i.e., age, medical history, occupation, etc. See what happens if the mask takes over—or do you resist the mask?

When approaching mask/character work, it is crucial to let the mask have its own voice and its own say. You cannot impose your biases and prejudices upon the mask. The mask must speak for itself.

In the same way, you cannot impose your viewpoint on a character; if you prejudge your character you begin your work with a strong moral filter that will color every choice you make. Instead of judgment, approach the character with positive curiosity. Your task is to create a full, rich, complex human being; contradictions are to be encouraged rather than ignored. Stay neutral and let the character speak for itself.

Putty Masks

Use this activity to become comfortable with physically endowing a mask.

1. Scatter around the playing space.
2. Mold and remold the features of your face with imaginary silly putty to form a mask for a new you.
3. Start with your forehead, then move to your eyebrows, eyes, cheekbones, nose, lips, chin, jaw, neck, and hairline.
4. When you are finished, turn and observe the mask in an imaginary mirror.
5. Leave the mirror and begin walking in the playing space. Retain the image of the mask. Let the mask dictate your walking tempo and rhythm.
6. As the mask begins to take over, give an interview to an imaginary interviewer. Reveal all the secrets of your mask's autobiography.
7. Shift your tone and pitch until you discover the mask's voice. Once you find the voice, you will always speak in that voice.
8. Freeze. Remove the mask.

Effort: Variable.

Observations. The putty and mirror are devices to stimulate your imagination. The mask guides its own formation. Checking in the mirror only reinforces the image.

Do not look at the mask in the mirror for more than fifteen seconds. You only want to create an impression of the mask rather than a specific, detailed portrait.

In the autobiographical interview, concentrate on facts that will lead you to strong physical choices: age, occupation, injuries, allegeries, disabilities, etc.

Endow yourself as you go along, and translate those endowments into physicalized specifics. You are defining your relationship with yourself, establishing the who in your who. Translate everything into physical sensory terms.

The voice is the most difficult aspect of the mask to locate. Once you've found it, it will always be there. It also reinforces your physical image of the mask.

There will be a specific moment when you must surrender to the mask and allow it to determine your action. You will sense this happening, and you must give yourself over to it.

The moment of removing the mask is especially powerful since it marks the return to self. Give yourself some time to re-establish yourself when you put the mask away. Walk or run around the room and shake off any after-effects of the exercise.

Variation No. 1. Work in teams of two, alternating molding the mask onto one another. Accept every offer.

Variation No. 2. Mold a specific mask for a character you are working on for a scene. Mold the mask for that character at a particular time in the character's life, either younger or older than the time of your scene. Do an entire life cycle over an extended period of time.

Variation No. 3. Body masks. This is an extension of mask molding. Once the facial mask is molded, continue to develop and mold the body mask with putty. Work with specificity to create all parts of the body. When you have molded the body examine your image briefly in an imaginary mirror. Turn to an imaginary closet and dress yourself. Once dressed, re-examine your fully clothed image in the mirror.

Move about the playing space and allow the character image to suggest the walk. Complete the physical transformation by finding the voice. Once you have established the voice, develop relationships with one another and play the scene.

Instant Characters

This flow activity strengthens transformational skills within the mask.

1. Begin in the Neutral Stance.
2. Start to move. Keep the parallel and perpendicular axes of your body intact.
3. Exaggerate the shape of your body as you move. Transform the shape until a full body mask image develops. Be specific and concrete in your transformation.

4. Add the face to the mask.
5. Develop the walk for the full mask.
6. Develop the inner voice of the mask. Give the mask a name.
7. Verbalize the inner voice. Conduct an interview with yourself.
8. Change the horizontal and vertical planes of your body. Advance the image, until a new mask begins to emerge.
9. Continue defining the mask until the image is fulfilled.
10. Continue and advance through three more masks.
11. Transform back into the original, named mask.
12. Freeze.
13. Return to the Neutral Stance. Breathe.

Effort: Variable.

Observations. Many subjects that might normally be taboo may now be released through the mask. Self-censorship diminishes when the energy released with the mask increases.

Instant Characters

The power of the image shapes your physical transformation. Your physical transformation will release the power within the image. The clearer the image, the easier the transformation.

The transformation is strongly inner directed. Intuitive rightness guides all choices. Trust your sense of flow.

Tension blocks are instantly visible in the mask. A tension block traps energy rather than allowing it to release and flow into that part of your body.

Play Instant Character quickly for best results.

Cloning

This exercise strengthens your observational skills as well as your ability to work from the outside in.

1. Decide who will be A, the cloner, and B, the clonee.
2. B: Stand in the Neutral Stance and allow yourself to be molded and shaped by your partner. Stay alert.
3. The cloner has one minute to mold and shape his or her body and stance onto the clonee. Time will be announced every fifteen seconds.
4. If you are molding, start at the feet of your partner's body and work up. Be specific in molding the way you stand, how you hold your weight and tension, the placement of your arms and hands, and the expression on your face. At the end of the minute you should be able to stand back and see yourself.
5. At the end of the minute, stand back and walk around your partner. Examine the body from all angles.
6. If you are the clonee, sink into the body and make it your own. You are in the midst of an action, frozen in time. Respond to the impulses your body is sending you about your frozen action. When you are ready, complete the action. Keep your inner monologue alive.
7. Trade roles and repeat the sequence.
8. Work in silence.
9. At the end of the second round, take a moment and talk to one another: What felt right? What didn't? What did you see? What did you experience?
10. Return to your original roles of cloner and clonee. You will have three minutes to clone your walk onto your partner. The time will be announced every fifteen seconds. You may talk to one another.
11. A: Clone your walk onto your partner. You may move around the playing space. Do whatever you need to clone your walk. Be sure to focus on the gait, the tempo, the rhythm, and the direction of your focus in space when you walk.
12. At the end of three minutes, stand to the side of the room. Watch your partner walk around the room. Watch in silence. Avoid the temptation to laugh.

13. If you are the clone, find a way to make the walk your own. Use the physical life of the walk to trigger your imagination. Try to capture the essence and spirit of the person walking. Don't worry about the precision of every detail.
14. You are late for an appointment. Move around the room preparing mentally for the appointment.
15. Stop. Make an inventory of every object in the room. Count shoes, bags, books, chairs, tiles in the ceiling. Be thorough and complete with your inventory.
16. Freeze. Let the mask dissolve.
17. Reverse roles and repeat the entire sequence.
18. Take a moment and talk about the process: Was there ever a moment, even if only for a second, when you saw yourself moving? When you felt you "got" the other person while you were moving? How did that happen?

Effort: Variable.

Observations.   Work without making value judgments about your body or your work. You are the material you work with.

Agree to mold, and to be molded. You both must say yes to one another during the initial phases of the process. Work towards the creation of a single image that will evolve into the mask.

When the clone accepts the mask, and begins to make it his or her own, the image will advance. The impact of the activity becomes more immediate when you transcend your everyday knowledge of one another and surrender to the impulses triggered by the mask.

You are attempting to recreate yourself. When you walk and move during the activity, the physical image triggers a strong internal response. You will experience being in another body and thinking like another person as long as you maintain the discipline of the mask.

Mirror Cloning

This mask activity is an exercise in observation and imitation, and a tool for drilling advancing and transforming action collaboratively.

1. Divide into two teams, A and B, and sit with your team on the floor.
2. Close your eyes and listen to a piece of orchestral music.
3. As you hear the music, create a series of pictures of environments—wheres—to be set to the music.
4. Listen to the music again and agree with your teammates on a series of communal images for an environment suggested by the music. Do not discuss character, action, or dramatic context. Concentrate solely on the

environment, and discuss it in terms of sensory images: hot, cold, wet, dry, light, dark, etc.

5. Begin to move in this environment. Concentrate on your individual response to the physical/sensory given circumstances. Use the music to trigger your imagination.

6. Select a partner from the opposite team.

7. Team A moves through the environment again, concentrating on the individual where and slowly adding a why—why each player is there.

8. Team B watches their partner in Team A. Team B will clone Team A. Duplicate the action in exactly the same order and in exactly the same manner each time you play. Team B will clarify their partner's relationship to the environment.

9. B clones the where, the why, and adds a who—who you are and why you are there. Advance all images.

10. Team A watches Team B, in order to clone them. Team A advances the interaction between the characters.

11. Continue cloning back and forth. Each team advances the action and makes it more specific. Always work with a stated focus: define the relationship with the environment, the relationship with the other players, the objectives, the given circumstances, etc.

12. Repeat the entire process, starting with Team B.

Effort: Variable.

Observations.   You will need clear and specific instructions before each round of playing.

Once you begin the cloning process, you and your partner will be working together to create one shared mask—an image of the character you are creating in tandem. The character belongs to both of you; neither can claim ownership nor seek to control the mask's development. This is a shared, collaborative effort, and you must be willing to surrender control of the mask's development in order to create something that will be much larger than your single imagination can conceive.

Once you understand and are familiar with Mirror Cloning you will be able to watch scenes transform with each round of playing.

Work to clarify the action. Make it more detailed and specific. Every move is an offer; accept and advance the playing. Keep the action alive and transformational.

The music is a tremendous trigger throughout the work process. In essence, it becomes your text. Once you are comfortable and confident with the score you have devised, try eliminating the music and see what happens to the playing. The music then becomes your subtext that you carry with you—it triggers your inner voice.

Mirror Cloning

When you finish working, take a moment and talk with your partner and evaluate the experience. You may be surprised to discover that you were both playing the same endowments and targets. This happens when the physicalization is strong and clear and the hurdles are high.

Variation. Once into the third or fourth round of the cloning, work simultaneously, so that both teams are cloning each other at exactly the same time. Eliminate the music and work in silence. Justify the use of silence with endowments.

LANGUAGE

Language is thought in action. In language you will examine the synchronicity between thought and action. You will learn to tune your body to intensify your involvement in the thinking process, and use molding and carving to deepen your engagement in action.

You will develop tools to isolate and separate body language from verbal language. You will experiment in developing a process to physicalize language, to own the experience of words in your body.

You will learn how to read a text to find clues for meaning through language—how sound groupings, vowel lengths, consonant patterns, image clusters, and punctuation reveal intent.

You will experiment with finding the inner flow of thought, either on the line or under the line.

You will learn to target language by stressing operative words that carry meaning and action. You will discover the shape and forwardness of thinking and language by using language substitutes.

You will refine your ability to translate patterns of thought into patterns of action by integrating dynamics and shaping/design elements into speech.

Language

1. Word Games
2. The Loop
3. Story Telling
4. Parallel and Paraphrase
5. Graphing
6. A/B
7. Punctuation
8. Eliminating Action
9. No Move
10. Crescendo and Cascade
11. Thinking Aloud
12. Departure Dynamics

Word Games

Use these two shape games to trigger your physical imagination about the nature of words.

Alphabets

1. Use your body to spell out all twenty-six letters of the alphabet.
2. You may write or print; use capitals or lower case.
3. Do not lie on the floor.
4. Spell out all the letters in one minute.
5. Repeat. Make the shapes more interesting.

Spell-Outs

1. Work in teams of four or five.
2. Spell out different words with your body. Each player creates one letter of the word.
3. Spell as many different words as possible within three minutes.
4. Select your most interesting word and present it to the other teams.
5. Design your presentation by giving each letter a dynamic and dramatic shape—one that helps convey the essence of the meaning of the word.

Effort: Quick and light.

Observations. Both these games require imagination and a sense of humor.

You will arrive at extremely interesting responses to the design problem if you take enough time to image thoroughly before you act.

You must strive for consistency in your individual as well as team presentation. You must agree on format, shape, and design, and work together for clarity of image as well as dynamic presentation.

The shape of the word must amplify its content. Determine the essence of the word's meaning and give it form, dimension, and design. Translate the sound into a physical shape. Make it a collaborative effort.

Word Games

If you are truly daring, have a spelling bee.

The Loop

This is a verbal variation of Continue and Advance.

1. Decide who will be A and who B.
2. A: Work with a sound and a movement in an abstract form. Do not try to make sense out of it.
3. Continue repeating the gesture until it has a clear beginning, middle, and end. Continue to replay this "loop" of action.
4. B: Add a complementary sound and movement to your partner. Join in the loop.
5. Together, transform the abstract sound and movement into a specific word and gesture.
6. As the action clarifies, make your relationship more specific.
7. Continue looping until your relationship is as specific as the physical activity.
8. Advance the action together. Jiggle it back into an abstract form of sound and movement. Do not repeat what you've already done. Let the specific physical action of the activity suggest a new, abstract pattern.
9. Continue to "loop" the action until you make the abstract specific and form a new word and gesture.
10. Loop and advance at your own rate of transformation.

Effort: Quick and strong.

Observations. Looping only works when you advance the action together. There can be no leader and no follower. Agreement and timing are crucial to the spontaneity of the activity.

Sound can become repetitious unless you focus on keeping it alive and varied within The Loop. The Loop is at its best when sound and movement are connected into one complete action.

Use sound to trigger your imagination. Work from the outside in and blend your physical action with your emotional response to the sounds of words. Once you merge the outer and the inner, the action will have a dynamic life of its own.

Variation. Play with a large group of players. Every time the action advances from the abstract to the specific or from the specific to the abstract, change your visual focus. Find a way to justify the change and incorporate it into your playing.

Looping is a repetition activity. You repeat and repeat until you no longer have to think about the form (or the structure) of the activity and are free to focus on its intent and inner life.

Looping is most effective when you work in concentrated bursts, focusing on a specific speech or activity. Work in depth for a short period of time. Continually repeat the word; work rapidly to overload your imagination through sound. Use looping to break down your preconceptions and trigger a fresh response to the text.

Story Telling

These exercises use verbal hurdles to heighten the emotional overload and intensify the dynamics of your playing.

Story No. 1

1. Sit facing a partner.
2. In one minute, describe a real encounter with someone. Talk simultaneously.
3. Repeat the story, with a different partner. Tell the story as if for the first time.
4. Repeat again, with a different partner.
5. With a new partner, stand and physicalize the story as you tell it, using physical and sound leads.
6. Repeat the story and begin to eliminate words. Pare the story down to essentials. Concentrate on heightening the impact of the major events.
7. Repeat without words. Let physical gestures carry the action of the narrative.
8. Return to your original partner. Repeat the story with words and gesture.
9. One at a time, tell your story to each other.

Effort: Quick and strong.

Observations. Talking simultaneously is the hurdle throughout the activity. You must make your partner listen and respond to you each time you speak. Stay within the one-minute time limit. Use the boundaries to spark your imagination.

Repetition gives you the opportunity to streamline and focus your story. The more you repeat it, the clearer it will become to you. Use the repetition to edit and shape, i.e., design, the experience of the story.

The entire story is a setup for the payoff. The payoff happens at the end of the story. Mold and shape the dynamics of the story telling to heighten the payoff. Use words that underline the drama, or humor, of your story. Make every word count.

As you reduce the variables in the story telling, color each word with emotional weight. By eliminating language altogether, the gesture has to carry the force of the action. Your gestures will be strong, dynamic, dramatic. You are starting to "carve" the space in your story telling. When you carve, you mold and shape the space around you. When you bridge, you link the gesture out from you to your partner. Bridging is a mark of involvement in the action; carving is an intensification of that involvement. Carving is an indication that you are at your most passionate, that your involvement is at its deepest level.

Notice how the language changes once you return to verbal story telling after carving. The words have been endowed with a sense of action. Has the story telling changed? Has the story itself changed?

Story No. 2

1. Sit facing your partner. Talk simultaneously. Tell a story to one another.
2. Tell the same story to a new partner, in one minute.
3. With a new partner, physicalize the story.
4. With a new partner, tell the story, without words.
5. With a new partner, tell the story in words, without movement.
6. Return to your original partner. Concentrate on receiving the story, even though you are still talking simultaneously.
7. Trade stories. Own your new story.
8. Add a physical life to the new story.
9. Tell the entire story in thirty seconds.
10. Tell the entire story in fifteen seconds. Use just three sentences: one for the beginning, one for the middle, and one for the end of the story.
11. Reduce the story to three key words, in five seconds. Use gesture.
12. Reduce the story to one sound containing the essence of each key word.
13. Repeat the sound and add movement to it.
14. Exchange sounds with your partner, so that you return to your original story.
15. Extend the "essential sound and gesture" you have been given into three key words that suggest the beginning, middle, and end of your story.
16. Extend the three key words into three key sentences.
17. Tell your story in thirty seconds, with the three sentences forming the beginning, middle, and end of your story.
18. Repeat your story, and never break eye contact with your partner.
19. One at a time, tell your story to each other.

Effort. Quick and strong.

Observations. Monologues are usually stories about the past told to someone to make a point in the present.

Exaggerate and overattack your story. By enlarging the size of the telling you will begin to unlock the emotional intensity of each image in the story.

Repetition forces you to discover the climax—or payoff—of the story. Organize the action around the payoff by working backwards to create the setup. Once you have a point of view, you can attack the telling with focused energy.

You must make the story yours. Trading stories demands instant endowment and ownership. Tell the story as if it happened to you. Build the facts around what you have heard. You will fill in the rest of the details, and invent what you don't know. You will have heard enough of the story, through its repetition, to grasp its essential meaning.

Now you are "acting"—you are creating a character and telling someone else's story as if it's your own. You must make it as personal, spontaneous, immediate, real, and truthful as your own story.

When you finally trade stories again, you are not really telling your own story anymore. You are telling your story as it has been reinvented by your partner. You have moved from nonfiction to fiction. Discover the truth of this new story.

Story No. 3

1. Divide into two circles.
2. Create a story as a group. The story evolves as each of you adds one phrase to the narrative. Concentrate on making the voice of the narrator fluid and unbroken.
3. Change the direction of the story telling. If you were telling to the right, now tell to the left.
4. Tell a new story, one word at a time.
5. Continue to tell the story, one word at a time, using gibberish.
6. Tell the story in gibberish phrases.
7. Tell the story in gibberish sentences.
8. Speak the same language.
9. Keep the voice of the narrator consistent from player to player. All sentences must sound natural.

Effort: Quick and light.

Observations. Overload is very strong. You will make the transition to gibberish quite easily.

The gibberish provides a release of energy, so that communication can become more direct. There is never a need to be clever. You must concentrate on keeping the action of the story moving forward.

Gibberish is a language substitute. It forces you to image clearly. Language either describes a mental image or illustrates it. Language substitutes, such as gibberish or no movement, help clarify the intent of the words. The language, whatever its form, makes you see the intent with precision and definition. You have to choose your words carefully in this exercise to describe or illustrate the image and communicate it to your partner.

Playwrights do exactly the same thing when they craft a script. They choose each word to help define the intent of their characters. Approach each text as if you are speaking your own words. Why did you choose this particular word to express this particular thought and intent at this particular moment in time?

The single voice of the narrator is extremely important. It requires a collaborative effort. You may not impose your own sense of order, or control the work. Since you are discovering the work as you go along, you all must be "present," sharing the same time and space. The narrative voice is a device to link you with one another, a way of connecting you with your partners and getting you all to move the action forward simultaneously. When someone isn't "present," you will hear it. Instantly.

Your focus is in the center of the circle, because that's where the story exists, that's where all of your attention goes. The narrative depends upon your contribution, yet, ultimately, it is larger than any one individual; it is the sum total of your collective effort, and therefore, larger than all of you. It exists within you, yet, paradoxically, outside of you.

Parallel and Paraphrase

This activity helps reveal the structure of a scene through its language.

1. Work with a prepared text.
2. Agree on a parallel situation, one that mirrors the text, but is taken from your own life. Mirror the endowments of time, place, and context, but play from your own experience so you can bridge to "own" the scene.
3. Agree on a parallel where.
4. Agree on parallel characters.
5. Play the scene in your own words. Parallel the action, frame by frame.
6. Return to the prepared text. Play the scene through as scripted. Note any differences or changes in the quality of the action.

Effort: Variable.

Observations. Parallel scenes must be extremely precise in adhering to the patterns of the text.

Choose a situation that comes from your own experience. Make everything you do and say personal; keep the playing close to your own world.

Use the parallel to own the text by bridging your world and the world of the play.

The structure of the scene must remain intact. If the parallel scene were imposed onto the text the intent of the action would remain the same, though the words would be different. Relationships must also parallel the text exactly.

Paraphrasing and improvising uncovers the action patterns and design of the scene. When you play the scene in your own words you begin to find out how much of it is really in your body and how much is in your head; how much you can truly commit to, and how much of it you are faking.

If you discover you are missing frames, go back and reincorporate them into your playing. Action always has its own cohesion and logic. Each frame grows logically out of the previous frame. If your thought patterns are not clear, your action patterns won't be clear.

After the parallel, make whatever internal adjustments you need to make. When you return to the text, see if it is any clearer, immediate, personal, or spontaneous.

Variation.   Play the parallel with A/B as a language substitute for added clarity (see A/B).

Graphing

Use this activity to physicalize shape patterns and to target a speech.

1. Work with dialogue from a scene.
2. Stand opposite one another and continuously repeat or "loop" the dialogue. Repeat the words until you no longer have to think about them.
3. Imagine the action while you talk. What are you doing, through the words, to affect your partner?
4. Use your hands to begin to graph—or illustrate—the shape of the action. Think of the action in terms of verbs. Are you pressing, jabbing, gliding, slashing? What are you doing from moment to moment, and can you graph, or translate, that action into a gesture?
5. Use your entire body to graph the action pattern in space. Then loop— or repeat—the graph.
6. Continue to graph and eliminate the verbal text. Play the scene only with graphed action.
7. Vary the effort factors and the playing dynamics. Play the score light and quick, strong and quick, strong and sustained, or light and sustained.
8. Play the scene again, verbally, without graphing. Stand still and just speak to one another.

9. Take a moment and talk to one another. Did anything change? How was the quality of the play between you? What do you want to keep? what discard?

Effort: Variable.

Observations. When you graph you will usually start with a generalized vague pattern and end with a score of highly specific, highly charged verbs. Everything will be much clearer to you.

Graphing is a means of defining, reinforcing and strengthening your sense of verbal action. You move from the mental image—a series of pictures created by the words you are speaking—to a physicalization of that image, making the language active. Then you reincorporate and absorb the physical image back into the text.

Once you have discovered that language is physical, and that speaking is active, your playing will be charged with a sense of visceral immediacy. You will be playing with your complete instrument.

Variation. Work without hands. Use your entire body to graph. Repeat the scene, but don't move. Maintain the image of the body graph and place that image into the language.

A/B

Use this language substitute activity to induce clarity and specificity of intent when playing a scene.

1. Work with a prepared text.
2. Play the scene once.
3. Repeat. Substitute these four "words" for the dialogue in the scene:

   A.
   B.
   A.B.A.B.A.B.
   B.A.B.A.B.A.

   You may speak these four words in any order you wish.
4. Try not to overgesture when you use A/B. Play the scene normally.
5. Repeat the scene, using the prepared text.

Effort: Variable.

Observations. A/B is a way of jamming your mind and breaking your predictable patterns of perception.

When you become so set or rigid in your way of looking at things that you stop having new or stimulating ideas, you need to provoke yourself into breaking out of your rut and see things differently.

In A/B you must really focus on what you are thinking; you cannot take anything for granted. If you get lost in the text, so much the better. Stop, ask your partner for help, and continue.

Like all hurdles, A/B makes you work harder, and therefore, work with greater accuracy and specificity. You will not be able to speak unless you know the intent of the language in its context. When you return to the prepared text, see if there is any difference in the quality and clarity of what you say.

Punctuation

This activity focuses on the direction in language.

1. Work with a prepared text. Have a copy of the text in front of you.
2. Graph the text. Physicalize and chart it out in space, using abstract body language.
3. Stress all verbs, nouns, and adjectives. Do not stress pronouns, unless they are used for comparisons. Build every list with a crescendo.
4. Pay special attention to the punctuation of each sentence. Use the punctuation to investigate how thoughts are bridged and linked together.
5. Pause for commas, stop for periods, take half breaths for semi-colons, hold your breath for dots and dashes.
6. Use "and" to link thoughts, "but" to contradict one thought with another, "or" to compare thoughts, and "if" to set up hypothetical situations.
7. Set off each new unit of thought by calling out "frame."
8. See if you can find the architecture of the speech, shape, structure, and design of its thought.
9. Repeat the speech as written, without graphing. Note any changes in the intent of what you say.

Effort: Variable.

Observations. Punctuation is a way of physicalizing and visualizing thought, and making thinking active.

Every thought has a shape. Shape involves balance. Ideas are balanced and counterbalanced, weighed one against the other. Pauses, or any break in the flow of voiced language, signals a shift or change in the balance and direction of the thought pattern, and must be played as if they were meant to be spoken.

Engaging yourself physically in the process of analyzing the text helps get it out of your mind and into your body. Thinking and speaking are physical activities. They must be crystal clear if the audience is to follow what you are saying—and doing—from moment to moment.

Eliminating Action

This is a verbal hurdle activity. It leads to heightened playing by compressing action.

1. Use a set speech from a text. Give it physical life by adding five physical movements—a walk, a kneel, a turn, a reach, a sit—to the text. Develop five frames of action within the speech, frames that can be repeated precisely every time you speak.
2. Repeat the frames. Connect the frames with a target to give them intent.
3. Repeat the frames again. Add sensory endowments to make each frame more specific.
4. Repeat the speech. Eliminate one frame. Retain the sense of the entire speech without using the missing frame.
5. Repeat the speech again. Eliminate a second frame. Compress and endow the remaining frames with the sense and sensibility of the missing frames.
6. Continue to eliminate frames until the speech is reduced to a single frame. The frame carries the history and meaning of the entire sequence.

Effort: Variable.

Observations.   Eliminating Action demands specificity and physical concentration. You cannot think your way through this activity; you must focus all of your energy into the execution of the action.

When you eliminate an action the remaining action grows in power. So does the inner voice. Strong hurdles require compressed and focused effort and lead to greater intensity when playing.

No Move

This variation of Eliminating Action strengthens the patterns of language by integrating physical hurdles into your play.

1. Stand opposite your partner.
2. Develop a physical score of action involving a change of arm position, a change of visual focus, a change of head position, and a shift of weight.
3. Each frame—or unit of physical action—must be specific and in response to your partner.
4. Develop a set sequence, a nonverbal dialogue, and loop, or repeat it.
5. Eliminate one gesture and substitute a change of level. Continue the sequence. Although the score of the sequence will transform, the intent of the "dialogue" must remain the same.

6. Adjust and adapt to the new score.
7. Add words to the sequence. Use language to extend and clarify the meaning of the physical action.
8. Once the verbal score is established, play it in tandem with the physical score.
9. Play the scene without physical movement.
10. Repeat the scene, but this time lean into one another.
11. Repeat and lean out from one another.
12. Introduce one gesture.
13. Introduce a second gesture.
14. Introduce a third gesture.
15. Eliminate all physical movement.
16. Play the scene once through, using only the words.

Effort: Variable.

Observations.   The continual substitution and elimination of physical activity forces you to heighten the intent and focus of your action.

The compression of meaning tends to emotionally overload each frame and forces you to work with heightened endowments in a very physical way.

Do not move your head during the course of No Move. Absolute still-ness will intensify the inner life and your experience of the flow of the activ-ity. Each added gesture becomes rich and powerful when seen in relief against a score of stillness.

No Move demands great strength and concentration. Maintaining the physical discipline of not moving means that the work will have a directness and a focus that you might not otherwise experience. Keep your focus on your partner.

Once you've established the score of action, and a clear sense of the rela-tionship, challenge your partner by changing the dynamics of the playing, yet maintain No Move.

Use the hurdle—not moving—as your trigger to clarify your intent through using the language. Hurdles force you to increase your effort by finding ways to overcome them. In so doing, the hurdle always makes the playing stronger. Strong playing = strong hurdle; a strong hurdle = strong playing.

Crescendo and Cascade

These pattern games give shape and dynamic to language.

1. Work in groups of four.
2. If you are the first player, establish a sound and movement phrase. Once you have established the phrase, offer it to the player on your right.

3. If you are the second player, accept the offer. Continue the action. Do not transform the phrase. Increase its intensity and dynamic by half a step. Then offer the phrase to the player on your right.

4. Each player accepts the phrase, increases its dynamic and intensity by half a step, and offers it to the next player.

5. Continue the "crescendo" by increasing the intensity until you reach the peak of the phrase.

6. If you are the first player, start a new phrase. Once you have established the phrase, offer it to the player on your left.

7. If you are the second player, accept the offer. Continue the action. Do not transform the phrase. Diminish its intensity and dynamic by half a step. Then offer the phrase to the player on your left.

8. Each player accepts the phrase, diminishes its dynamic and intensity by half a step, and offers it to the next player.

9. Continue the "cascade" by diminishing the intensity until you reach the bottom of the phrase.

10. Try the same two patterns with a prepared speech or scene. Each player helps build the crescendo or the cascade. It is a group effort. Everyone contributes to moving the speech forward.

Effort: Quick and strong.

Observations. Each player adds one new element to an already existing structure and, in so doing, transforms the pattern.

Crescendos and cascades are "topping" patterns. One adds energy, the other reduces it. Each step in the pattern must be smooth and fluid; you cannot skip a step.

Once you are comfortable with a single speech, try using a crescendo throughout a scene. Each player tops the other so the scene has a quality of energy and momentum.

Do not worry if the scene does not make sense at first. Adjust and adapt the endowments to justify the crescendo for the sake of the exercise. Do the same with a cascade. Alternate between the two, and see how they affect the intent of the language in the scene.

Thinking Aloud

Use this activity for insight into the power and effect of the inner voice.

1. Improvise a scene.

2. While your partner speaks, verbalize your inner voice. Speak to your partner directly only when you are ready to speak.

Effort: Variable.

Observations. The inner voice is your thought process. It is the voice you hear at all times inside your head. It tells you what you are thinking as you think it. It is usually reactive. When working with a spoken inner voice, respond only to what your partner does or says. Don't feel obliged to manufacture a running commentary; you are simply speaking your thoughts to yourself aloud. Allow the inner voice to grow and develop spontaneously as a natural part of the scene. When you know what you are thinking, you know what you are doing.

The inner voice is conditioned, like everything else, by the endowments. It will change from moment to moment, as the playing changes. Adjust and adapt the inner voice throughout; it must always be operative if you are to be alive and present in a scene.

Variation No. 1

1. Divide into teams of two.
2. Each team works in tandem with a second team.
3. Play an All Yield scene. Accept every offer. Make as many offers as possible.
4. If you are on Team A, play the scene, without dialogue.
5. If you are on Team B, speak your partner's inner voice aloud.
6. Repeat the scene, reversing roles.

Effort: Variable.

Observations. Yield to your partner's offers. Accept each new idea and endowment without question.

When the scene is really working, you will have the sense of advancing the action together. Try to sustain your direction within the scene. A target will emerge as the scene progresses. Shape the scene so that it has a beginning, a middle, and an end.

When the scene is repeated, try to retain the individual frames and endow them with freshness and spontaneity, as if you are playing the scene for the first time.

Variation No. 2. Play a scripted scene. Use the inner voice when your partner is speaking. Respond to what is being said. Use it to define the link between your partner's line and your own.

Departure Dynamics

This is an exploratory activity for speeches involving highly imagistic or poetic language.

1. Use twelve lines of a Shakespearean text or a sonnet.
2. Walk around the playing space. Silently work through the speech.
3. Mouth the speech, without sound.
4. Voice the speech.
5. Without sound, send the speech to someone at the edge of the room. Send to the roof. Send outside the building.
6. Using sound, work through the speech word by word, sound by sound. Support and define each sound with a physical image. Build the images sound by sound, frame by frame, line by line.
7. Group words together into image groups. Develop one physicalization for each image. Engage your entire body in the physicalization.
8. Eliminate sound. Hear the sound with your inner ear. Concentrate on your physical action. Endow it with the power of sound.
9. Add sound. Transform the images into sound and movement phrases.
10. Work through the entire speech with sound and movement. Work from image group to image group.
11. Stand still. Without moving, work through the entire speech once, using the text.
12. Send the speech to another player.

Effort: Variable.

Observations.   Action is contained and played on the line, not under it.

Translate and transform the power of thought into the power of language. Let the sounds of the words reveal their power. Give sound physical shape and place it in space. Let the sounds explode in your body. Vary the dynamics. Chew, bite, tear into and spit out each sound, word, phrase. Exploit and make the most of the text. Dare to do too much and go over the top.

Then reverse the process. Do the opposite and see what happens. Stand perfectly still. Contained. Don't move a muscle. Place all of your focus and energy on stillness. Allow the sounds of the words to resonate on their own. The physical experience of each sound and word is now stored and coded into your muscle memory. It will inform your speech if you don't get in the way. Relaxation is crucial in allowing the speech to happen on its own. Release.

SET SEQUENCES

Set Sequences drill skills in collaboration, observation, interpretation, and integration of technique.

They exercise your ability to uncover, discover, and play action, linking frames of action forward into scores of action, with direction, intent, and purpose.

In Set Sequences you will focus on the three phases of action cycling: initiating action, engaging in action, and completing action.

You will be required to play individual cycles of action and then link them with a magnet into a score of action.

You will move from the outside—the formation and creation of a "text"—to the inside—interpreting the text—to the outside—performing the text.

You will work on team problem solving. You will tune your skills in transforming an idea into action. You will use provocation to generate new ideas when you are stuck or blocked. You will exercise collaboration in both creating and playing the score of action.

You will rehearse the rehearsal as you move through the set sequence, working with targeted focus, intensified endowments, heightened hurdles, and a mask.

You will transform the score from the general to the specific in each round of work.

In Set Sequences you will build endurance and stamina in sustaining your sense of flow by learning to collaborate with and "read" an audience in performance. You will develop skill in adjusting and adapting your playing technique with an audience without sacrificing the integrity of your mask.

You will begin to approach style by learning to edit your choices for consistency and synchronicity with the world of the play.

Set Sequences

1. Collage and Instant Performance
2. Sound Scoring
3. Tag-In/Tag-Out
4. Cartoons and Animated Features
5. Portraits
6. Perfect and Imperfect People
7. Silent Music
8. Silent Movies
9. Silent Tension

Collage and Instant Performance

This set sequence embraces all phases of the transformational process, moving from random images to a designed pattern of action in twenty minutes.

Collage

1. Sit in a circle on the floor with a sheet of newspaper in front of you.

2. Tear the newspaper into five different pieces. Arrange those pieces into as many different patterns as possible in two minutes.
3. At the end of the time period, stand up and walk around the collage. Find a different way of looking at the pattern. In one minute, rearrange the newspaper pieces to clarify the intent and design of the pattern.
4. Work in teams of two. Without discussion, combine your two separate collages to create one new work. Work together for one minute.
5. At the end of the minute, study the collage from a new point of view. Talk with your partner and agree on a concept for the design.
6. Rearrange the collage until the pattern is clear, specific, and expressive of the concept. Work for one minute.
7. Form into two large teams. Each team has ninety seconds to agree on an approach to making the group collage. Agree on a means of organizing the material and a concept for the work.
8. Work for ninety seconds to execute the collage. At the end of the time walk around the work and find a new point of view.
9. Discuss the work with your teammates for one minute. Talk about any changes you may wish to make in order to clarify the concept. Work for one minute to make those changes in the design. Change your point of view and study the collage again.
10. You may eliminate one piece of paper from the design. Change viewpoints. You may replace the piece of paper in the design if it will clarify the concept from this new vantage point. Find a new point of view.
11. Look at the entire collage. Use one finger and trace a pathway through the work. Start at any point and work through the entire design until you arrive at an exit.
12. Repeat the tracing pattern and duplicate it as precisely as possible.
13. Turn away from the collage and repeat the trace pattern.
14. Clear away the collage. Begin with an empty playing space.

Effort: Variable.

Observations.   Acting is a creative process that uses exactly the same tools you used in creating the collage.

You begin with raw material—the script—and you examine it to discover its shape and meaning. You know there is an underlying intent unifying all the elements and that your initial task will be to discover the intent and see how all the parts fit together.

You keep changing your point of view to approach the work with new imagination and energy. You focus on the endowments, the targets, the hurdles, and the relationships. You exercise your perception. To keep things in focus, you examine all angles and all possibilities; you enter the MAP from any point.

You do all of this perceptive analysis—your "homework"—alone, and at an early stage in the process, you begin to collaborate with your partner. You work together, changing points of view, to reach a series of agreements. You work by offering and accepting, triggering one another's imaginations, creating a shared image of the design of the work. You each have your tasks and your individual part in the effort, yet you are united in approach and what you wish to say with the collage.

The next stage of the process involves moving out of your head and into your body. You have done your analytical work, you have circled around and around and have changed your point of view many, many times and now you are ready to act. You trace your pattern—you determine your score of action—and you focus on what you have to do, and you move to the rehearsal as the next step in your MAP.

Instant Performance

1. Both teams will work simultaneously, though separately. Each team will work within its own imaginary proscenium arch, and will not invade the other team's playing area.
2. Scatter to your separate stages. Move across the floor in a physical pattern that corresponds to the pattern you traced through the collage. Physicalize every turn, circle, squiggle, dot, and dash in the "collage" pattern. Repeat the pattern exactly as you traced it on the floor through the newspaper.
3. Freeze at the end of the pattern. When everyone on your team has frozen, return to your starting point. From now on, you will work with a set sequence, in which the physical pattern will remain exactly the same, although the inner flow may change from round to round.
4. Repeat the entire sequence. Concentrate on making eye contact with other players.
5. Repeat. Every time you make eye contact, change your effort factors. The playing dynamics of the score may change from round to round.
6. Repeat. Exaggerate the changes in the dynamic. Connect outer and inner, so that changes in the effort/playing dynamic correspond to changes in the inner flow. Begin to develop an inner voice.
7. Repeat and justify each change of action and dynamic. Every change must involve a change of status.
8. Team B sits and watches Team A perform. If you are on Team A, focus on playing the score at performance level. Work full out.
9. If you are on Team B, create a title for what you have just seen. This is your offer to the other team.
10. A: Repeat the performance, now that it has been titled. Clarify, amplify, and expand the images suggested by the title. The theme of the title will

give the work a central focus and condition the effort involved in playing.

11. Repeat and clarify your individual magnet. Make sure every move is justified and motivated by a target. Make the relationships more specific and keep the status transformations alive and active.
12. Exaggerate your body shape and define your mask. Concentrate on the physical elements of time, place, clothing, endowments within the environment, and your hurdles.
13. Perform the score full out as a fully developed performance piece. Do not be afraid to play large for clarity.
14. Reverse roles. Team A watches Team B perform. Repeat steps 8 through 13.

Effort: Variable.

Observations.   The creation of the image is more important than the end result of the performance. The collaborative process is also larger than any single individual.

Performance is a natural culmination of the working process. You began with a series of squiggles on the floor, and in twenty minutes, you've developed a performance piece that has a beginning, a middle, and an end, and that has a logic and sensibility of its own, unique and consistent within its own world.

In this working process, you didn't have much time to think. There was only time to do. Each repetition helped you organize random and seemingly irrational factors into a sequence that had logic, order, design, and meaning.

The inner voice is closely tied to your sense of synchronicity and inner flow. When the inner voice is blocked, or has gaps, you can isolate those single moments and work to connect the dots, i.e., figure out how you get from point A to point C by going through B. The inner score of action connects all the separate elements and makes them work as one.

All actions evolve in response to the other players. The focus is continually on offer, accept, offer. The score of action is only as clear as the moment-to-moment balance of the relationships. You must have a tangible sequence of actions to perform, and each action must be fully justified and fit into the overall design of the piece.

Once you know the rules and boundaries of your world—once you are secure in the structure of your score—you are free to play spontaneously, and with energy. All of your choices are firmly rooted in your "text" and work to amplify and clarify the central concept of that text, as you have named it and agreed upon its image.

Playing, acting, and performing are sensory experiences. You rely on your senses for your timing, on your feeling for the action from moment to moment. Performing is an experience in which all of your senses are open and alive, in which you respond with your deepest levels of intuition. When you are "inspired" you "breathe in the air of the gods." You allow the mask to take over, to guide and direct you, to release the stored energy of your intuition, the energy of your impulses, the energy of your imagination.

Sound Scoring

This set sequence drills internalizing and justifying endowments in order to strengthen targets and hurdles.

1. Work with a "found musical instrument," i.e., coins, shoes, a comb, books, etc. Any object in the room.
2. Sit in a circle and improvise a musical phrase with the instruments. Work together to compose a piece of music with two figures, or sections.
3. Compose and then repeat the first figure—a set sequence of sound— until the pattern is set and the figure can be repeated precisely and specifically.
4. Repeat the scoring process with the second "figure."
5. Perform both "figures" as one composition.
6. Physicalize the score without sound. Use your body as your instrument. Translate the sound pattern into a physical pattern.
7. Work with the first figure until it is complete. Then move on to the second figure. Repeat the pattern twice, working for clarity and specificity of image.
8. Extend the physical form by adding vocalization. The sound must grow out of the dynamics of the action.
9. Connect the outer with the inner.
10. Once you've set the physical score, and added the playing dynamics, endow the score with a strong sense of intent. Connect the playing to the people around you. Work to affect them through the action.
11. Add more and more endowments about your relationships with the other players. Adapt and play the score accordingly. Respond to each offer.
12. Add circumstances of time and place. Adapt and play the score accordingly.

Effort: Variable.

Observations. Once the score is set and the endowments are introduced, stay focused on one another. Offering, accepting, adjusting, and adapting are the keys to playing the score, and they are all based on exploring the dynamics of the relationships with the other characters.

You spend the first half of the exercise establishing a fixed score, and the second half of the exercise in playing the score precisely. Be firm about the first half—this is the "text" you will be speaking, and you must not veer from it.

Once the score is set, repeat each set of endowments two or three times to adjust and adapt your playing to the new conditions. Allow the scene to emerge. The scene will gain clarity, focus, and intensity once you take the time to find your way through it.

You will also have to endow rapidly as part of the playing process. The endowment is your offer. You tell your partners who they are to you, and they, in turn, define who you are to them. Accept the endowments and incorporate them into your playing.

You will become utterly dependent on one another for the development and playing of the score. Anything less than a group effort is impossible.

The score becomes inviolate. You will discover you cannot alter the score once it is set with your partners, since everyone depends on fidelity of the sequence for cues and action.

The manner in which the action is performed may vary as the endowments change. The internal logic of the situation always remains constant.

In working from the outside in, you will gradually begin to connect all the individual frames and arrange them into a sequence that has meaning, logic, and a strong sense of purpose. It is impossible for us to work in chaos. Therefore the repetition gives us a chance to ascribe meaning to everything we do. An inner throughline—a flow—and a magnet—a purpose—will emerge to organize and arrange all of the information into a consistent and meaningful pattern of action.

Variation No. 1.   Create a score using three short figures. Work in two teams. Develop the scores into vocalized scenes and perform them for the opposite team. The opposite team "clones" the performing team. Continue to advance the action back and forth with Mirror Cloning until the scene is specific and clear. Introduce language substitutes into the scene until it becomes a spoken scene. Once the verbal intent is specific and tied to the basic internal action the scene can advance from language substitutes into true dialogue.

Observations.   This approach allows you to discover the true meaning of language, how it is tied to thought and action. Language becomes an extension of the inner process and grows out of a sense of immediacy, urgency, and intent. When you develop the language yourself, and see how strongly it is tied to the endowments governing the relationship, there can never be an extraneous sound or a false moment. Every moment counts in carrying the action forward. Keep this experience alive with you when you begin to approach a previously formed text, and seek to make your approach to language as immediate as if you had created it yourself.

Variation No. 2.   Work with the images of specific writers: Tennessee Williams, David Mamet, Lillian Hellman, Sam Shepard. Adjust and adapt the timing of the score to meet the givens inherent in each of these worlds. It may take more time to play a Mamet version of the score if the pauses are truly observed yet all the frames and action must be played out in their entirety according to the givens of the style and the score.

Observations.   When you work within a set "world" observe all the rules of the endowments of that world. Look especially at the grammatical notations for pauses in commas, dots and dashes, exclamation marks, etc. These become the musical codings that tell you how the dynamics of the "language" are to be played. Adhere to them and see what kind of a world you can create.

Tag-In/Tag-Out

This activity focuses on understanding the audience's role as an active participant in the process.

1. Work with music.
2. Play a transformational pattern game, such as Melted Architecture or Musical Combines, in which you continually endow one another with character and relationship.
3. One player remains outside the group and observes. She is the audience.
4. If you are the observer, whenever you are ready to play, tag yourself into the scene by tagging someone out.
5. The Tag-In/Tag-Out continues until you have all had a chance to observe the action.

Effort: Variable.

Observations.   Almost everyone is fascinated by the prospect of watching the group perform.

Tag-Out gives you the opportunity to observe the group dynamic in process. Chart the changes in status between the players as they work—who jockeys for position, and how the jockeying happens. Note, again, that status is fluid and constantly changing; there will be a great deal of movement within the group, and the pecking order and hierarchy will continuously transform.

Observe from a neutral point of view. Do not feel obligated to play the role of audience or draw unwarranted attention to yourself through self-conscious inappropriate responses.

When you tag in, you choose the role you wish to play, since you are tagging out a specific player. Offer something new when you join in—use your audience insight to transform and advance the quality of the play.

Cartoons and Animated Features

1. Choose a "line"—i.e. a straight line, a dash, a dot, a curve. This line forms the key for your character mask.
2. Move in the manner of your line. Make a series of consistent choices about how to move.
3. Use the floor as a sheet of paper and draw a pattern with the line.
4. Form a relationship with another line.
5. In groups of three, examine the relationships between the lines. Create a score of action. Let it evolve while you work. The score must have a beginning, a middle, and an end. Do not discuss the content of the score until it has evolved. Work for three minutes.
6. Repeat. Work for two minutes compressing, editing, and eliminating one minute of action from the score.
7. Repeat, eliminating action and playing the score in one minute.
8. Each team performs its score for the other groups.
9. Each team must title its work.

Effort: Variable.

Observations.   This activity forces you to work with specificity and economy of action.

The compressed time factor forces clarity of detail and charges the playing with energy and immediacy.

Create your own soundtrack for the performance. Verbalize, or vocalize, as your character while you perform. Integrate the sound score into the overall design of the performance.

Portraits

(Music: Chopin Etudes)

1. Work with a scripted character.
2. Focus on the target and character needs as they are described by given circumstances in the text, i.e., what the character wants and why he wants it.
3. Develop a facial and body mask for the character.
4. Develop a repetitive abstract gesture that expresses the character's need.

5. Continue the gesture. When ready, advance the abstraction into a gesture associated with a specific action.
6. Include this gesture in all transactions.
7. You are all in a communal environment. Use Melted Architecture to create a short score of action.
8. Repeat, making the score more specific and the relationships more immediate. Keep the gesture alive throughout the playing of the score.
9. Repeat until a narrative begins to emerge. Add No Move into the score until the scene has greater clarity, definition, and focus.
10. Eliminate the music and play the score again.
11. Play the score as a scene of Silent Tension.
12. Gradually add the text to the score and play the score as a new scene.

Effort: Variable.

Observations.   Repetitive gesture is a direct connective tool for bridging the inner life of the character with an external physical form. It is also a device for keying into the character mask and for defining behavioral patterns that are connected to inner hurdles.

Use the gesture excessively when placing it within a score of action and then pare it away and use it only when needed for punctuation or emphasis. Once discovered, the gesture becomes a strong key for the character. It triggers a series of psychological associations and emotional responses that will unlock your imagination.

Perfect and Imperfect People

Use this Status Body exercise to define the relationship between the inner and outer lives of a character.

1. Begin in Parallel and Perpendicular. Move around the playing space. Hold the image of one vertical line crossed by five horizontal lines.
2. Advance the image to a perfect person walking. Let your walk transform into that of a perfect person. As the image gains clarity, develop a perfect person body. Link the body shape with its status.
3. Verbalize the inner voice of your perfect person. Include your name and the autobiographical details of your life as you give an interview to an imaginary interviewer.
4. Greet other perfect people. Make all your moves, gestures, and actions consistent with rank and status. Find your voice.
5. Move slightly off the perpendicular. Adjust your status to fit the new image.

6. Move off the parallels and tilt to one side. Adjust your status to fit your new body.
7. Exaggerate the tilt. Move as far offcenter as possible.
8. Move around the room wearing the perfect person face with an imperfect person body.
9. Maintain the shape. Greet one another.
10. Find a partner, your best friend. Share a secret with one another.
11. Separate. Find a place to sit.
12. Sink into the imperfect person body. Let the face transform to match the body.
13. Stand and move as the imperfect person. Make the inner voice more specific.
14. Keep the imperfect person alive and move back onto the parallel and perpendicular planes.
15. Wear the imperfect person face with a perfect person body.
16. Let the character dissolve.
17. Freeze. Release.

Effort: Variable.

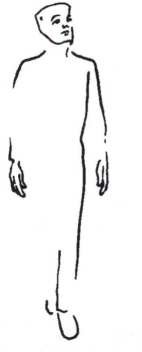 

Perfect and Imperfect People

Observations.   The perfect person tends at first to be extraordinarily rigid and almost impossible to play or make interesting. Images of Barbie and Ken, or the Stepford Wives, abound.

Once the mask goes offcenter and ventures into the realm of the imperfect person, something unique and extremely active develops: conflict. Who you are inside does not match who you are outside. Your outer and your inner do not "fit." There is a need for change in your relationship with yourself. When you try to maintain the perfect person mask with an imperfect person body, the inner conflict often triggers psychological insights into personality structure and behavioral patterns.

Inner and outer are almost always in opposition to one another. The outer always works as a cover for the inner, masking, shielding, and protecting its true essence.

Imperfect does not necessarily mean low status, nor does perfect mean high. Status is always relative to its context.

There is a tendency with imperfect people, at first, to play grotesque extremes. Exaggeration is a powerful tool, but be willing to abandon it if it makes you a cartoon and you lose the humanity of your character.

Perfect outers, with imperfect inners, are not necessarily rigid or difficult to play. Imperfect outers with perfect inners can have depth, humanity, and a clear inner purpose. Outer and inner can feed one another in a complementary fashion.

Start the process with a physical image and a physical key. Work from the outside in; connect the outer shape with an inner image, then move to a state of action. As you begin to define your relationship with your inner and outer status—the "gap" between your outer and your inner—use that gap as an inner hurdle. Use the hurdle to help create and define a target for yourself.

What the character wants for itself is usually the connective thread that links all the small moment-to-moment targets together. The only way the character can change its relationship with itself is by changing its relationship with the people around it. Everything the character does must "land" on your partners to alter your relationships with them. As your partners adjust and adapt to your actions, your character's relationship with itself will transform and its status will change. This is part of the inner movement pattern of the scene.

The linking thread, the throughline that drives all of the action forward, is called the magnet.

Silent Music

This ensemble activity is an exercise in additive playing, building each frame one step at a time.

1. Begin in the Neutral Stance, standing in a circle.
2. Shift your eye focus from the front to the side. Move your head to follow your eye focus.
3. Continue the eye shift/head shift sequence and make a box pattern with your focus: shift from the right to the upper right to upper center to upper left, down to middle left, to lower left, then to lower middle, lower right, middle right, and back to center.
4. Repeat and reverse directions, working to the left.
5. Add your body as you change the focus. Focus, shift, move. Use your body to add line and direction to each move.
6. Use the other players as points of focus.
7. Use No Move to create and change rhythms. Syncopate rhythms when possible.
8. Develop conversational rhythms.
9. Add touch.
10. Try touching without using your hands.
11. Change the spatial relationships yet always keep the space charged with action.
12. Add more than one focal change in each move. Begin to create phrases.

Effort: Variable.

Observations.   In Silent Music you artificially create a sense of order and structure, and you fill the structure with meaning and intent. You move from one specific image to the next. Each unit of action has a focal point and a beginning, middle, and end. You build the score of action slowly, deliberately. It is a long additive process.

Preserve the pattern whenever possible so the progression of the activity is clear during all of its various phases.

The activity becomes more interesting when you are adventurous and daring. Complexity develops through repetition—filling in the details, adding more and more endowments to the relationships, more variety and nuance to the playing.

Control the complexity of each frame by varying your use of time and space.

Maintain the eye pattern once the flow is established. Use physical stillness as an active element in the "music." Being physically still does not mean you are inactive.

Silent Movies

This set sequence tests the synchronicity between action and its physical manifestation in space.

1. Play a prepared scene.
2. Repeat. Speak, but without making any sound, as if someone turned down the volume control to zero.
3. Play the scene without overcompensating or exaggerating.
4. Really listen to one another with your eyes.
5. Repeat the scene, with volume, and make whatever adjustments are necessary.

Effort: Variable.

Observations.   Working without sound demands total attention and focus. The scene must be played with exactly the same dynamics and intensity as when spoken. Do not whisper; simply eliminate all sound from the scene.

When you watch the scene played as a Silent Movie see if you understand the relationships and the actions of the scene as they exist in space. Are the words necessary to tell the story? Are there times when the actors are lying? When are they saying one thing and their bodies are saying something else? If so, is it appropriate for the endowments and context of the scene? Do the players need to adjust to one another in any other way?

The moment-to-moment playing without sound needs as much clarity and focus as the moment-to-moment playing with sound. If the relationship is not clear and understandable without sound, it will never be clear with sound.

Silent Tension

This is another additive set sequence that exercises your ability to use different points of focus as a provocative tool in problem solving.

1. Take the following moves and combine them into a set sequence:

   One step forward
   One reach
   One kneel
   One turn
   One rise

2. Repeat the set sequence three times. Always begin and end in the same place, wherever your sequence takes you.
3. Justify each move in the pattern. Repeat the pattern once.
4. Think of each move as a frame.
5. Emphasize and change the effort factors for each frame.
6. Divide into two teams. As a team, establish your own playing space and, simultaneously with your teammates, repeat your score of action.

7. Establish eye contact with a different player for each frame. Adjust and adapt your playing to each other.
8. Endow one another and establish a series of relationships.
9. As a group, create a piece of Silent Music.
10. Give and take the focus within the score until a narrative emerges. Work for clarity and specificity of focus. Tell the story together.
11. Add BADs to inform and condition the playing.
12. Clarify your targets and heighten your hurdles. You are almost ready to speak.
13. There is a reason why you don't speak to one another. Incorporate that reason into your playing.
14. Play the score as a scene of Silent Tension.

Effort: Variable.

Observations. This activity combines Instant Performance, BADs, Silent Music, and Continue/Advance.

The score becomes a performance "text." The "third eye" of the audience takes you into a greater awareness of what you are doing, and how you do it. You begin to adjust and adapt, not only to your teammates but to your audience as well.

You started with a random series of unrelated moves. You arranged them into a set sequence. Through the simple process of repetition, you began to give the set sequence meaning and order. You moved from the general to the specific, from the random and chaotic to the ordered and sequential. This process of connecting disconnected elements, of finding the hidden relationship between parts, is a natural function of the brain. You don't have to force it; it happens on its own.

You added focus to the sequence by dividing the units into individual frames. Each frame had a beginning, a middle, and an end. Each frame was connected, through eye contact, to another player. Each frame involved a target—something you wanted from the other player—and action—what you did to the other player to get what you wanted.

The score evolved, from an individual effort to a team effort. You had a sense of playing the score together as music, and integrating design elements to give the music shape, definition, and clarity.

You justify the playing as a scene of Silent Tension through endowments. You do not use language substitutes to speak, but you use direct focused action. You focus on the relationships and the shifting patterns of status within each relationship. You work as a team. You are all in the same world, playing with a shared sense of time and place.

Each round of working is informed by a specific focus. Focus is a way of directing your attention and engaging your imagination. When you are focused you move the attention to a specific area and examine it in detail. It is your point of entry into the larger fabric of the work. It is impossible to focus on all of the fabric at once. Instead, you work in small units and let one unit lead to another. Once you are engaged and in a state of flow, you are working on all of the elements all the time. The trick is to create a point of engagement that helps you overcome your natural resistance and takes you into the work. Rehearsing is a process of eliminating obstacles that inhibit your concentration and disrupt your sense of flow.

PART THREE

MAP CLASSES

Hamlet, by William Shakespeare, Yale Repertory Theatre, New Haven, Connecticut, 1992.
Photograph © 1992 by T. Charles Erickson.

MAP CLASSES

The following twelve sessions are a reference guide illustrating how the MAP works. The modules can be combined in any sequence to deal with specific areas of the training. You also can mix and match the modules according to your needs in the rehearsal situation to solve whatever problems are presented.

The sessions organized and presented here link directly with one another to introduce the basic concepts and vocabulary of the MAP. Once the MAP vocabulary has been established it is possible to combine the modules, first with improvisational performances and later with a predetermined score of action—a script—as a means of making the process specific.

The conceptual work and the skills work always need a focus—a target—to challenge creative flexibility. The ultimate goal of the MAP is the creation of a practical, physical process that you can use with confidence in any working situation.

If you drill the modules—focusing on what you do and how you do it—and then mix and match by mapping, your creative skills will grow in proportion to your technical proficiency.

Work with Instant Performances—creating and shaping a score of action—will drill your ability to surrender into pure action. When you work nonverbally, everything must move forward without stalls or idles. The Instant Performances grow out of your imagination and life experience. They are structured to exercise creative skills in problem solving, MAP sequencing, and collaborative effort.

The work with a script will apply the MAP in a different way. You will work through language to discover the text's underlying patterns of action, and then use the rehearsal process to transform those patterns into dynamic, focused playing.

MAP provides a methodical way of seeing all the components of action, and then combines those components into a fluid sequence that can meet the creative demands of the moment. The MAP is a consistent and accurate process that will take you from any starting point from the page to the stage.

The two approaches to action—the imaginative, improvisational route using Instant Performances, and the structural, analytical approach using language and pattern analysis—are complementary. The MAP creates a fluid process that embraces and integrates both ways of working into one solid technique.

Sessions

   I. Flow
  II. Release
 III. Patterns
  IV. Transformations
   V. Balance
  VI. Status in Action
 VII. Scoring
VIII. Bridging the Text
  IX. Solo Speeches
   X. Approaching a Scene
  XI. Syncing
 XII. Style

SESSION I: *FLOW*

The first MAP session focuses on playing with a strong sense of physicality and flow.

1. Equidistance
2. Changing Tempo
3. Cross Thru
4. Balloon Breathing
5. Yes Game
6. Gift Giving
7. Blind Offers
8. Melted Architecture

Warm-Up:

1. Equidistance
2. Changing Tempo
3. Cross Thru
4. Balloon Breathing

Notes to the Players.   The first four activities should be played without pause back-to-back. Focus on the flow within each game and the quality of interaction with your partners. During the first three games you will endow one another and begin to bridge with one another by using strong and direct focus.

Engage your imagination with Changing Tempo; create histories that define the nature of your relationships. Let the endowments color the quality of your play; work with and off of one another.

The more you use and engage one another in the process, the easier the process becomes. Always integrate your imagination into the work.

In the Cross Thru justify the change in playing dynamics by shifting focus and transforming your relationship with the other players.

Balloon Breathing allows you to calm down after strong physical exertion. It is a recharging activity used continuously during your training.

Evaluation.   Examine these activities in terms of engagement: During these four activities did the quality of your playing change? Were you able to justify the changes and transformations of time and space through the use of endowments? Did you focus on creating relationships first, and then manipulate the externals to fit into your plan? Or did you focus on action and use that to trigger the justification?

Abide by the rules of play. The rules provide a context and structural framework for each activity. In essence, the rules give the playing shape and form. You fill the structure with meaning. When the outside and the inside are "in sync"—when the form of the playing merges with and expresses its content—you are engaged in flow.

5. Yes Game
6. Gift Giving

Observations.   These two games establish the basic playing patterns for all subsequent games: offer, accept, offer. You will drill these patterns repeatedly during the course of the training until the patterns become second nature to you. The pattern is the structural shape of the game.

The focus of the playing is always on triggering your partner's imagination by **bridging** to establish a direct path of communication and action.

7. Blind Offers
8. Melted Architecture

Observations.   These two activities are variations of the basic offer-accept pattern. They incorporate the use of far reach space: all gestures should begin from the center of your body and stretch out into the farthest corners of your personal space. The playing should be swift and spontaneous; don't take too much time to think. You will be working with a strong overload. Use the overload to trigger your impulse; act directly on the impulse.

Evaluation.   Did the quality of your interaction become stronger as the playing continued? What does intuitive rightness feel like? Did you experience a strong sense of flow? What happens when you act to trigger one another? Did you control the playing or did you experience playing "in the moment," and from "moment to moment?" What does it feel like to, quite literally, go with the flow?

Notes to the Trainer.   This is a fast-paced and physical session. Players may be apprehensive at first or they may have strong preconceptions about the nature of playing and "acting." Remember that part of your plan for each session is to remain deliberately unpredictable; you want to provoke the players and throw them off guard, yet build each session by introducing and then reintegrating concepts from previous sessions.

In this first session players come into contact with one another in a non-threatening environment. They begin to collaborate to experience concepts directly rather than intellectualize them.

Emphasize playing and responding to the impulse in the moment. Bridging is a physical process; players will be able to feel it as it happens. Bridging changes the quality of the play within each game.

Within each session, move players from perceiving analytically to perceiving intuitively by focusing on physical activity. Be on the lookout for habitual physical patterns favored by each player. Suggest areas for growth and change; leave the responsibility for making change to each individual player.

Every player develops at a different pace. As a trainer your primary task is to create an environment in which change is possible. You set the tone for each session; if the work seems tedious and dutiful to you you will see that reflected in your students. You are there to observe, guide, and coach the players; they will absorb discoveries when they are ready, and then move on to the next level of awareness. Maintain the discipline of the drills; the skills will follow.

Use the evaluations at the end of each sequence to monitor awareness. The questions you ask, and the answers you receive, will determine the observations you make about the process. The evaluation period should help players link experience with concepts; the MAP vocabulary always must be anchored by tangible reference points rather than isolated theory.

The primary goal of the initial session is to make players aware of their inhibitions by providing alternatives to release blocked energy. Once players are in a state of flow, anything is possible; they will be directing themselves through the activities. Your task will be to observe their growth and progress, and to continue to offer alternative paths that will provoke new directions for them.

In the next session you will continue to focus on the experience of flow while developing physical awareness of stress, tension, and release.

SESSION II: *RELEASE*

This session focuses on surrendering tension and releasing inhibition to develop a sense of collaboration and play.

1. Wholeness Isolation
2. The Elevator
3. Solo Stretch
4. Body Shapes
5. Kinetic Sculpture
6. Talking Dolls

Warm-Up:

1. Wholeness Isolation
2. The Elevator
3. Solo Stretch

Notes to the Players.   These three activities involve sustained focus, coordination, and physical awareness. To truly engage, place your focus on an image outside yourself. You cannot be self-conscious and play freely; self-consciousness inhibits the release of energy.

Keep your focus on the external image. In the Wholeness Isolation activity focus either on the mobile or the stable part of your body. In the Solo Stretch focus either on the vertical or the sagittal planes in your body and the shapes you are making. Breathe into each shape and lengthen your spine.

As you become comfortable, take more time. Use the physical warm-up to tune and engage your imagination. Expand your awareness to include areas where you are holding tension. When do you release? Can you integrate your breathing into each of these warm-up movements?

How do you ground your physical support and how have you learned to compensate for inert body parts?

Throughout, try not to compress your spine by collapsing your neck or allowing your chest to crumble into your waist. Lengthen your spine by lifting your sternum; release your pelvis by unlocking your knees. Expand awareness of your body in space.

Take time with the stretches. Move from The Elevator into the Solo Stretch with a sense of flow. Connect one activity with the next, so that you develop a feeling of forwardness and direction in your motion. Linking and connecting physical activities also strengthens your mental alertness and builds stamina.

4. Body Shapes
5. Kinetic Sculpture

Observations. These two activities require strong offers and accepts with your partner. Your focus should always be physical. You will be working with different parts of your body as leads to guide your direction in space. As you work, endow one another, and allow the endowments to transform your response to the different leads.

Work for a strong sense of connection with your partner; play without leading or following. Work together to discover the pattern, direction, and flow of the activity.

Add Freeze/Go to break and alter your action patterns. Establish a rhythm to the playing, then vary the rhythm. When possible, see what it is like to inhibit rhythm. Create a reason for the inhibition—add either a penalty or a reward, so that there are consequences if the evenness of the tempo is broken.

Change your positions in space often. Vary your levels and let the change in level suggest different situations and different relationships. Work to engage, provoke, and expand your imagination. Respond with your first impulse; physicalize your response. Experiment with what happens when you move through your initial inhibition and bridge with your partner.

6. Talking Dolls

Evaluation. Examine these activities in terms of flow: did the experience and quality of the playing change as the activity progressed? Did the playing become easier when you knew the structural pattern of the game? Did the rules of the game make the game more specific? If they did, was it easier to release into the playing, or do the rules make the playing more challenging and difficult?

How wedded is the internal to the external, and the external to the internal? Do they work together to help trigger and deepen your involvement in the playing? When were you collaborating with your partner, and when were you separate? Were you able to surrender your own desire for control and allow yourself to be led into something unexpected? If so, what happened once you got there?

Observations.   If you are the manipulator, you must work with your partner to give the doll life and movement. Maintain eye contact throughout the playing.

If you are the doll, you must surrender to your partners and allow them to guide you. Be willing to go into the unknown. When you speak, let the words grow out of the physical lead. Speak only when necessary.

As you recreate the physical pattern on your own, work to give it a context and a sense of forwardness. Fill in the blanks of time and place by responding to the clues your body is giving you. Work from the outside in. As the image begins to emerge and you gain clarity, adjust and adapt your physical score to suit the context you have created.

You are now beginning to work with a creative, transformational process, continuing and advancing the image. Work with and through one another in a collaborative manner to unlock the impulse that propels this process forward. Integrate reason into the action, and let it inform and color your playing. This will lead you into another form of release, in which you play from a heightened and personalized core.

Notes to the Trainer.   This session is built around additives and steps—each activity builds upon and expands the previous one. The shape and flow of the energy in the session involves a gradual build to Talking Dolls. Abruptness and dynamic shifts are inappropriate. Make the experience of the session smooth and even; think in terms of one long, smooth arc of action, rather than abrupt, jagged steps.

The initial activities are warm-ups for the rest of the session. As such, they are meant to focus the players' attention and prepare them for what will happen next. While the point of attention is primarily physical, players must engage mentally. Help guide and intensify this aspect of the process in your coaching.

Work with a specific focus to engage and direct attention. Focusing is merely a starting point for the activity; as the players engage, they will intuitively change their point of focus to suit the task at hand. Help them integrate the physical with the mental as soon as possible.

Integrated playing is the foundation upon which you will build all other activities. The sooner players begin to experience this form of concentrated flow and associate it with released, focused energy, the stronger and faster the work will progress.

Help players begin to develop an awareness of how they carry stress in their bodies and how stress, in excess, shuts down and inhibits the creative impulse. The stretches and releases offer a series of alternatives that bypass and circumvent creative and physical blocks; they help release power and energy within the player's imagination. Once that power is unleashed it can inform the quality of the playing. Focused energy is the creative fuel that propels the playing process.

The concept of release in this session operates on three levels: the physical level, which enables players to engage in action with less tension; the creative level, which allows players to experience the power of their imaginations once they are physically engaged; and the emotional and psychological level, which involves surrendering and engaging on a deeper, more personal level.

The physical is, once again, the guide to monitoring the psychological. Stay alert for the clues and signs of suppression of energy: shifts in eye focus, moments of broken contact between players, or any time the flow pattern seems erratic, abrupt, or fluctuating. Most importantly, stay alert to players who want to guide and control the direction of the playing. These patterns must be acknowledged and broken if the player is to grow.

The next session expands the concept of release by working on patterns. While continuing to develop a physical vocabulary you will shift the focus to the player's work process, formally introducing the initiating concepts of the MAP process.

SESSION III: *PATTERNS*

The focus of this session is on defining how rules create structural patterns.

1. Spinal Walk Down
2. Spinal Float
3. Group Jump
4. In Nine
5. Hit the Mark
6. Changing Places
7. Squat Ten
8. Mirror Cloning

Warm-Up:

1. Spinal Walk Down
2. Spinal Float

Notes to the Players. The warm-up activities focus on releasing stored energy within your spine and pelvis. They are designed to minimalize your effort in stretching and maximize the amount of contact and interaction between you and your partner.

Surrender to your partner and allow yourself to be guided through the activity. The less you do and the more you surrender control and responsibility, the farther you will be able to release and stretch.

At the end of The Float, take a bit of time to walk around through the playing space. How does it feel to experience length and release in your spine? Do you feel lighter? Taller? How does your pelvis anchor your walk?

Take another moment and talk with your partner. When were you working together? Were you able to stay connected through your breathing? How did the two of you communicate nonverbally?

3. Group Jump

Observations. This is a pattern game. Learn the pattern of each sequence and observe your process in learning the pattern. Focus on yourself first, as you learn to image the pattern. The focus then shifts onto your partners—to bridge and link with them—so you can play the game together. In the third round you begin to refine your playing, making it more specific by intensifying the factors that condition and affect the quality of your play.

The steps in this sequence mirror the four primary steps involved in the MAP. First, you prepare alone, looking for clues and patterns of action that will propel you forward. Next, you work collaboratively with your partner to find the collective patterns of action—the score of action—within the scene. Then you define and refine the score through repetition, heightening and intensifying the playing of the score. Finally, you perform the score of action for an observer.

As you work the Group Jump, stay aware of the rules of the game. You must begin and end together. Once you have integrated and absorbed the pattern of the game into your body you can play without having to think about it. Focus on the quality of your interaction with the other players; this is when the playing begins to transform.

4. In Nine

Observations. This is a framing game. Each unit of action has a frame, which defines its shape and content. By counting out each frame, you'll have a clear idea of where you are heading every time you move. As the structure and shape become more obvious to you, and as time compresses, you can fill each frame with more interesting and engaging action.

5. Hit the Mark
6. Changing Places
7. Squat Ten

Observations. Focus on defining the frames to know your boundaries. You must be willing to go beyond the mark in order to define it; then go to its furthest possible limit before moving on to the next mark.

As you play Changing Places focus on agreeing with your partner by making eye contact with one another before you move. Fill the "frame" as you move across the floor by engaging in an exchange with your partner. Complete the cycle by transforming once you arrive at your destination.

You are drilling the action cycle, in which you initiate, engage, and complete an action. Every action has its own frame—its boundaries in time and space which give the action shape and definition.

First, discover the pattern of the action and its structure; then, as you continue to play, make the relationship with your partners more and more interesting. Endow one another with more complex qualities, and let those qualities infuse and inform the quality of your playing. Complete each action before you begin the next cycle.

Squat Ten is deliberately designed as a no-win game. Your focus of attention is on the quality of the playing. You will have to shift continuously between offensive and defensive playing. Observe how the framing devices—the rules of the game—become increasingly complex from round to round. Does this transform the experience of the playing?

Evaluation. Examine these activities in terms of the quality of your playing: Did your playing have a sense of destination and purpose? Were you ever able to define for yourself a clear point of focus that guided and directed you forward or did you "idle," marking time without a sense of advancing the action? Did the quality of the flow change or was it constant? What did you use as your trigger to initiate the action? How did you engage in the action? What did you do to complete the action cycle?

As you played these games was your focus on what you were feeling or on what you were doing? How does emotion fuel and propel action rather than be the action?

If you began to experience a sense of destination in your playing, moving from one edge of the frame to the other, what did you change along the way, or what changed along the way, to make the journey from edge to edge more interesting, dynamic, and exciting?

8. Mirror Cloning

Observations. If you are the cloner, make your instructions specific and direct. If you are the clone, follow the instructions without hesitation. Surrender to the physical shape and see if it triggers your imagination.

Evaluation. Are the inner and the outer related? Since you are developing an awareness of the interrelationship of all the parts, what stimuli can you use to trigger and engage your imagination? Does the shape of the character inhibit or release your engagement in the flow of action?

Notes to the Trainer. This is a varied session, focusing on the concept of patterns. Throughout the session, be specific in setting up the "frames" of each activity. Focus the player's attention on a specific task that will take them from one edge to the other. How they get there is how they fill the structure and engage in the creative process.

The warm-up involves patterns of resistance and release. Players will always resist before they surrender; in your coaching focus on making them aware of their individual patterns of holding and withholding. Once the body knows what to expect of itself, it can surrender and release.

The next three activities, Group Jump, In Nine, and Hit the Mark, focus on establishing boundaries and setting obtainable targets. Each frame must be clearly defined. It must be easily obtainable. As players become more and more confident and comfortable with small frames—and can mark out beginnings, middles, and ends within the action cycle—they can begin to link the cycles together into larger frames with more complex patterns of action.

In Changing Places and Squat Ten keep the dynamics of the playing swift. Overload the playing so players don't have much time to think; they must respond to one another, yet they must maintain the discipline of the rules and structure of the game. If they break the rules, in an attempt "to win," they violate the game and sidestep the process for a quick, easy result. If this happens stop the playing, restate the rules, and begin again.

The cloning exercise is the first major point of integration in the training sequence. It allows players to exercise their observational skills, their communicative skills, and their transformational skills. It can provide a deep release of inhibition if players surrender and allow the mask to take over.

These first three sessions are physical and focus on the processes of release, shape, flow, and patterning. Each session begins with a physical warm-up, followed by a series of activities that examine and investigate a specific concept or group of related concepts. Each session ends with one final activity that integrates and reincorporates all the previous concepts into a performance game. Evaluation and discussion are vital components in the process, linking experience with theory to develop a practical, collective working vocabulary.

With the MAP, skills are introduced cumulatively and are examined and worked on individually, from session to session. Progress will be unique to each player, and the dynamics of each session will vary from group to group, even if the same structural sequence is used over and over again.

In the next triad of sessions the thematic focus shifts from physical processes to interactive processes, examining three major elements of interaction—transformations, balance, and status. You will continue to focus on flow, individually and interactively, but you will expand the focus of attention to include the patterns and dynamics of changing relationships.

SESSION IV: *TRANSFORMATIONS*

This session focuses on defining action patterns.

1. Back to Back Elevator
2. Duet Stretch
3. Giants and Elves
4. Zig Zags
5. Transformation Circles
6. BADs
7. Nonverbal Yield Scenes

Warm-Up:
1. Back to Back Elevator
2. Duet Stretch

Notes to the Players.   This warm-up is a variation of the solo stretch, but it requires skills in bridging, sustaining flow, and nonverbal communication. The playing is more subtle and complex and the teamwork needs to be clearly focused.

Work for a gradual and sustained release. Stay connected with one another through your breathing. When you feel resistance in your body, exaggerate the resistance—let it swell up and grow out of proportion until you have no choice but to surrender and let go.

The quality of flow between you will improve as the stretching progresses. When you repeat the pattern, stay alert for changes in body tension. Do the shifting patterns of tension affect the nature of the communication between you? When do you hold and when do you release tension? Does the release change when you surrender control to your partner?

3. Giants and Elves

Observations.   Use this game to refocus and redirect your energy after the sustained stretch. Play rapidly and with strong, dynamic shifts and contrasts. Locate and use specific physical **keys** to trigger the image of each mask.

4. Zig Zags
5. Transformation Circles

Observations. These two patterning games are a form of physical free association. They rely on one image triggering another without you predetermining the outcome. Simply respond to what your partner offers you, sink into it, and allow it to change until it defines itself, and then offer the new action to the next player. Do not judge the action or question it; simply accept, respond, offer.

As you become comfortable with this process, work to integrate your inner life with your physical playing. Infuse the outer dynamic with immediacy and urgency. At the same time, avoid tension. Stay open to all possibilities. Allow the outer to trigger your inner and then use your inner to transform and trigger the outer. When your playing is intense and passionate you will begin to experience an action drive.

In the Transformation Circle focus on the movement from one "frame," or unit of action, to the next. Each unit of action is important as is the linking process that connects the units. The links have equal focus in the playing pattern. Find them together as a group, and complete each link before initiating a new action cycle.

Evaluation. What happens when you play with "full action"—when the outer and the inner are connected? What happens when a player jumps without going through the entire developmental process? Do you feel the dynamic of the action as you observe others playing? How do you respond to it as an observer? How does nonverbal communication affect you? What is the impact of body language, body dynamic, and the transformation of energy? How does this impact affect your skills as a communicator?

6. BADs

Observations. Each of the BADs creates a unique pattern of action. The patterns are tied to psychological cores which define your individual essence in specific, nonverbal terms. You usually move into an action drive as a scene progresses and reaches its climax.

The BADs are useful for organizing your approach to action within a text. You can read a text initially looking for patterns of action—is the character direct or indirect, strong or light, quick or sustained? Even if the choice is arbitrary, you can organize these impressions and act on them. Once you move from the page to the stage your perception and understanding of the effort patterns will grow and transform through experience.

Analyzing the BADs is one way of initiating action. Your choices are based on an exploration of the text rather than random and isolated hunches and guess work. Every choice based on the text strengthens the quality of your playing and your confidence in the work process.

7. Nonverbal Yield Scenes

offer / accept
continue and advance the narrative action
transform the action within each frame
shift the dynamics of the effort with each transformation

Observations.   The final exercise of this session reincorporates and integrates all of the concepts and skills in the first four sessions. Structurally, you must initiate, engage, and complete an action cycle. Each cycle forms a "frame" that has a perceptible beginning, middle, and end. The frame must change every time your thought and action change. Change of action = change of direction in the course of the scene. Every frame must link up and connect with the next.

The action can progress only by a series of offers and accepts in which you endow your partner and examine the nature of your relationship with the other character. You must work with a sense of forwardness in playing the action from one edge of the frame to the other. Because you are working without words you may not stall or idle in time. Everything must take you forward until the scene finds its logical conclusion.

The quality of the teamwork is crucial for the development of the narrative. Work together to discover the patterns of action within the scene. Play the scene as honestly and directly as possible. Keep your sense of movement alive—not necessarily your physical movement, although that may be part of it. Rather, focus on the inner movement within the scene, the progression and transformation of your relationship with your partner, and how changing the relationship propels you forward into acting and reacting.

Evaluation.   What is the experience of transforming action? How do you engage when you play an action? How do you respond when you observe action? Can you sense when the action moves into a drive? Does the quality of the play change when this happens? Are the shifts in effort patterns visible or invisible? How do you know when something is changing and transforming? How do you know when the transformation is complete?

Notes to the Trainer.   This session is the first formal introduction to the concept of action and the processes of interaction. Work to trigger the players by guiding and directing their physical responses; focus on the players' individual use of effort as well as their collaborative effort when playing together. Vary the effort patterns within each segment of the session to trigger a deeper, more dynamic sense of flow within the playing.

The warm-up should be sustained and strong. Giants and Elves is a fluctuating activity with rapid shifts of effort. The Zig Zag will involve abrupt shifts, while the Transformational Circle will involve gradual changes. The BADs will vary, and the Nonverbal Yields should include a wide variety of effort shifts, shapes, changes, and patterns.

This is a fast-paced session. Coach the players to complete each action cycle and to complete each link. As players develop strength in playing small units of action they can begin to link the units together into larger and larger cycles, each with a clear beginning, middle, and end. The patterns will gradually organize and form a score of action. This score defines the structure of a scene.

Continue to focus on clarifying the rules and structure of each activity. The players are developing skills in endowing, releasing, integrating their imaginations into the work, offering and accepting, and therefore, playing together with outward focus and a sense of forwardness. In short, they are learning to fill form with content and meaning.

The focus must always stay on fulfilling the structure of an activity, on finding and defining the things they must do, not on what they must feel. Feeling is not a process; it is a result of the doing.

Action is experiential. Do not overanalyze at this stage in the training process. Help players to engage in action, and then get out of their way and allow them to play the action fully. Coach them when they get stuck or blocked, and then get out of their way again. As they get stronger, they will be able to sustain longer segments of uninterrupted and uncoached action. Your task is to continue to look for the inhibiting factors that prevent players from fully engaging and releasing into the action. Note when the blocks occur and share your observations with the players. Enlist their aid in devising individual plans of attack, unique to each of them, to break their patterns and habits. They must participate in the process if they wish to unlock the range of creative possibilities open to them.

In the next session you will focus on the concept of balancing action. While balance is a physical process, it also has structural and psychological ramifications. Players will focus on developing their skills in using weight, and with weight, their ability to sense and act on intuitive rightness.

SESSION V: *BALANCE*

The session focuses on relationships and status.

1. Goosenecks
2. Scrape the Bowl
3. The Whip
4. Triangles
5. Status Bodies

6. Verbal All Yield Scenes
7. Add: Compliments/Insults
8. Status Transformations
9. Maxi Gap

Warm-Up:

1. Goosenecks
2. Scrape the Bowl
3. The Whip

Notes to the Players.   These three warm-up activities focus on shape. Work to connect the outside to the inside and focus your attention on creating "line" in space with your body.

Observe, once again, the relationship between your spine and your pelvis. Keep your knees slightly bent to unlock your legs, and allow your pelvis to release forward. Once your pelvis is released, your spine will lengthen. Make sure you do not compress your neck by lifting your chin; work the opposite way, tucking the chin and lengthening the nape of your neck.

Gooseneck, The Whip, and Scrape the Bowl require length within the body. Focus on becoming aware of your own vertical axis; emphasize your up and down directions rather than your side to side or front to back directions.

Thinking and imaging in terms of planes and axes—directions in space— become increasingly important as you describe your observations of how people engage in action.

These three activities also engage you in postural rather than gestural action. Gestural activity does not require weight shifts or changes within the central axis of your body, whereas postural activity does. When you shift your weight you engage both your pelvis and your spine—your centers of gravity and balance—and you work on a more complex physical level of engagement.

The activities also take you into carving space—working with a strong sense of engaged flow. Carving, especially when combined with postural action, is a sign of intense, in-the-moment involvement. It is similar to playing an action drive. Drill carving, even if it is artificially induced, to recognize the sensations of action driving. Remember, you always work the outer to trigger the inner; once you engage the inner, you can transform the outer. Trigger your imagination by endowing your partner and create a specific, detailed relationship.

4. Triangles

Observations.   Triangles require balance, trust, surrender (to the unknown and to each other), and endowment. Once you learn the structure of this activity endow your partner with elements of intrigue, danger, attraction, or allure. Make the rewards or penalties for a loss of balance meaningful enough to require precise and specific action while playing. Go to the edge—hit the mark—as you balance and counterbalance, and define for yourself the thin line between abandon and control.

5. Status Bodies

Observations.   Continue to endow one another throughout the reunions and gatherings. Remember that your eyes are the key to unlocking your imagination in this activity.

Your shape will determine your status. Status is always relative to context. The high status body usually requires length, postural engagement, and stillness. Work in intermediate to far reach space. The low status body usually requires compression and gestural business. Work in near space, close within your physical sphere.

One of these shapes will feel more comfortable than the other. Focus on the uncomfortable shape. By developing flexibility within the shape (and confronting your instincts about why the shape is uncomfortable) you will begin to stretch into playing someone other than yourself. You must be able to move up to the character as well as pull the character down to you. The mask lives somewhere in the space between the two.

Separate yourself from the mask. It is the mask who has high or low status, not you. Try on and wear as many different masks and status bodies as you can while you are in the safe playing environment. The more you risk—the more you release into the playing—the more you will discover on your own.

6. Verbal All Yield Scenes

Observations.   In a Verbal Yield scene, speak only when you need to speak. Begin with a physical activity and stay with the activity as long as possible. Define yourself and your partner by what you do, not what you say. Make words an extension of the action, rather than a substitute for it.

Drill the Verbal Yield scene carefully. Become comfortable with its structure. The less you have to think about making an offer—the more automatic it becomes as a way of playing—the freer you will be in surrendering to the action of the scene and moving the narrative forward.

7. Add: Compliments/Insults

Observations.   By complimenting or insulting your partner, you automatically have something to do in the scene. You either raise your partner (and lower yourself), or lower your partner (and raise yourself). The scene becomes a verbal extension of The Triangle you played earlier.

Scenes are about the moment-to-moment balance—the status shifts—in your relationship with your partner.

All scenes are about relationships changing and transforming in front of our eyes. It's not what the characters say, it's what they do that engages us. The saying is contained in the doing. The patterns of action within a scene chart the transformation and balance within the relationship; as one character rises, another falls, whether slightly or dramatically.

Structurally, scenes are about characters jockeying for position with one another. What characters say to one another—the information they reveal about themselves—forms the content of the scene. Play the intent of the language—what it does to shift the balance—not its emotional content.

Drill raising and lowering. Learn to recognize and see the patterns immediately. Raising and lowering are structural actions; as you see the structure and surrender to it, you will be able to release into the playing without inhibition or hesitation. It is not you, but the mask, who rises and falls.

Evaluation. You endow, i.e., build bridges, in the early part of a scene to establish the patterns of action and behavior within the relationship. Then you break these patterns. These moves: pattern, break the pattern, new pattern, break the pattern, new pattern, break the pattern, form the action sequence of the scene.

Each action sequence has a beginning, a middle, and an end. Each sequence is made up of moment-to-moment "frames" in which you see and chart the progression of the transformation within the relationship. The isolated frames link together to form a sequence. The sequences link together to form the larger score of action.

Each frame, sequence, and score has its own flow pattern, its own movement of effort and tension. Focus on examining the moves the characters make, through their use of language, and how those moves force the relationship to evolve. Once you know the structure of the scene you can play it fully, from moment to moment, with a sense of forwardness in the action.

Every relationship involves a gap of tension between the characters that changes as the scene progresses. It is possible to chart the pattern of action within a scene in terms of how the gap expands or contracts; this movement describes the relationship between the characters. When you focus on defining the gap you focus on what you do to affect your partner, not on what you feel.

8. Status Transformations:
   Matching
   Seesawing

Observations. These two activities are gap games. In Matching you establish a gap and work to maintain it. Keep the gap even at all times. Inhibit any impulse to change the gap. Eventually, the playing will become static; the scene will grind to a halt.

Seesawing involves shifting and changing the gap. You and your partner agree to switch positions whenever you can. The scene is about the raising and lowering of positions, the shifting of balance between the two of you. Make the moves as even and gradual as possible. Focus only on transforming your position by either raising or lowering your partner. Participate in the move in either direction; do not resist being lowered. Let the gap fluctuate.

9. Maxi Gap: Master-Servant

Observations. The easiest way to examine the gap is to blow it out of proportion until it becomes visible and unavoidable. Master-servant is an exaggerated Maxi Gap relationship: it involves the largest possible gap between the characters. Who occupies which position is always relative to the context of the scene; sometimes the master is high, sometimes low. The infinite variety of possibilities makes the scene interesting.

Surrender to the needs involved in fulfilling your role. If you are low servant raising your master, release into the action; either lower yourself unashamedly or raise your master unapologetically. Do whatever you need to do to fulfill the structural requirements of the scene. Initiate the action, engage in the transformation, and complete the pattern. Once it is completed, look for the transition into the next action cycle. Fulfill the rule of the activity—keep the gap moving.

Evaluation. Did the action within the scene advance, or did you stall for time? When do you stall? What do we want to see happen in a scene? What are our expectations during the course of the scene? What happens when they are fulfilled and when they aren't? Can you see and feel the difference between inhibited and uninhibited playing? How does this difference contribute to the quality of the play during the course of the scene?

Notes to the Trainer. This is another additive session. Each activity links into and feeds the next. There is a constant and steady progression throughout the session that takes the players first into themselves then out to one another, moving them from exercise to scene work. The session advances the previous work with nonverbal action and expands it into the verbal.

Throughout, focus on players establishing and developing relationships with one another. Bridging is crucial at this stage of development.

Whenever players get lost or blocked, it is because they don't know who they are to one another. Their status is not clear. When players know who they are and where they are in the arc of the relationship, they know what they can or must do to one another to move the action forward.

It is only when we wrestle with finding a solution to a difficult problem that we discover how much we know. Remember that the MAP deals with problem solving: players learn to identify a problem, seek alternative solutions to unblock their locked imaginations, and then experiment with applying those solutions until their energy is released and they move forward again.

The Verbal Yield scenes are always difficult and, therefore, are loaded with opportunities for discovery. Players may talk too much; they may lose the sense of action they had with the nonverbal work when they suddenly have something to say. Rather than doing, they'll ramble, idle, or stall.

Get them to focus on their relationship with their partner. Make them bridge. Make them make offers about their relationship, which either raises or lowers their partner's status. The focus must always be on triggering their partner's imagination.

Whenever possible, make the players do more and say less. They will want to describe action rather than engage in it. It is vital, at this stage in the training, that players learn to see language as thought in action. Language and the process of speaking involve bridging—one player linking to another—and then working from the outside (what the character says) to the inside (what the character wants) in order to understand what the character does.

Once players understand this process, language will be used only when necessary. The words are infused with action and have a reason for being in the scene. Continually coach the players to stay on the thought, to keep the thought on the line, and to keep the line moving forward.

Players do not have to be clever or original, but they do have to be alive and in the moment. When players become inhibited verbally, they need to shift their focus from content (what they are saying) to intent (what they are doing). This shift in verbal focus is a skill players will continually refine in their training and is a major tool in the MAP.

The concept of balance is a key to understanding the processes of patterning and defining structure. Balance is tangible, observable, practical, experiential. If you are in a state of dysbalance, you concentrate on coming into balance. If characters are in a state of dysbalance with one another, they focus on trying to make the other character compensate for them by either taking more or releasing less weight—and stress—into the scene.

Balancing is the metaphor for the psychological jockeying for position between characters in a scene. Every move has a countermove; every action a reaction. Looking at the patterns of the moves—the flow and sequencing of the expansion and contraction in the gap—is one way of determining the structure of the scene.

When players are out of sync with one another coach them into looking for the shift in the pattern their partner is making, and counter that move with an offer of their own. Keep the focus on the structure and the pattern, not on the content of the scene. Balance the scene move by move. This shift in focus physically is another skill players develop in their training and is another way to trigger engagement and release.

The sixth session develops the concept of balance by focusing on complex patterns in group dynamics. Once again, if players focus on fulfilling the structure of a scene within the context of the endowments, the content takes care of itself.

SESSION VI: *STATUS IN ACTION*

This session continues to focus on the dynamics of status.

1. Cloud Hands
2. Air Ball
3. Energy Ball
4. Narrative Patterns: Status Transformations
5. Maxi Gaps
6. Mini Gaps
7. Pecking Orders
8. The Squeeze

Warm-Up:

1. Cloud Hands
2. Air Ball

Notes to the Players.   These warm-up activities continue to drill skills in release and flow.

Shift your point of attention as you play. First, focus on your partner; then focus on releasing a held or inert body part. Shift your focus back to your partner. Move together with perfect synchronicity. Shift your focus to release the tension stored in your lower back. Maintain your vertical axis as you move. Shift the focus to the reach space you are using with your partner; keep the space equidistant and constant.

This continuous shifting of focus will prevent you from drifting mentally as you work. The intent of the warm-up is to root you firmly in the here and now; abandon all other thoughts and considerations. Your body is your key to engaging and focusing your attention.

Sustain and intensify contact with your partner. Moving your focus back and forth between two points of attention keeps you in a constant state of inner movement and activity. You have specific boundaries for your focus—a frame—and you move within it. This gives direction to your work.

Keep the flow smooth and even; balance and physical control are extremely important. Work without leading or following. All countermoves between you should be small. Share the process of the evolution of the action, each taking the activity forward one small step at a time. Let the process "jiggle," or bounce back and forth, between the two of you. Use peripheral vision when you work side by side.

3. Energy Ball

Observations. Play with swift and dynamic effort changes. Take all the accepts into the center of your body; play posturally. Make all offers in far reach space. Work with a strong overload, so there is no time to think, just to respond. When all three balls are moving simultaneously, keep your focus of attention as open as possible.

4. Narrative Patterns: Status Transformations

Yields—Yes, And
Blocks—Intent and Content
Shelves—Yes, But

Observations. These patterns focus and direct the shape of narrative action. They describe movement in thinking patterns and therefore, movement in action patterns.

Yielding accepts the offered thought and counteroffers with another offer. The action continues to move forward. This pattern is heightened with "And Then You ...," which forces you to loop and engage your partner in your reply. Yield to your partner by giving your partner what he or she wants in terms of intent and content.

Blocking accepts neither the intent nor the content of an offer. You must make the distinction between the two. If you block the **content** of your partner's offer you yield to your partner's intent—you don't accept his or her premise because you want to continue the argument. If you block the **intent** of your partner's offer you might accept his premise because you want to end the argument.

Shelving accepts the basic offer but moves it aside for the moment. It is not completely blocked; you might reincorporate it at a later date.

At all times work to trigger one another's imaginations.

As a challenge, and as a means of breaking preconceptions about action patterns, work with two coaches—one to call directions to you, one to call directions to your partner. Your coach will tell you when to yield, block, or shelve. You may not make a move on your own. Respond only to the instructions given to you. Work to fulfill the structure of each move; the content will take care of itself.

Keep the playing physical. Do not become talking heads in the course of the scene. Use the physical action to trigger your imagination. Remember that the point of the scene is to engage in an exchange that transforms your relationship.

Spend the first frames of the scene jockeying for position, establishing the boundaries of the relationship. Then engage in transforming the relationship. The scene ends when the transformation is complete and a new pattern is established. Status becomes an active element in the scene.

Use blocks and shelves sparingly. They change the direction and pattern of action in the scene. Each pattern needs time to establish itself before you change it. Yielding involves endowing and bridging. Be generous in giving your partner information about who you are to one another.

Evaluation. Examine the narrative action of the scene: how does a scene work when you have more than one point of focus? When do you respond to your partner and when to your coach? What's the difference between being inside the scene and having to make quick decisions while in overload, and being outside the scene, observing it in an unpressurized way? How important are your offers? Do they take you deeper into the relationship and give you information you can use or do you use them to stall for time? Is the quality of your teamwork growing? Is it any easier to get up and play?

5. Maxi Gaps with Yields/Blocks/Shelves
   Review: Seesawing

Observations. You are now integrating many different components of the training process. You are defining and establishing the mask of the character through shape. The playing must have flow. You must engage in complete action cycles, and the cycles must link together into an action sequence. You also are working with overloads, rewards and penalties, and complex patterns of action.

At the same time you are structuring the narrative while you are creating it. You are linking the outer with the inner to create language that is active. You are transforming relationships and playing within a highly defined world of rules and boundaries. You may not predetermine or control the direction of the action.

Make the status transformations smooth and even. Match your partner move for move, offer for offer. Begin and end simultaneously within each frame; do not jump in the course of the transformation. Remember to breathe.

6. Mini Gaps with Yields/Blocks/Shelves
   Review: Matching

Observations. In the Mini Gap, all moves are small and perfectly bal-anced. If you get stuck in the course of the Mini Gap, match or mirror one another physically. When you match you continue to neutralize one another and stay on an even keel. You will also have something to do—a point of focus outside of yourself to give your playing direction.

In a Mini Gap the moves are never quite as dynamic or dramatic as they are in the Maxi Gap. The transformation of the pattern usually happens over a longer period of time because the moves are small.

Use Yield/Block/Shelve to give the scene extra momentum. Varying the narrative patterns will break the status pattern and give the scene unex-pected direction. Let the relationship transform in order to fulfill the struc-ture of the scene.

7. Pecking Orders:
   Hierarchies and Pyramids

Observations. Status is always relative to its context. You may be in the high position in one relationship, in the low position in another. Moving back and forth and making rapid adjustments between the two extremes requires mental as well as physical dexterity. The MAP encourages this form of flexibility.

Focus your attention on areas of resistance, either mentally or physically, and work to release and expand these areas to develop more range within your work. Remember, when you raise and lower your partner's status, you are also expanding or contracting the status gap between you.

Every group has a pecking order that determines hierarchy within the group. You must know where you stand, who is above you and who below, in order to know how to act appropriately in any context. Your position in the pecking order determines who you bridge with and how you endow your partner.

Your physical shape is a strong element in determining where you fit into the pecking order. Your shape must be appropriate for your status; so must your verbal skills (or lack of them) depending on your level in the hier-archy. As in all work with masks and status, do not confuse your own status with that of the mask you are wearing.

These activities are meant to increase and expand your skill in observing and articulating the dynamics of group behavior. Man is, by nature, a pack animal; we travel in packs, we socialize in packs, we seek out like company and participate in pack activities. Status is constantly moving and fluid within the pack. Status becomes more complex and dynamic when it moves from one-on-one playing to a larger social context.

8. The Squeeze

Observations. Body language is a key to the dynamics involved in The Squeeze. Play with stop motion and freeze/frame; observe and analyze the physical relationships and how they outwardly mirror the inner structure of the action from moment to moment. Note how players turn into or away from one another, or physically link and bridge with one another. At what point is this physical life a subconscious response to the action, and at what point does it become a conscious tactic to stay in the game?

Discussion. The Maxi Gap and Mini Gap activities involve fixed points of reference; you know what the gap is in the relationship at the beginning and at the end of the scene. The focus of the scene—its structure and form—involves discovering how you move from one point to another, and how you link these points together.

The Pecking Order scenes involve both fixed and fluid positions. One and four—high and low in the Pecking Order—are fixed; two and three are fluid. Develop flexibility by playing all four positions at different times. Do not specialize.

The Squeeze demands fluidity; you must fight to stay in the game at all times; you must play with forwardness and physicality or you will be squeezed out. The group will intuitively determine its own pecking order, although the order will change and fluctuate as the playing progresses.

Evaluation. Do these activities accurately mirror group dynamics and interaction? Do all transactions between people involve shifts in status? Does status ever have negative connotations? Does status ever have positive connotations? Does the quality of your play change according to your status? How do your offers determine your status? What is a status endowment? Can you endow yourself with status? Can you endow an environment with status? How does status lead you into action?

Notes to the Trainer. Like the previous session, this session starts with sustained activities and gradually builds momentum. It moves from the physical to the verbal to the transformational; it exercises proficiency of skills in seemingly isolated areas and then combines these areas as a means of creating an ever-expanding field of attention.

You are training players to become aware of all the factors involved in the creative process; the more players see, the more they can do with the

MAP. Each area of focus is a "visual aid" to promote perception. As the areas combine and expand, players get the larger picture in bite-sized and digestible pieces. The process will gradually reveal itself as they are ready to see it. By focusing on the physical the process stays direct, immediate, and accessible.

You are demystifying the creative process and, at the same time, strengthening the players' confidence in their ability to create. The training process is built on a series of specific steps; each session is a miniature of the entire process. The sessions start with a single point of focus that expands as the playing progresses. The additive steps take the players forward and allow the action to emerge and evolve.

At this stage in the process players are playing out of their own imaginations and life experience. Their focus is on defining and then mixing, matching, and combining the various MAP components to create action with forward motion.

Keep the focus on the elements of action: the factors involved in establishing relationships, the moves involved in transforming the relationships, how those moves form the structural patterns of the scene, the stakes involved in each action that intensify the quality of the play, and how characters emerge to move the action forward.

These elements examine the concepts of action fundamental to all contexts and situations, whether improvised or scripted. You will return to them over and over again as the training progresses. Continue to drill them now for clarity and precision. The more the players see, the more they can do. Their playing will grow if they have a solid technique and an expanding vocabulary to express themselves as they create and play scores of action.

Continue to encourage bold choices. If a scene isn't working, focus on clarifying the status between the players. Make the players do something to define their status. Get them to embrace the obvious. Encourage them to experiment with narrative patterns and use blocks and shelves to reveal the intent of action and thought. Make sure the status mask has a physical shape and that the shape engages the pelvis. Check that players are working to continuously trigger one another in the course of a scene.

The focus of the training shifts in the next triad. You will apply the MAP vocabulary to the process of rehearsing. In doing so you will begin to link the imaginative world of improvisation with the more formal structural needs of a script. Proficiency in previous skills, especially Cloning, will be tested and challenged; players will use their acquired structural skills to investigate specific targets within a text, and then integrate their discoveries into a score of action.

Remind players that the discovery and learning processes take time and patience. The MAP is a gradual process; it reveals itself with time and practice. Growth will be apparent in some areas, and slower to manifest itself in others.

Be flexible in using the MAP modules; mix and match, return to previous sections, or jump into new ones as the need arises. These twelve sessions are only one possible combination of the modules meant to provide a model to trigger your imagination in ways of using and investigating the process.

SESSION VII: *SCORING*

This session focuses on transforming improvisation into a set sequence.

1. Curve, Straight, Arch
2. Monkey Walk
3. The Worm
4. BAD review
5. Plastique
6. The Dolly
7. Instant Performance: Fairy Tale

Warm-Up:
1. Curve, Straight, Arch
2. Monkey Walk
3. The Worm

Notes to the Players.　The three warm-up activities involve articulating the spine and pelvis to create shape. Integrate awareness of shape in all of your work.

Move on the breath. Release the breath with sound as you stretch. Anchor each move with an image. Imagine the shape before you move into it. Let the image trigger your impulse to move. Lead with your pelvis and let the spine follow. Keep your neck and head released; avoid compressing, shrinking, or collapsing.

Think in terms of wholeness; move the front and back, right and left, and top and bottom simultaneously. Each component contributes to the totality of the shape. Continually shift your focus from one element to another to deepen your engagement.

4. BAD review

Observations.　Focus on connecting the outer with the inner. Stay engaged in the action. Use the other players as your focal point and at all times work off them; keep your focus outer-directed. Always bridge, always endow, always create and transform relationships as you move. Exercise your imagination as well as your body.

5. Plastique

Observations.   The Plastique begins by isolating each body part. Gradually the isolated parts combine to form a sequence that has direction and focus. Connect the outer with the inner as you work expressively and integrate the BADs into your playing.

Keep varying the time and weight of your effort. Be careful to avoid mirroring one another. Accept the offer and then move it into a different part of your body. Avoid repetition, even if you must arbitrarily change physical leads. Whenever you become aware of falling into a pattern, break the pattern and initiate a new one. Play vigorously; play "all out" for the last thirty seconds of the activity.

Focus on your partner. Do not root yourself in space; adjust and adapt to one another by moving through space. Choose a specific target and send to that target; make sure your actions land. Your eyes are the bridge in The Plastique; "listen" to one another by sustaining eye contact. Change your playing dynamic as you transform your relationship; your effort will either trigger the transformation or be a response to it.

When you feel stuck or don't know what to do, do nothing; wait for your partner to trigger you.

6. The Dolly

Observations.   Find the relationship through your partner; you may not predetermine or impose a relationship arbitrarily. The image must come from a specific trigger in space. Surrender to it. The image may transform as the space transforms.

Stay attuned to the signals and messages you receive as the space changes. As you move from far to intermediate to near reach space, the relationships will transform dramatically; stay open to all the nonverbal factors that create dialogue.

Evaluation.   Examine the physical processes of bridging and creating relationships in space: How does direction in space affect your relationship? How was moving apart from one another different from moving in to one another? What are the differences in leading with the right side of your body and the left? Does positioning in space define status? Which spatial relationship felt awkward or uncomfortable? How did that affect or inhibit the quality of your playing?

7. Instant Performance: Fairy Tale

Observations.   This is the first full scoring activity. You move from a series of random physical actions to a performance of a fairy tale you will create in twenty minutes. You both participate in and observe the process because you not only work, but watch the other team work as well.

The scoring process involves repetition. You create a pattern of action and then recreate it. Each round of playing has a specific focus with a targeted task to accomplish. The target gives the playing direction and guides your attention. Every step links into and feeds the next. The "text" of the score gradually reveals itself if you are patient and persistent.

The score of action will also gradually transform. This is part of the process; you want to establish a general pattern of action and then jiggle it—move it back and forth between you—until it becomes specific and repeatable. As the specificity grows, the structure of the scene will reveal itself.

As you repeat the score you will be able to intensify and tune the playing by manipulating those factors that influence and condition your relationship. The more you begin to see the relationship, the more you will be able to do to transform the relationship.

Observing the other team work is a vital part of the process. You will be able to recognize all the steps in the process, see them in operation, yet feel no pressure to perform.

Evaluation.   Did the score begin to make sense to you? Did you know who you were and why you were there? Were you able to work collaboratively to discover the narrative action of the fairy tale? How did your effort transform from frame to frame? How did that transformation affect your relationships with the other players? Was your status constant or did it change within the sequence? What happens to your focus when you have to repeat the same action repeatedly? What did you see and recognize when you were observing the other team work?

Notes to the Trainer.   This session initiates a new sequence in the training. You are integrating the various components into more complex patterns that prepare players to investigate a text.

The Instant Performance combines and exercises all the elements of non-verbal communication: effort, status, transformation, release, shape, and flow. Players must offer and accept, endow and bridge, adjust and adapt to one another throughout the playing.

At the same time the new element of repetition takes them into experiencing the rehearsal process. Players work in an additive manner, moving from the general to the specific, from the outside to the inside, and then, from the inside to the outside. They focus on creating a score of action from their own experience—improvisation—and then, by repeating the score, apply their skills to shape, design, and refine the score of action until it is expressive of content.

The score of action is the text. Once the text has been established, it can be investigated for clarity, content, and structure. Players work in isolation at first, "preparing" their roles, and then come together to discover the shape and intent of each "frame" of action. They then focus on linking the frames together into a sequence that has flow and forwardness. At all times the players work to discover the impulse for action, and then embrace and play that impulse fully.

All of the other activities in the session are preparatory for the Instant Performance. The warm-up focuses on flexibility and shape; it demands release and a sense of inner flow. The Plastique expands the sense of flow into space, requiring contact and connection with a partner. The BADs exercise endowing and bridging as well as transforming energy. The Dolly takes the endowments one step further and deals with shape in nonverbal communication—shape in space.

As you work the Instant Performance, stress the linking movements—how one step leads to the next. Your focus is on the additive process, not on the performance; the players are rehearsing proficiency with the individual components and how they link together to create flow, pattern, and action.

Players are developing a methodology for their work. They create their own MAP, working one step at a time from the beginning of the process to the end. The more they practice and rehearse the process, the more confident they will become in their work. You are training actors who are fearless because they have a process that enables them to investigate any text with thoroughness and accuracy.

The next session examines bridging into the text. Players will exercise their nonverbal skills in shaping, mask, release; their creative skills in transforming and balancing; and their interpretive skills in transforming images into action within the social context of the world of the play.

SESSION VIII: *BRIDGING THE TEXT*

This session focuses on interpretive skills and the collaborative process.

1. Back to Back Elevator
2. Duet Stretch
3. Spinal Float
4. Two As One
5. Talking Hands
6. Collage with Mirror Cloning

Warm-Up:
1. Back to Back Elevator
2. Duet Stretch

3. Spinal Float

Notes to the Players. The three warm-up activities should be played without pause or interruption; link them together into one sequence. Note resistance in the spine as you begin. After completing the sequence look for changes in tension within your body. If you feel longer, how did you get that way?

Tension inhibits; it makes us compress, contract, and withhold. In the warm-up, target specific areas of tension in your body. Focus on releasing into those areas. Once the energy is released it is possible to experience length, expansion, and openness. Tension is usually fear trapped inside the body.

4. Two as One
5. Talking Hands

Observations. The next two activities are flow drills. They require outward focus, offering and accepting, working in synchronicity with your partner, and openness. Use the physical to trigger the mental; integrate and use the mental to transform the physical.

In Two as One, use the Mini Gap to work on moment-to-moment balance and evenness in playing. If you are in sync with one another it will be difficult to determine who leads and who follows. The action should have a sense of intuitive rightness to it.

In Talking Hands compare the first round with the second. Was the quality of the play different when you used the hands as a lead rather than as a follow? Did the balance of responsibility shift and a sense of collaboration and mutual discovery evolve?

6. Collage

Observations. Use a collage to create a score of action. The score will eventually tell a story. You will discover the shape and form of the narrative collaboratively. It is crucial that you begin the process with concrete and specific images—with a strong, clearly defined outer. The physical pattern will help you develop the score of action.

As you create a collage, exercise your problem-solving and design skills. Work alone and then with a partner to establish, define, and refine a pattern. Transform the pattern into a physical score of action. Each step links and flows into the next. Every step works to clarify your perception of the pattern. Repeat the pattern until you don't have to think about it anymore; you are then free to play within the pattern and interact with your partners.

7. Instant Performance/Mirror Cloning

Observations.   In Instant Performance you and your partners share ownership of the score of action—you all collaborate on its development and performance. When you add Mirror Cloning and clone members of the opposite team, the performance process is both objective (observing the score) and subjective (duplicating the observation).

The creative process inches forward, one step at a time, in the Instant Performance. There is no way to predetermine what will happen within each round of playing. The action literally jiggles back and forth between you and your partners.

As you translate the score of action into an instant performance, the structure may never vary or change. However, you may change how the score is performed, the status within the relationships, and the patterns of transformation that shape the action.

You no longer play out of your own experience when you mirror clone. You are playing someone else's experience, a score they created. Part of the investigative process focuses on finding a way to "own" the action—to take the score and make it yours. You are now beginning to exercise your ability to interpret as well as create action.

You will have to "read" the score you are cloning for clues about action patterns, relationships, targets, rewards and penalties, endowments, and context.

Repetition of the score demands discipline and precise playing. You must duplicate the shape, mask, effort, and flow patterns of your partner; at the same time you must remain spontaneous in the quality of your play. Focus on discovering the impulse for the action. Every action must involve a shift—either a mini or a maxi—of your partner's status.

Each discovery you make is a moment of insight that reveals more of the score's structure and inner action. Incorporate these changes and at the same time continue your progression through the text.

Finally, perform the score full out. Intensify the way you play the score by adding penalties and rewards, so you play with high stakes from frame to frame. Because you are playing without words, make sure each move involves postural, rather than gestural, action. Carve rather than mold. Check body positioning and direction in space. Be specific with your visual focus.

Each frame also must involve a change in effort; change the effort as your thoughts change within the score. Give yourself enough time to think each thought. If there are gaps in the thinking process, focus on linking and bridging the gaps, rather than ignoring them. If the patterns and score shift slightly because of the bridges, let the score evolve and transform.

Evaluation.   Examine the rehearsal process: Did the score of action take on a clear shape with a beginning, middle, and end when you cloned? How did you discover the patterns of action? Did you anchor those patterns to any of the BADs to form a core for your character? Did this core lead you into shape and mask? Were you collaborating with your partner to create the initial score? How do you approach playing a score you haven't created yourself? How do you interpret and own the action? What do you do to link and bridge with the character?

Notes to the Trainer.   As the training sequence begins to examine working with a text, players move away from their own experiences and grapple with interpreting someone else's score of action. Guiding players into recognizing structural elements of the prepared text becomes an important addition to coaching for creativity, collaboration, and transformation.

The session begins by returning to the concept of surrender and builds on this theme throughout the session. Players must rely on one another to find their points of departure and their points of release. They do not have to do the work alone; coach bridging, offering and accepting, exaggerating resistance, and, finally, surrendering to one another. Fear will always force a player into holding and inhibiting flow.

While the warm-up stresses body length, it also begins to focus on a secondary physical axis: width. Coach players into opening their chests and expanding their rib cages in the Spinal Float. As they align, look for signs of shrinking in the horizontal plane: pinched shoulders, compressed chests, tight elbows, rolled-in ankles, or locked knees. Players can release into their elbows to help promote a sense of width in their upper bodies, or, to promote width in the lower body, roll out onto their outer ankles by lifting their insteps off the floor.

Two as One and Talking Hands depend on complete collaboration. Psychological surrender and openness are as important in these activities as physical synchronicity. Both activities promote a sense of open flow and humor.

Playfulness is an important tool in creativity; players should be willing to be "messy" and not worry about getting it right.

The Collage is a tool for scoring action with visual triggers. Tracing the pattern gives the action shape and a visual reference. It also clearly marks out a literal path to follow that takes them forward in space.

Each round of playing in the Instant Performance should define another aspect of the inner structure of the action. Keep the coaching specific and additive: focus on eye contact, marking out the frames, setting the status transformations within each frame, marking each frame with a shift in effort, linking the frames together into an action sequence with flow, determining the shape of the character, building the character mask, or anchoring the mask with a BAD core.

With each transformation, check to see if the player's thinking is becoming more specific. You will see the moment when the thought clicks into place and intuitive rightness takes over. There may be gaps in the pattern, but for the most part it will have a beginning, a middle, and an end; and a strong sense of moment-to-moment action, direction, and focus. Make sure players take enough time to think each thought and complete each action before moving on to the next.

By reincorporating Cloning, an activity introduced in the third session, you keep the players off guard. Cloning moves them forward because their focus, once again, must be on someone else and not on themselves. The clones also have a vested interest in the activity—they see themselves in instant replay; they have an opportunity to see what it is they have communicated, and how they looked as they played.

It's important that players do not comment on the mask when they clone in the Instant Performance. The temptation always exists to exaggerate the mask and joke at another player's expense. Players are always vulnerable when they perform, especially when they perform their own original work. All players must respect and honor each other's effort.

Coach the Cloning very specifically. Players work from the outside in to discover both the inner score of action and the thinking patterns that inform each action. Move from the outer manifestations of the action—shape, mask, effort, and flow—to the inner manifestations of the action—thought, direction, and intent. As these reveal themselves, the players will have discovered the impulse for action that infuses each frame.

Coach the players in integrating this impulse into the score of action. Repeating the score involves coming into continual contact with the trigger.

When you evaluate this session with the players, focus their attention on problems associated with approaching a text. They must learn to "read" the text for clues about the endowments, the relationships, the factors conditioning effort, and the rewards/penalties—the stakes—coloring and intensifying each action.

Although the next series of sessions will focus more and more on language, text, and the process of experimenting in rehearsals, players need to continue drilling their skills in nonverbal action. If they can collaborate and tell a story without words they will be able to embrace the challenges of a text. They will be expanding, through language and text, the fundamental processes of creation, collaboration, and action that they have been drilling in these first eight sessions.

SESSION IX: *SOLO SPEECHES*

This session focuses on analyzing and investigating language as a means of defining action.

1. T'ai Walk

2. T'ai Circle
3. 2/3
4. 3/4
5. Body Shapes:
   Door/Table/Wheel
6. Solo Speeches:
   Framing
   Transformations
   Connect the Dots
7. The Loop:
   Punctuation
   Operatives
   Emotional Adjectives
   Weighted Conjunctions
   Punchlines
   BAD core w/body type

Warm-Up:

1. T'ai Walk
2. T'ai Circle

Notes to the Players.   The warm-up is extremely concentrated. It requires physical control, sustained release, openness, and partner flow.

Maintain the vertical axis and length in your torso; do not sink or collapse into your chest. Check to see if you are tilting forward or backward. Check that you bend your knees and that your weight on the forward moving foot does not extend beyond your toes; if it does, you will place extra stress on your knee. Maintain accuracy in the form.

In the circle, keep the distance between you and your partner equal at all times. Work to counterbalance each other in every move. Be aware of excess tension in your hands and crunching in your knees and lower legs. Bend your supporting leg in order to lower your center of gravity.

Keep the contact with your partner alive and fluid, even as you focus on maintaining correct form. Rely on one another for guidance and direction. Stay within the shape of the circle; do not pass another couple. Use your peripheral vision to stay connected with the other couples in the circle. Gauge the gait of your steps. Keep the dynamic and tension flow even between you.

3. 2/3
4. 3/4

Observations.   These two pattern activities are also strong overload devices. Surrender control and let your body take over. Choose one point of focus and stay with it. You may change the focus at any time. Do not try to do everything at once.

When you are in overload, you must always find a specific focus to direct your attention. Once you've taken the first step, the rest will follow. The pressure to perform, especially when working an exercise for the first time, let alone perform a difficult task perfectly, can be overwhelming. This pressure creates excess tension that causes you to shut down and inhibits your flow of energy.

The single focus, no matter what it is, allows you to release and get moving again. Work in small units; let one frame lead you to the next. Eventually, as you pass through overwhelm, you will be able to assemble all the individual pieces and see the large picture.

5. Body Shapes

Observations. These three body shapes and four body types form the seven basic physical masks of character. They are shapes and types that, when embraced, lead you from the outer to the inner; their form contains and reveals character.

Door/Table/Wheel are body shapes based on space and direction in space. They always involve moving the body with distinct points of orientation—either vertical/horizontal, horizontal/sagittal, or sagittal/vertical. These shapes are outer directed; they deal with action and states of action. They trigger completely different inner responses. One shape may be more difficult for you than the others. This, then, is the shape to embrace first because it will require more practice, flexibility, and surrender.

Shape—direction and organization in space—is a component of mask. The BAD cores and body shapes move from the inner to the outer. Mask work blends outer and inner to reveal character.

Evaluation. Examine the relationship between the outer and the inner: Which shapes and types felt comfortable? Why? Where in your body did you experience resistance? Which shape and type are you? How do these shapes and types synthesize and integrate inner and outer? Do you experience flexibility in moving from one type to another? Is it possible to use one type as a core of a character, but cover and mask it with another?

6. Solo speeches

Observations. The next three activities focus on approaching and structuring a monologue from a contemporary American play. Even though you are working alone on a solo piece, you will use similar MAP when investigating a scene with a partner.

Divide the speech into a series of frames. Each frame marks the beginning and end of a unit of thought. Every time the thought changes, one frame ends and another begins. Clearly delineate and define the units of thought.

Set off the frames physically. Every time one frame ends, change either your weight, your body direction in space, or your visual focus. The physical notation may change every time you work the text; use it now to help bring clarity, order, and structure to your work.

Each frame must have its own beginning, middle, and end. Look for the impulse that initiates the thought; engage it and then complete it. Each frame involves a transformation of thought and, therefore, action; it may be a major change or it may be a minor one. The frame must always contain this movement and shift in dynamic.

Work through the speech again. Focus on transforming the effort within each frame. Make the dynamics subtle or obvious; they can be wildly fluctuating and abrupt or even and gradual. The more there is for you to do, the more engaged you will become in playing the score.

Once each frame has shape and definition, focus on connecting the frames—how do the small pieces fit together? As you work through the text again, take enough time to find the links—the triggers at the end of one frame that propel you forward into the next. Really think the thoughts and play the action between the frames.

Work through the speech again. This time look for larger units and create bigger frames. Give each larger frame a beginning, middle, and end. Examine the links between the frames. Give them equal attention. Then connect the frames and link them together to play the entire sequence.

Extend the process one step further. Look at the entire speech and see it as one frame of action. Give it a beginning, a middle, and an end. See the pattern of transformation in the entire unit and play its larger shape as you work through the text one last time.

Evaluation.   How do the little pieces expand into the larger ones? Is it possible to have an image of the big picture while playing the smaller ones?

Focusing on the small frames makes you play the speech moment to moment. Yet the moments must always connect and have a sense of forwardness. The actor always must know the larger shape and direction of the speech and focus his or her energy on getting there; both the big and the little picture exist simultaneously.

Use this process to give clarity, order, and structure to your work. Always maintain the structure of the speech; the emotional content will take care of itself. Focus on how you move from frame one to frame two to frame three and intensify the factors that condition your playing by adding rewards and penalties to create stakes.

7. The Loop

Observations.   These five activities explore the text to uncover its action and meaning by examining form and structure. Work from the outside in, and then from the inside out.

Musicalize the punctuation within the speech. Stop at periods, pause at commas, suspend at ellipses, etc. Observe each notation and follow its musical direction. How do the notations guide and mark the directions of the thought and action?

Focus on the operative words within the speech. Stress the verbs and nouns: verbs carry action and nouns carry the focus for the action. Do not stress pronouns unless you are making a comparison.

Color each adjective, even if you make arbitrary choices. How do the adjectives condition the nouns? What kind of images and pictures do they create? What does this information tell you about what you are doing? Why do you choose to color the image that way?

Turn your attention to the connecting words—how do the thoughts, actions, and frames link together? "and" links; "but" moves in an opposite direction; "or" weighs opposites. Physically change direction whenever the conjunctions change the direction of the thought.

Drive through each line to the end. Make the end of the line more important than the beginning; give it more emphasis, more energy, and more weight. Think of the end of each line as a punchline. Set up the punch at the beginning of the line; when you arrive at it, hit it. Work through each frame this way; then connect the frames and play the larger units this way. Finally, play the entire speech this way. Create a set-up at the beginning, and deliver the punch at the end.

Don't be afraid to exaggerate and overemphasize. Be willing to do too much. As you put the pieces together, you are literally carving out the structure of the speech. Work for clarity, shape, and definition. Once you've uncovered the shape, you will be able to retain it; it exists on the line as you speak. Release and surrender into the line and let it carry you forward. You won't have to work as hard; you can let it happen rather than make it happen.

If you really take as much time as you need to think every thought, you will never get ahead of yourself. Eventually, you will be able to think faster so the speech has dramatic momentum and immediacy.

Finally, add shape and mask to the text. Are you a table, wheel, or door? How do these shapes and types influence the text? Do they change what the punchline is? How do you play the punchline? Do they explain why you use the operative words? Do they help reveal the intent of the speech?

Evaluation.   How do all the pieces fit together? Does focusing on the structure of the speech inhibit or release your energy? How do you make creative choices? Where do you find the impulse for action?

_ When you work a solo speech, remember that you are usually speaking about something in the past to affect and transform someone in the present. How does this speech help you change the status of the person you are speaking to? Where do you direct the punchline? Does it help you shift and transform the status? How does the speech land on the listener?

Notes to the Trainer.   The focus of this session is process and methodology. Players repeatedly drill various ways of moving from the general to the specific, playing from moment to moment and connecting the moments into a larger design and pattern.

At all times the playing must have forwardness and purpose. Work the warm-up with this in mind; don't let players bog down or drift. Keep them on track and connected to their partners with outward focus. Make sure they maintain eye contact with one another.

Push the players through the overload section. Reinforce and strengthen their determination to make it all work. While players may want to obsess on conquering every detail in the pattern, it is more important to first work for direction and shape of the large picture, no matter how tentative the individual parts may be. Sometimes seeing the larger picture will release and liberate the player.

Body shapes and types work both the inner and the outer. One provides a sense of direction (action); the other triggers emotional complexity and hurdles. These activities move the focus of the session onto character and action, synthesizing outer and inner.

The text work shifts the session once again. This is the first time players confront someone else's words. The physical approach to text analysis puts the focus on doing rather than feeling. Players work through the text in depth and detail to discover how the text's structure reveals its content. All of these exercises can be used as preparation for rehearsal.

All investigative work begins and ends with the text. It is the conduit, the treasure map, the source of all information regarding the scene you are working. It is crucial for players to begin their formal scene work with a healthy respect for the text, and an orientation that continually takes them back to the text as their primary source of information. If they truly explore the text, their work will be built on a solid foundation, not supposition or guesswork.

The framing section deals with analyzing and breaking the text down into patterns and small units, and then linking the pieces together to get back to the large picture. The looping section examines the language within each frame. Again, stress forwardness, even if it is arbitrary, at this point in the process.

Drill the players in playing through to the end of the line. The ends of thoughts—the completion of each action—must be more important than the initiation. As the frames link, the playing will gather momentum and drive; constant repetition will help clarify the shape of the speech.

Your task, as always, is to create an environment for the players in which change is possible. The players must collaborate in the process of their training; it is not something that happens to them. At times you will lead the collaboration; at times the player will. Because you are always the objective observer, you will need to either lean in to the player and apply pressure to move them over a hurdle, or lean back and away from the player to let them discover the process on their own.

The next session focuses on collaborative investigation. Players will be working with a scene from a contemporary American play and experimenting with approaching the scene from many different points of view to discover its action.

SESSION X: *APPROACHING A SCENE*

This session focuses on the investigative process in rehearsing.

1. Solo Stretch
2. Spinal Float
3. Spinal Walk Down
4. Yes Game
5. Gift Giving
6. Putty Masks/Body Shapes/Thinking Aloud
7. You Never/You Always
8. Remember When
9. Text: Yield, Block, Shelve
10. Parallels and Paraphrase
11. Silent Movie

Warm-Up:
1. Solo Stretch
2. Spinal Float
3. Spinal Walk Down

Notes to the Player. In returning to these activities, focus on release, flexibility, sustaining breath, and surrender. See if the quality of the stretch has changed since you began in Session I. What feels different? Is your approach different? What is your focus when you stretch? How do you counterstretch?

Is the quality of the flow different when you work with a partner? Are you aware of collapsing through your spine, or do you lift through your sternum? When do you tend to sink and when do you tend to rise?

4. Yes Game
5. Gift Giving

Observations. Focus on release, offering and accepting, and challenging your partner.

Is the quality of the flow different now than in Session I? Is your awareness different of how the process works and how the pieces fit together?

Evaluation. The first five activities are reviews. You have a chance to return to early concepts and principles and see them from a new perspective. Everything is always clearer in hindsight. Although you are still moving forward in the process, it's important to stop at each step of the way and see where you have been.

How has the quality of your playing changed? What feels stronger? What do you need to strengthen? Has your perception changed about structure? What is the difference between the intent and the content of an action? What do you focus on when you play an action: intent or content? Which propels you forward? How do you create forwardness?

6. Putty Masks/Body Shapes/Thinking Aloud

Observations. While it is always possible to work completely from one's imagination, these activities work best when you have a specific, predetermined focus; therefore, use a character from a contemporary American play as a point of departure.

Use a putty mask to trigger your imagination about the physical life of the character. Body shape and body type will help define both the inner and the outer manifestations of the character. Work from your knowledge and impressions of the text. Is the character a thinker, a doer, or a maker of things? Is the character inflexible, overloaded, helpless? How do the various inner and outer aspects come together to determine the character's physical shape and body type?

Gather clues about the character from the text. Look for what the character says about himself or herself, and what other people say about the character. Look for patterns of repetition in thought and action. Look for biographical information that will also affect shape and type—occupation, age, status.

Once you mold the shape and find the walk of the mask, begin to speak. Give an interview to an imaginary interviewer. State all the facts of your biography. Be specific in filling in details. Rather than just thinking the biography, whisper it, so it is voiced and placed in space. Do not censor your impulse as you speak; let your imagination guide you.

7. You Never, You Always
8. Remember When

Observations.   Two more endowment activities to be played with your scene partner.

Focus on the quality of the offers; be specific in creating your history. Remember, you must accept every offer; the more you offer, the more you have to build upon. Play within the putty mask.

Remember When deals with the past—your history together, the events and circumstances of your relationship. You Never, You Always focuses directly on your relationship and how you see one another in the present. In the process, you are telling your partner who she is to you. Do not worry about being logical or consistent in how you present information. When you are looking to gather information, contradictions are extremely helpful. Use the text as a springboard for your imagination.

9. Yield, Block, Shelve with Text

Observations.   Focus on the structure of the text. Look for patterns of action. How does the text change when you block or shelve? Does this take the action forward? Are you continually offering new information to one another? Does the information take the relationship forward?

Experiment with the patterns. Try them in various combinations. Look at all the possibilities before arriving at a final choice. Do the patterns of action—and thinking—become clearer as you analyze the structure of the interaction? Why do you block or shelve? Why do you yield to one another? Are you yielding to intent or to content?

10. Parallels and Paraphrases

Observations.   Create a different context for the scene, one close to your own life experience. This new context must parallel the situation in the text. Parallel all the factors that condition the action.

As you play the scene, use your own words. Play the scene frame by frame. Be specific in the moment to moment playing; do not use any words of the text. Work to clarify intent, thought, and action, but in your own manner and in your own way. Play without hesitation. Focus on the doing.

In a Parallel and Paraphrase, try to accurately mirror the structure of the scene. If there are gaps—missing frames, sections, or sequences that are not clear to you—you will discover them. Don't be afraid of making mistakes; you are trying to discover what is unclear so that you can give it clarity and fit it into the pattern.

If necessary, go back and play the Parallel and Paraphrase two or three times until all the pieces fit together and take you forward. Remember to drive towards the punchline of every frame—complete each action.

Play the scene one more time; use the text.

Evaluation. Examine the rehearsal process: Does the scene seem different to you now? Is the action clearer? Do you understand its progression from moment to moment? What is "ownership" of a text? Do you feel you are playing from yourself? Are the words yours or do they feel disconnected? Are the thoughts yours, or do they feel uncommitted? Are the actions yours, or do they feel foreign?

11. Silent Movie

Observations. Play the scene again. Play full out without sound. Play within the mask, the type, and the shape of the character. The Silent Movie is a texted nonverbal pattern scene, a variation of the All Yield scene.

Finally, play the scene one last time. Repeat everything you've discovered in the Silent Movie, but add sound; speak the text aloud.

Evaluation. Were you listening to one another? Were you able to find the trigger for each frame in your partner's offer or were you inventing it for yourself? Were you "in sync" with one another, continually adjusting and adapting to one another as you played? Are the spatial relationships appropriate for the action from frame to frame? Does the status transform from frame to frame? Does the status transformation affect your spatial relationship with one another?

Notes to the Trainer. The focus of this session is on the sequencing and scoring of action. Reincorporate earlier activities to provide a launching pad for new ones. Once players realize how far they've come, they will continue the journey with renewed energy and commitment.

The warm-up, once again, deals with release and flow. The pattern games reinforce basics: offer-accept-offer, working with openness, and a willingness to experiment before arriving at a final solution.

The mask/shape/type work directs the players' attention to factors that make up the world of the character, as defined by the text. In the previous session the players worked without a strong textual context; in this session, they are working to investigate context.

The focus is still on the processes of exploration and experimentation. Players need to be kept off balance so they don't gravitate too early into concepts of how a scene should be played. They must discover the shape and the score of the scene collaboratively.

No matter how thoroughly the player prepares for each rehearsal, he must to be willing to abandon that preparation the moment the actual process of working with another actor begins. The homework is a launching pad; it provides information and a context. The script is always the treasure map, the guide; the score of action is the treasure the players want to find.

The endowment activities are linking and bridging activities—they take the players deeper into one another and help fill in the gaps in the history of the characters. They build shared memories and should be used to develop past events alluded to in the text.

In the same way, the players should agree on a common history and image for each off-stage character referred to by the text. The more specific each image is, the easier it becomes to release into the playing. The actors must play in a context that has reality for them; they do not exist in a void.

If there is tension in the playing of the Yield, Block, Shelve or the Parallels and Paraphrases, ask the players to examine the source of their inhibitions. What are they withholding? What are they afraid of if they release? Most importantly, is it appropriate for the character at that moment to withhold? These activities are ways for the players to link and bridge, not only with other players, but with the text. These activities involve "ownership," playing out of one's own experience and finding the points of empathy and compassion with the character through the structure and context of the script.

More importantly, it gives you an opportunity to see if the players understand what they are doing in the scene. In the Parallels and Paraphrases, players will want to use the text rather than their own words. They must stay with the paraphrase and be specific in their use of language until they discover that there is no better way to express themselves than in the words given to them by the playwright; ownership is achieved when this process happens.

Finally, the Silent Movie is an opportunity to return once again to a form and structure the players are familiar with, and to use it in a new context. The scene should have clarity, direction, and focus. If the players are out of sync with one another, note those moments as you watch and return to them afterwards to uncover the blocks in communication.

When players return to the scene for a final round of playing, on voice, they should be able to repeat the physical score accurately. Spatial relationships and patterns in space, especially when discovered while players are in a strong state of flow, should always be reincorporated into the playing.

However, players must not focus on merely duplicating the outer form of what they've done. The task, when repeating the score, is to continually discover, play, and respond to the impulse for the action, rather than recreate its shape and the form. This process of engagement is what makes the playing seem fresh and spontaneous in performance, rather than by rote.

In the previous section the players focused on uncovering structure. In this session, players focus on building a context and integrating that context into the structure of the scene. In the next session players will focus on intensifying the context to create immediacy and dramatic tension in their playing.

SESSION XI: *SYNCING*

This session focuses on the dynamics of playing a fixed score of action.

1. Follow the Leader
2. Felt Tip Pens
3. Obstacle Course
4. The Hunter and the Hunted
5. A/B Loops
6. Back to Back Scenes
7. Sound Leads
8. Physical Leads
9. No Move
10. Silent Tension
11. Touch and Talk
12. Go

Warm-Up:

1. Follow the Leader

Notes to the Players. Change the time, weight, and space constantly. Jump all the transitions; make every transformation abrupt, startling, dynamic, dramatic. Play with a sense of forwardness and immediacy. Clone accurately. It should be impossible to tell who is leading.

2. Felt Tip Pens

3. Obstacle Course
4. The Hunter and the Hunted

Observations.   Play these three activities back to back; try not to pause between them. Keep the focus and energy crisp and strong.

When you play Felt Tip Pens keep your focus and direction in space direct. Know where you're going and get there. Your point of focus (your destination) is the "punchline." Play through to the end of the line and "punch it" when you arrive; don't give up as you cross the room. Use the change in the time factor to intensify and condition your playing, even when the playing becomes difficult.

In the Obstacle Course, when you don't know what to do, do nothing. Wait for instructions; always find the impulse for action through your partner. Keep your target firmly in mind. Whatever happens, keep your sense of forwardness, no matter how many hurdles you encounter or how many times you stop and have to start over. Use the hurdles to intensify and condition the quality of your play.

When you play The Hunter and The Hunted, play in the center of the circle rather than along the sides. Make the playing dangerous; play for high stakes—life and death. Use the time limit to heighten and intensify the quality of the play.

Evaluation.   How do outside factors color and condition the quality of your play? Do they help strengthen your target? What happens when you add rewards and penalties? Do they strengthen or diminish your target?

Once you have determined the score of action, add intensifiers to elevate, strengthen, and transform the quality of the playing. By changing the outside factors—the time, the stakes, and the need to reach your target—you add immediacy and urgency to the playing. You don't have time to think, you only have time to do.

Intensifiers help transform the action from "a state" into "a drive." By narrowing your focus, you have no choice but to become more specific in your playing. You'll find clues about the intensifiers in the text.

5. A/B Loops
6. Back to Back

Observations.   Examine a scene from a contemporary American play. Play it through once with the text. Repeat the scene a second time using the A/B language substitute. Loop the scene; once you are comfortable with the language substitute, move directly into Back to Back and continue looping.

Play quickly. Maintain physical contact throughout. Keep varying the A/B pattern; whenever you find yourself falling into a repetitive A/B pattern, break and change the pattern. Try not to pause. Make your responses to your partner quick and direct. Move around the playing space. Vary your levels. Turn and face one another. Begin working with Leads.

7. Sound Leads
8. Physical Leads

Observations. Continue using the A/B Loop. When it is your turn to speak, respond to your partner's trigger with open sound. Let the sound "lead" you into the line; release your response, whatever it may be, and let your response initiate your action. Do not predetermine your response or try to guide or control the direction of the scene. Be willing to abandon the previous score and go wherever your impulse takes you. Your task now is to follow your impulse.

Work in the same way with the physical leads. When your partner makes her offer, respond first with a physical gesture; engage the center of your body in the gesture. Let the gesture trigger your response. Play in far reach space.

9. No Move
10. Silent Tension

Observations. Deliberately break the pattern and do not move. Do not use sound or physical leads. Place all of your focus and attention on the verbal action in the scene. Speaking is everything. Justify No Move by using Silent Tension.

With Silent Tension, speak only when there is a need to speak. Wait until the tension between you becomes unbearable before you speak. You may adjust, adapt, and move when you speak. Then return to No Move, and begin the Silent Tension cycle again.

11. Touch and Talk

Observations. Play the scene without the A/B language substitution. You may talk only when your partner touches you. Your partner may talk only when you touch her. Follow the sequence and structure of the text; do not skip speeches. Work line by line, even if you break the line by withdrawing contact. You do not have to touch with your hands to make contact with your partner.

12. Go

Observations. Finally, play the scene one last time. Play the text in its original context. Do not pause in the course of the scene. Whenever you pause the coach will call out "Go" to keep you moving forward.

Evaluation. How do all these exercises affect your understanding of the text? Is the action more specific? Is your playing more immediate or direct? Do you feel more spontaneous? Are you responding to your impulse from moment to moment? Are you able to sustain the overall arc of the scene—its forwardness—yet play moment to moment? Did any of the moments surprise you? Were you able to break any of your patterns, expectations, or preconceptions about the scene? Did you discover anything new about the text, the relationship, or the score of action?

Throughout this session you've been working to unlock your imagination and find new ways to examine the text. Once you have established a set way of seeing the action, break the pattern and experiment, if for no other reason than to confirm the choices you've already made, or to let them transform and evolve into even more interesting choices.

The work process is in a state of continual evolution. Find a solution for a problem, arrive at the solution, and refine your solution. Then make the choice more specific and interesting as you play. One way of doing this is to add intensifiers (Felt Tip Pen No. 3). Another is to raise the stakes (The Hunter and the Hunted). Another is to to deepen the need (The Obstacle Course). Another is to use substitutes to make you think on the line (A/B Loop). Another is to change your orientation in space (Back to Back). Another is to break your normal pattern of synchronicity (Leads). Another is to eliminate and withhold part of the pattern (No Move and Silent Tension). Another is to break the normal perception of the pattern by adding irregular rhythms (Touch and Talk). And yet another is to compress the pattern (Go). At all times, the text is your conduit into the action.

By using these pattern breakers, you must rely on your partner; you cannot play the scene alone. Every variation of the intensifiers takes you deeper and deeper into your partner. The more you connect, the stronger the synchronicity, the more enjoyable the experience of playing can become. After you've determined the score, your task is to play it on the impulse every time you play. You always must find the impulse through your partner. Your task, as always, is to trigger your partner's imagination.

Notes to the Trainer. This is a fast, intense, and dynamic session. Stay alert for signs of synchronicity.

Synchronicity for the individual player manifests itself as coordination between the verbal and the physical. Speech and gesture flow together. In most instances, players use bridging gestures. In this session you want them to move into carving, which is a more intense, passionate sign of involvement. Working with far space usually triggers players into the appropriate intensity.

Felt Tip Pens, Obstacle Course, and The Hunter and The Hunted all involve targeting; players must set targets and strive towards them. This focus is fundamental to the quality of the play. Targeting and playing for the target gives the action intention, direction, and purpose. The path—the score of action heading towards the target—becomes instantly visible to the player. Once a direction has been determined it is easy to add hurdles and overloads to make the journey more interesting.

Throughout the scene work, check to see if the players are in sync with one another. Body language is a key to syncing. For every move, there should be an equal countermove. The scene, if played without sound (Silent Movie), will look like a dance. The move/countermove pattern is subconscious; however, if players are not in sync, you can add the move/countermove pattern to induce synchronicity.

These activities involve a tremendous release of energy. When one activity flows directly into the next, without time for recovery, players expand and open to one another. As always, look for signs of resistance: artificial or repetitive sound leads that have nothing to do with the trigger, A/B locks, when the language (and therefore the thought) never progresses, disconnected physical leads that do not trigger new responses, jumping the silences in Silent Tension, or sluggish playing in Go. Whenever you spot one of these patterns, make the player aware of it, and get him to collaborate with you in breaking the pattern.

Players often get lost in the text, especially when they use the language substitute. This is another way of breaking their predetermined set patterns. A/B makes them return to the impulse to speak and to act. Throughout, you are maneuvering the players into listening and seeing As If for the first time. It may be uncomfortable for them initially but it is a necessary component of the process.

Monitor the quality of the playing. When the intensifiers are added, the target becomes clearer. This is another way of working from the outside: add more pressure from the outside and the player must use more effort to arrive at her destination. All of these activities will bring the player to greater clarity about where the character wants to go and what stands in the way of getting there. Players are in sync with their training when they use the MAP to arrive at their destination and repeat the journey with consistency and freshness.

In the next session players will begin to investigate the factors that create style. Players will examine language and endowments to expand their skills in creating the world of a play.

SESSION XII: *STYLE*

This session focuses on integrating context and content to determine style.

1. Energy Ball

2. Changing Places
   Frames:
      Triggers
      Hooks
      Completers
   Links:
      Down Endings
      Sustained Endings
      Rising Endings
3. Scoring the Scene: Sound Score
   Frames
   Status
   Transformations
   Endowments
   Links
   BADs
   Status
   Targets and Hurdles
4. Endowment of the Mask
   BAD Core
   Invisible Envelope
   Thinking Aloud
   Go

Warm-Up:

1. Energy Ball

Notes to the Players.   Play quickly and stay alert. Play posturally rather than gesturally. Engage your imagination in the activity.

2. Changing Places

Observations.   Use this activity to review Framing and the action cycle. Play the first round as a review of the game's structure. Move only when you find the impulse through your partner. Abide by the rules of the game.

In the next round of playing think of each move as a unit of action within a frame. Shift your focus to the beginning of the unit. Emphasize and highlight the trigger—the impulse that initiates the action.

In the next round, maintain the trigger but shift your focus to the hook—the section within the frame in which you come together with your partner. Initiate and engage; stress the trigger and the hook within the frame.

In the next round, maintain the trigger and the hook, but focus on the transformer—the moment at the end of the unit when you are affected by your partner and change. The transformation is triggered by the hook.

Play again with a trigger, a hook, and a transformer—initiate, engage, and complete the cycle of action. At the end of the cycle, let the energy drop. Return to neutral and start another cycle. Continue playing this way, with down endings at the end of each frame.

In the next round, do not drop the energy at the end of the frame. Sustain it; keep it on an even keel and use it to link directly into the next frame.

In the final round, lift the energy at the end of the frame. Let it **rise;** each frame links upward, so the end of one unit is higher than its beginning.

Evaluation.   Examine the structure of your playing: How did the quality of your playing change when you focused your attention on the trigger? The hook? The transformer? How did the links change when you moved from a down ending to a sustained ending? From a sustained ending to a rising ending? Did your sense of forwardness change in the course of the game? If so, how?

3. Scoring the Scene: Sound Score

Observations.   Work this activity to review the framing process and integrate it into the scoring process. Work from the outside to the inside to the outside. Set the score musically then transform the music into action. Work from the physical action and discover its inner structure; once you understand the structure, adjust and adapt the playing of the score to better express its inner structure.

Begin by creating the set sequence—the series of activities that make a pattern—with Sound Scoring. Always play each musical unit in the same place in the sequence; the sequence may never vary. Then give the music physical life and shape; transform the musical score into action.

Add: Frames. Each frame has a trigger, a hook, and a transformer. The frame defines each unit of action within the set sequence.

Add: Offers and Accepts. Each frame contains an offer and an accept. When you offer, endow your partner. Give him status and adjust your behavior accordingly.

Add: Links. Eliminate down endings. Add sustains and rises. Justify using a rising ending. Use the links to connect one frame with the next.

Add: BADs. Adjust your effort pattern within each frame. As the action cycle progresses, let the inner transform with the outer and the outer with the inner. The adjustments may be subtle or dynamic, depending on the nature of the relationship with your partner.

Add: Status. Continue to endow your partner. Make the changes in effort mirror the shifts and changes in status within each frame. The changes may be mini or maxi. Your character's status may change from high to low from frame to frame, or it may remain constant.

Add: Targets and hurdles. Make sure each frame has a target. Move to hit the target. The target must be tied to your relationship with your partner and how you want the status to transform. Add hurdles to make the playing more interesting.

4. Endowment of the Mask

Observations. Focus on developing your mask. Briefly review everything you do within the score. How do you use time? Is everything quick? Or sustained? When does the time change? Do you use one time quality more than another?

Is your weight predominantly strong or light? Is your focus in space predominantly direct or indirect? Are you a presser, puncher, flicker, dabber, slasher, wringer, floater, or glider? Which of these eight BADs best describes the core of what you do? Integrate the core into your pattern. Don't be afraid to vary what you do, but link everything to this BAD center. Move and play from this center; use it to organize and structure your thoughts and actions.

Add: Invisible Envelope. Use the Invisible Envelope to help shape your body. Slip into the envelope while you play; use it as a key to trigger your imagination about who you are. Move from the key; stay consistent within the mask. Adjust and adapt as necessary to suit the action. The Envelope may transform once you start to use it.

Add: Shape and Type. Extend the BAD core: are you a door, wheel, or table? Play consistently within the shape and type. Fuse it with the Invisible Envelope and the BAD core. Are shape and type revealed or concealed by the mask?

Return to the score of action. Focus on linking all the frames together into one large set sequence. Make sure each frame feeds into and triggers the next. Each target should lead you forward. The sequence should flow.

Add: Thinking Aloud. Verbalize your thoughts as you play. The thoughts should be in response to each trigger and propel you forward. If there are gaps in the logic of the sequence, you will discover them now. Focus on the gaps and make whatever adjustments you need until Thinking Aloud has consistency and flow.

Add: Go. Use intensifiers to elevate and heighten the quality of your playing. The Go will help you define the magnet—the target at the end of the score. Every action moves towards this magnet; the frame-by-frame targets link up to direct you forward to the magnet, and the shifts in status and action propel you to the magnet. When you add the Go, try to move directly towards the magnet, yet play each frame with enough time to complete every action. Incorporate Thinking Aloud into the score. Do not voice the thoughts, think them.

Focus on clarifying the narrative. Adjust and adapt the playing so that you do not all play at the same time. Offer and accept the focus. Find the direction of the overall story and adjust and adapt your individual sequence accordingly. Determine where you fit into the world of the story; what are the rules of that world and how do those rules color and condition your behavior?

Perform the score.

Evaluation. What determines style? Is it something artificial? Is it imposed on the action from the outside? Does it grow out of the impulse towards action? How do you know if you are all in the same world? Why do you need rules when you play? Who determines the rules of the world you are in? How does the text figure into all this? What happens if you don't play by the rules?

Notes to the Trainer. After focusing on language and text for the past two sessions, this session marks a return to nonverbal action. You will be integrating previous work and taking it forward by focusing on rules and how rules help create the style of the world players are playing in.

Use Energy Ball to overload and energize the players. Stimulate their imaginations as well as their bodies. Help them focus and keep them moving, without pause, throughout the rest of the session.

In the framing activity, stress playing by the rules. Repeat the rules often to avoid confusion. Make sure the focus of each round is stated simply and directly. Players won't be able to play if the rules aren't clear.

Guide the players through Sound Scoring/Instant Performance. You will see the work transform from round to round, moving from the general to the specific. Once players start to focus on the frame-by-frame playing, reinforce the concept of forwardness by stressing linking through the use of the magnet.

In the mask section, stress organizing patterns of action. Use the BADs, the Invisible Envelope, and Thinking Aloud to determine the structure of the inner world. Anything that appears to be inconsistent should be discarded or adapted to fit into the overall pattern. Help players see rules as guidelines to release their imaginations rather than inhibiting factors that limit or restrict flow.

Once the players have done their individual work, bring them together to focus on the collaborative effort—the discovery of the overall narrative. They will have to adjust and adapt what they do to fit into the larger pattern. This moves the process forward by expanding the focus of attention.

As the narrative emerges, stress economy of action. Players should do only what they need to do without elaboration or embellishment; they play to drive the action forward and tell the story. The intensifiers streamline the playing and re-energize it.

As a variation, add Mirror Cloning to reintegrate observation and interpretation. Or the players may speak, transforming this score into a Verbal All Yield scene. Use Thinking Aloud to help propel players into dialogue. Players should speak only when they need to; the use of language should be active rather than descriptive.

Players should be in sync internally, coordinating body and speech, and in sync externally, playing with one another. Use Silent Movie as a means of checking the sync. Return to playing the score with language one last time, as a full-out performance.

Add playwrights and writing styles. Vary the playing by making the score Shakespearean or Chekhovian. Ask: How is it different with each playwright? End the session by focusing the discussion and evaluation on the processes of style: What determines and creates style? Are rules external or internal, or a fusion of the two? How do the rules of a given time and place affect and condition behavior? Is it important to know the rules? When can you break them?

PART FOUR

MAP REHEARSALS

Del Close and Philip Seymour Hoffman in the Goodman Theater's 1994 production of William Shakespeare's *Merchant of Venice*, directed by Peter Sellars.

Photograph © 1994 by Liz Lauren.

MAP REHEARSALS

All actors want to convince their audience that what they are saying and doing is true. You arrive at an appreciation of those truths during the rehearsal process. Rehearsing enables you to focus and integrate your training. By preparing a scene that has a clear beginning, middle, and end, you will apply the MAP to transform words on a page into living, breathing actions on a stage.

The process moves through three distinct phases: preparation, rehearsal, and performance.

PREPARATION

Preparation is a time for daydreaming about character and action. It is a time to begin building bridges between yourself, your character, and the world of the play.

This is the time you work alone, reading and studying the script for clues about the play's world and the world of your character. You will want to know who you are, where you are, and what your relationship is to the play's action and themes. You'll focus on the why and the what of the play's world, as given by the playwright.

In the earlier stages of the training process, working with improvisation, cloning, and Instant Performance, you prepared for the first "reading" by observing your partners and gathering information about the score of actions or "text" they created. You learned to read the score of action to determine what they did, how they did it, and why they did it.

Now as you begin to rehearse, you will be working with the same process, only instead of reading and performing a score of action created from your own life experiences and those of your colleagues, you will be working with a written score and translating it from page to stage.

When you read the script for the first time note in its margins your impressions, images, and associations. Your first reading of the script is parallel to an audience's first exposure to the play: it is an adventure, a journey into the unknown, a time to form impressions.

As you continue to read the play, envision and respond to the shape and scope of the entire play's action. Look at the large picture, rather than the smaller, moment-to-moment pictures of your own scenes. Question the play's theme and what the writer is saying about human potential and the human condition: why the play was written. Having a sense of the whole will strength your sense of being an individual part of the whole.

As you study the script in detail, during your second reading, ask yourself four questions: Who am I? Who am I with? What do I do? Why do I do it? The what helps determine the why and the why leads to a more specific and interesting who.

To heighten the immediacy of the situation you will have to bridge into the play's world. Use your own life experiences and your imagination as your links into the script. Develop an image of who the character might be—an Invisible Envelope to trigger and release the power of your creative energy.

In your third reading of the script hunt for information about your endowments and history: your age, occupation, medical history, relationships, and psychological factors that you can manifest physically in your mask. Look for what the character says about himself, what other characters say about you, and what the character actually does. Remember, actions speak louder than words.

At this stage of the process accept any and all impressions. Do not edit or inhibit yourself in any way. You are gathering and collecting a series of associations that you can act on. You also are forming an all-encompassing image of the world of the play. Take into account any and all possibilities of behavior. The image of who you are is your springboard into action, the trigger that sets you in motion. Forming this image is the first step in the acting process, not the final one.

When you go into rehearsal your creative circle of attention will expand from the near—from yourself—to the intermediate—to encompass your collaboration with the other actors and the director. You will be transforming images into actions, and it is vital that you collaborate during every step of the process.

In rehearsal you will need a vast reservoir of courage to try anything, do anything, say anything. You will need to work in an environment where you are not afraid of failing, where you can make a fool of yourself and not be castigated or chastised for it—in short, an environment where you can shed your inhibitions and are free to act on your impulse.

The first phase of rehearsal usually begins with a "read" of the script. It is an opportunity to come together and discuss the play's themes and issues as well as your impressions of the characters and the play's world. In this first rehearsal period you all must agree on your rules—how you'll work, the focus of your working methodology, what you will be seeking to create together. You cannot play the game unless you all speak the same language and play by the same rules. This usually evolves intuitively.

At the same time you will begin shaping—finding a physical form for the mask of character. You will experiment with endowments, creating a personal as well as a shared history and context for your relationship with your partner. You also will begin to build the perimeters and rules of context that condition and create the world of the play.

In the second phase of rehearsal, you will be up on your feet, structuring the action. You will discover your individual scores of action as well as the collective patterns of interaction. You will work from the outside in—from the content of what you say to uncover and determine the intent of your score of action—and then from the inside out, translating that intent into specific physical actions that illuminate in space your relationship with your partner.

The score will take on a physical shape. You will create a score of action as you play the scene. Where and how you are in space will reveal the moment-to-moment balances in your relationship. Your focus is targeting your intent with your partner, and then offering and accepting and offering again to provoke your partner into responding to your action.

In the third phase of rehearsal you will refine the score of action by focusing on playing. You will work frame to frame to determine the targets and the magnet pulling your action forward. By focusing on the magnet you will link the frames together and enlarge the playing pattern. Those pieces that are inconsistent will be discarded and new alternatives will be found, prepared, and inserted into the score.

The more the score is performed the clearer your overall vision of it will become. You will want to perform the score without restraint or hesitation. The score should be so firmly lodged in your body that you won't have to think about what comes next. You will want to play spontaneously within the fixed perimeters and rules of the world you both have created.

In the fourth phase of rehearsal you will focus on ways of clarifying and intensifying the score by incorporating and integrating hurdles, rewards, and penalties. You will focus on making choices for the mask that are consistent with the rules of behavior found in the endowments of time, place, and context. You also will focus on playing the score collaboratively.

In the fifth and final phase of rehearsal, as you prepare for performance, you will focus on the quality of your playing. You will determine the dynamics of the score and the shape and structure of the patterns of action, giving them musicality and energetic muscle.

As the rehearsals near performance, your focus will expand once again from the intermediate to the far space, for you will be incorporating the objective observer into the process and she will once again affect your perception of the process.

In performance, confrontation with an audience will transform the playing into an event. Your skill will expand to include playing the score of action for maximum effect. Playing a fixed score requires the ability to erase any previous response and to begin anew at every performance without expectation or anticipation. For the actor, the audience is part of the play's experience each night. No two audiences are ever alike.

Performance demands adaptation in response, flexibility in timing, focused release, and a sense of play. The mask is never completely realized until you develop the ability to listen to an audience for their response without sacrificing the integrity of your action. While an audience continually tells you how you're doing through the intensity of their attention and the quality of their listening, you will never acquiesce fully to the demands of the audience. You must play the score of action as it was set and rehearsed and always perform with an ongoing eye for consistency.

First exposure to an audience will lead to insight and a sense of renewed discovery. Repeating the performance allows you to fine tune it, exploring it for subtlety and nuance. When the focus of a performance is renewed with specificity, the playing is charged with clarity and energy.

The MAP will guide you through the entire process, from the first moments of preparation to the final moments of performance. You will always select a specific point of focus at each stage of the process and pursue that focus until you are ready to advance and move on to a new focus. Because you are attuned to the process of transformation you know that at every step of the way, your insight and perception of the score of action will change and grow, moving you from the general to the specific.

You will begin with the large picture of the script, move to the smaller frames of action within the scene, and gradually link the frames back up into a new, all-encompassing pattern of action. You will play the large pattern frame by frame; each frame will have a magnet that links and pulls the frames forward.

The mask will be consistent with the endowments of time, place, and context found in the script. Your experience of playing will be based on outward focus; your target involves transforming the moment-to-moment balance in your relationship with your partner. The content of what you say is linked to the intent of what you do, and that intent is released forward in action.

You will collaborate with your partner on creating a score of action that has rhythm, energy, dynamic shape, and focus. You will release into playing action and focus the action on affecting your partner.

With the MAP you have a flexible approach that enables you to cover all points in the process in a graduated, orderly way, yet one that allows for spontaneity, creativity, flexibility, and discovery. Your focus is on experiencing first, analyzing and discussing after. The play process must be experienced through your body, not just your mind. In rehearsal with MAP you will move from the intuitive to the analytical, from the imaginary to the experiential, from the page to the stage.

ANALYSIS OF PREPARATION

There are many ways of preparing a scene, but the purpose of all of them—whether it be around a table or on your feet—is to ask the right questions of the scene, and discover what kind of scene you are in. As John Gielgud has said of style, "Style is knowing what kind of play you are in." You need to know what kind of endowments the playwright has given you, so that you will be able to play the action, status, hurdles, targets, and world of the play, all the dynamics that form the structure of scenes in their physical and verbal shapes.

As a means of applying the MAP directly to a text, work on preparing and rehearsing a scene from a modern American play. To help focus the MAP, we will examine the opening scene of Sam Shepard's *Fool for Love*.

During the preparation phase of the process, read, re-read, and daydream about the play. To focus your attention, examine and analyze the text in the margins of your script or in a rehearsal journal. How does this scene fit into the total shape and structure of the play? What part of the journey are you pursuing in the scene? How and what do you want: power, security, money, sex? What tactics do you use to achieve your targets? What are the personal, social, and ethical endowments of the time and place the playwright has written about—the "clues of the script"—that will inform and condition your action?

Begin by dividing the scene into frames of action and examine the shape of the action within each frame. As you write about your character, always use the first person ("I want") instead of "Eddie wants" or "May wants." We will focus on Eddie and May throughout the scene, although the Old Man is on stage during the scene.

ANALYSIS

FOOL FOR LOVE (The Magic Theatre of San Francisco production) was presented by the Circle Repertory Company, in New York City, in May 1983. It was directed by the author, the set was by Andy Stacklin, the costumes were by Ardyss L. Golden, the lighting was designed by Kurt Landisman, and the sound was by J. A. Deane. The associate director was Julie Herbert, the production stage manager was Suzanne Frey, and the lighting supervisor was Mal Sturchio. The cast was as follows:

MAY .... Kathy Baker
EDDIE .... Ed Harris
MARTIN .... Dennis Ludlow
THE OLD MAN .... Will Marchetti

Frame One Text

This play is to be performed relentlessly, without a break. Scene: Stark, low-rent motel room on the edge of the Mojave Desert. Faded green plaster walls. Dark brown linoleum floor. No rugs. Cast iron four poster single bed, slightly off-center favoring Stage Right, set horizontally to audience. Bed covered with faded blue terry cloth bedspread. Metal table with well worn yellow formica top. Two matching metal chairs in the 50's "S" shape design with yellow plastic seats and backs. Also well worn. Table set extreme down left (from actor's P.O.V.). Chairs set Upstage and Down Right of table. Nothing on the table. Faded yellow exterior door in the Center of the Stage Left wall. When this door is opened a small orange porch light shines into the room. Bathroom door Up Right of the Stage Right wall, painted red. This door slightly ajar to begin with, revealing part of an old style porcelain sink, white towels, a general clutter of female belongings and allowing a yellow light to bleed onto stage. Large picture window dead Center of Upstage wall, framed by dirty long dark green curtains. Yellow-orange light from a street lamp shines through.

Extreme Down Left, next to the table and chairs is a small extended platform on the same level as the stage. The floor is black and it's framed by black curtains. The only object on the platform is an old maple rocking chair facing Upstage Right. A pillow with no slip-cover rests on the seat. An old horse blanket with holes is laced to the back of the rocker. The color of the blanket should be subdued—grays and blacks. Lights fade to black on set. In the dark, Merle Haggard's tune, "Wake Up," from his "The Way I Am" album, is heard. Lights begin to rise slowly on stage in the tempo of the song. Volume swells slightly with the lights until they arrive at their mark. The platform remains in darkness with only a slight spill from the stage lights. Three actors are revealed:

The Old Man sits rocking in the rocker facing Up Right so he's just slightly profile to the audience. A bottle of whiskey in a brown paper bag sits on the floor beside him. He picks up the bottle, pours whiskey into a styrofoam cup and drinks. He has a scraggly red beard, wears a straw Mexican gardener's hat with a flat brim (not a sombrero), a sun-bleached dark quilted jacket with the stuffing coming out at the elbows, black and white checked slacks that are too short in the legs, no socks, Mexican sandals, an old vest, and a pale green shirt. He exists only in the minds of May and Eddie, even though they might talk to him directly and acknowledge his physical presence. The Old Man treats them as though they all existed in the same time and place. May sits on the edge of the bed facing audience, feet on floor, legs apart, elbows on knees, hands hanging limp and crossed between her knees, head hanging forward, face staring at the floor. She is absolutely still and maintains this attitude until she speaks. She wears a blue Mexican-type full skirt, baggy white T-shirt, and bare feet with a silver ankle bracelet. She's in her early thirties. Eddie sits in the Upstage chair by the table, Down Left, facing May. He wears muddy broken down cowboy boots with silver gaffer's tape wrapped around them at the toe and in-step, well-worn faded dirty jeans that smell like horse sweat. Brown western shirt with snaps. When he walks he limps slightly and gives the impression he's rarely off a horse. There's a peculiar broken-down quality about his body in general, as though he's aged long before his time. He's in his late thirties. His right hand is covered with dirty adhesive tape. He is applying resin to the handle of a bucking strap and glove. Song fades at end of first verse. Eddie stares at May. He ignores the Old Man. May stays still.

Frame One Analysis

Many actors don't count this essentially expositional frame as their concern, regarding it as the director's or designer's business. But it includes a huge amount of information for the actor about the play's action, shape, and intent, as well as clues about the status and endowments of the characters.

Shepard calls for a "relentless pace." This is important information about the forward movement of the scene. Is it a contest, a fight, a tournament? Are actor and audience never to be let off the hook?

The whole environment reflects the social, psychological, and emotional dynamics of the scene. The color of the room is essentially drab: dirty greens, browns, grays, blacks. It seems a barren world on the edge of the desert, where nothing flourishes. Occasionally, oranges and yellows bleed through, but nothing as dangerous as red. Once or twice the blinding, artificial light of the outside world slashes through the room. What is it like to live in such a space?

The textures of the furniture in the room—metal, formica, and plastic—underscore the lack of warmth, and help re-enforce the unwelcoming effect of the environment. The four-poster bed is made of cast iron; it's cold and sterile. The bed dominates the room, suggesting that sex might be an important element in the action, but the bed is offset in the room, implying that something is out of balance. The only other piece of furniture in the "reality" of the room is a table. May is on the bed, Eddie at the table. They are separate and far apart at the top of the scene.

May seems to be in the central dominant position, on the bed, which implies higher status; however, her despondent posture undercuts this. Her legs are apart, suggesting sexuality, but her head and body are collapsed between them; she is looking down at the floor. Her skirt and T-shirt do not reveal her body; they are part of a casual, uncaring, unsexual mask.

Eddie gives the impression of a classic working cowboy, dressed for riding and always on the move. He walks with a limp; he too is slightly off-balance, which wouldn't matter on a horse or in bed, but makes for difficult maneuvering in everyday life. Seated at the table he seems to be in the low status position as the scene begins.

The Old Man exists only in the minds of Eddie and May. He is down left, with his back to the audience. He seems to be looking at the scene in the same way as the audience. He acts as a playwright for the audience: he constructs and creates a "reality" and context for the action of the scene—he can place it against any emotional, physical, or psychological landscape he wishes. He is seated in a rocking chair, which is unstable, but he can create a counterpoint rhythm to Eddie and May by rocking.

The overall effect of the environment is drab, despondent, sterile. Is the room a cell, or a boxing ring, or a playground where only a fool for love would look for a fulfilled, hopeful future?

Frame Two Text

EDDIE. (*Seated*) May, look. May? I'm not goin' anywhere. See? I'm right here. I'm not gone. (*She won't look.*) I don't know why you won't just look at me. You know it's me. Who else do you think it is. (*Pause.*) You want some water or somethin'? Huh? (*He gets up slowly, goes to her, strokes her head softly, she stays still.*) May? Come on. You can't just sit around here like this. How long you been sittin' here anyway? You want me to go outside and get you something? Some potato chips or something? (*She suddenly grabs his closest leg with both arms and holds tight.*) I'm not gonna' leave. Don't worry. I'm not gonna leave. I'm stayin' right here. I already told ya' that. (*She squeezes tighter to his leg, buries her head in his knee, he just stands there, strokes her head softly.*) May? Let go, okay? Honey? I'll put you back in bed. Okay? (*She shakes her head violently, keeps holding tight to his leg.*) Come on. I'll put you in bed and make you some hot tea or somethin'. You want some tea? (*She shakes her head, keeps holding on.*) With lemon? Some Ovaltine? May, you gotta' let go of me now, okay? (*She releases his leg and returns to her original position.*) Now just lay back and try to relax. (*He starts to push her back gently on the bed as pulls back the blankets. She erupts furiously, hitting him to Upstage of Stage Left door. Eddie backs off. She takes a quick retreat to head of bed. After pause.*)

Frame Two Analysis

Eddie seems to play low status. He attempts to close the Maxi Gap by endowing May: she needs care. Why? Is Eddie's target contradictory—to both keep and let go of May?

May seems to have a parallel target: to keep Eddie, which puts her in a position of lower status, but not on his terms, which leads her to change status often, and with the change of status, to shift her BAD.

The gap in the status seems to swing drastically between mini and maxi. They both seem attached in a lethal, hopeless clinch. The bed seems to be in the middle of a boxing ring with a game of constant shadow boxing, feinting, striking out between the two characters.

Frame Three Text

You want me to go?

MAY. (*Shakes her head.*) No.

EDDIE. Well, what do you want then?

MAY. You smell.

EDDIE. I smell.

MAY. You do.

EDDIE. I been drivin' for days.

MAY. Your fingers smell.

EDDIE. Horses.

MAY. Pussy.

EDDIE. Come on, May.

MAY. They smell like metal.

EDDIE. I'm not gonna start this shit.

MAY. Rich pussy. Very clean.

EDDIE. Yeah, sure.

MAY. You know it's true.

EDDIE. I came to see if you were alright.

MAY. I don't need you!

EDDIE. Okay. (*Turns to go.*) Fine.

MAY. Don't go!

EDDIE. I'm goin'. (*Eddie exits.*)

Frame Three Analysis

There seems to be a fight for status within the frame. Information about Eddie's infidelities leads to a verbal sparring match.

The language becomes full of jabs, its verbal sparring. The tongue becomes fist. The monosyllabic language suggests the social status of each character. May is more restrained than Eddie ("pussy," not "cunt"), which may give her either higher or lower status in this situation.

Does May lose status by admitting her need with "Don't go"? Eddie is capable of leaving, which gives him permanently higher status, irrespective of the moment-to-moment playing.

Eddie seems to be a puncher who floats. May seems to be a floater who tries to punch.

Frame Four Text

(*Eddie re-enters.*)

EDDIE. What am I gonna' do? Huh? What am I supposed to do?

MAY. You know.

EDDIE. What.

MAY. You're gonna erase me.

EDDIE. What're you talkin' about?

MAY. You're either gonna' erase me or have me erased.

EDDIE. Why would I want that? Are you kidding?

MAY. Because I'm in the way.

EDDIE. Don't be stupid.

MAY. I'm smarter than you are and you know it. I can smell your thoughts before you even think 'em.

EDDIE. May, I'm tryin' to take care of you. All right?

MAY. No you're not. You're just guilty. Gutless and guilty.

EDDIE. Great.

Frame Four Analysis

There is a suggestion that the only way the relationship can be resolved is lethally—but is this part of May's fantasy?

"Erase" seems an odd word in this frame. It can mean "rub out" in Mob language. But here it seems to mean wipe from the memory of the mind in the fantasy they both live out. May raises the fantasy stakes.

Frame Five Text

(*Pause.*)

MAY. (*Quietly.*) I'm gonna' kill her ya' know.

EDDIE. Who?

MAY. Who.

EDDIE. Don't talk like that.

MAY. (*Stays calm.*) I am. I'm gonna kill her and then I'm gonna kill you. Systematically. With sharp knives. Two separate knives. One for her and one for you. So the blood doesn't mix. I'm gonna' torture her first though. Not you. I'm just gonna' let you have it. Probably in the midst of a kiss. Right when you think everything's been healed up. Right in the moment when you're sure you've got me buffaloed. That's when you'll die.

Frame Five Analysis

May raises the stakes further in her fantasy.

Eddie practices lassoing the bedposts in a later scene in the play. The bed is a metaphor for where Eddie keeps and uses May—he has her tied up when he wants to.

"Blood doesn't mix": there is to be no bond, even in death. There is also the possibility that the Old Man is the father of both Eddie and May—their blood is mixed. This is another hurdle in the relationship.

Frame Six Text

(*Pause.*)

EDDIE. You know how many miles I went outa' my way just to come here and see you? You got any idea?

MAY. Nobody asked you to come.

EDDIE. Two thousand, four hundred and eighty.

MAY. Yeah? Where were you, Katmandu or something?

EDDIE. Two thousand, four hundred and eighty miles.

MAY. So what! (*He drops his head, stares at floor. Long pause. She stares at him.*)

Frame Six Analysis

Eddie is still playing low status to close the gap and hit his target. He seems to be waiting to make his next status move.

Does May glide here?

Frame Seven Text

EDDIE. I missed you. I did. I missed you more than anything I ever missed in my whole life. I kept thinkin' about you the whole time I was driving. Kept seeing you. Sometimes just a part of you.

MAY. Which part?

EDDIE. Your neck?

MAY. My neck?

EDDIE. Yeah.

MAY. You missed my neck?

EDDIE. I missed all of you but your neck kept coming up for some reason. I kept crying about your neck.

MAY. Crying?

EDDIE. Yeah. Weeping. Like a little baby. Uncontrollable. It would just start up and stop and then start all over again. For miles. I couldn't stop it. Cars would pass me on the road. People would stare at me. My face was all twisted up. I couldn't stop my face.

Frame Seven Analysis

The action seems to be similar to Frame Six. Eddie raises the stakes. He uses his sexuality while playing low status. May seems to move from gliding to wringing.

"Neck" is what you usually see when you turn away and leave someone.

Frame Eight Text

MAY. Was this before or after your little fling with the Countess?

EDDIE. There wasn't any fling with any Countess!

MAY. You're a liar.

EDDIE. I took her out to dinner once, okay?

MAY. Ha!

EDDIE. Twice.

MAY. You were bumping her on a regular basis! Don't gimme that shit.

EDDIE. You can believe whatever you want.

MAY. I'll believe the truth! It's less confusing.

Frame Eight Analysis

May attempts to punch, but because she is basically a floater she dabs. There is a precise reference to Eddie and the Countess's infidelity.

Frame Nine Text

(*Pause.*)

EDDIE. I'm taking you back May.

MAY. I'm not going back to that idiot trailer if that's what you think.

EDDIE. I'm movin' it. I got a piece of ground up in Wyoming.

MAY. Wyoming? Are you crazy? I'm not moving to Wyoming. What's up there? Marlboro Men?

EDDIE. You can't stay here.

MAY. Why not? I got a job. I'm a regular citizen here now.

EDDIE. You got a job?

MAY. Yeah. What'd you think, I was helpless?

EDDIE. No. I mean—it's been a long time since you had a job.

MAY. I'm a cook.

EDDIE. A cook. You can't even flip an egg can you?

MAY. I'm not talkin' to you anymore. (*She goes into the bathroom, slams the door.*)

Frame Nine Analysis

The action seems to rise to a crisis.

May asserts her own fantasy of high status and leaves. Does she go into her own haven where she can be who she wants to be, and adopt whatever mask she needs?

Eddie tries to endow and engulf her with his own fantasy.

May attempts slashing action.

A return to the Maxi Gap?

Frame Ten Text

EDDIE. May, I got everything worked out. I been thinkin' about this for weeks. I'm gona move the trailer. Build a little pipe corral to keep the horses. Have a big vegetable garden. Some chickens maybe.

MAY. I hate chickens! I hate horses! I hate all that shit! You know that. You got me confused with somebody else. You keep comin' up with this lame country dream life with chickens and vegetables and I can't stand any of it. It makes me puke to even think about it.

EDDIE. You'll get used to it. (*May enters.*)

MAY. You're unbelievable!

EDDIE. I'm not lettin' go of you this time, May.

MAY. You never had a hold of me to begin with.

Frame Ten Analysis

The crisis continues until May lowers her status by returning to the room— to the boxing ring.

Eddie seems to stop playing low status; he becomes a presser.

Frame Eleven Text

(*Pause.*) How many times have you done this to me?

EDDIE. What.

MAY. Suckered me into some dumb little fantasy and then dropped me like a hot rock. How many times has that happened?

EDDIE. It's no fantasy.

MAY. It's all fantasy.

EDDIE. And I never dropped you either.

MAY. No, you just disappeared!

EDDIE. I'm here now aren't I?

MAY. Well, praise Jesus God!

EDDIE. I'm gonna' take care of you May. I am. I'm gonna' stick with you no matter what. I promise.

MAY. Get outa here.

Frame Eleven Analysis

Back to the standoff, with both Eddie and May sparring by using dabs and punches. They both want the relationship, but on their own, separate terms.

Is this a fantasy game of love?

Both Eddie and May need the fantasy. Both need what the other cannot give.

A possible hurdle: they are umbilically tied, which makes it impossible to get away but impossible to stay.

Frame Twelve Text

(*Pause.*)

EDDIE. What'd you have to go and run off for anyway?

MAY. Run off? Me?

EDDIE. Yeah. Why couldn't you just stay put. You knew I was comin' back to get you.

MAY. What do you think it's like sittin' in a tiny trailer for weeks on end with the wind ripping through it? Waitin' around for the butane to arrive. Hiking down to the laundromat in the rain. Do you think that's thrilling or somethin'?

EDDIE. I bought you all those magazines.

MAY. What magazines?

EDDIE. I bought you a whole stack of those fashion magazines before I left. I thought you liked those. Those French kind.

MAY. Yeah. I especially liked the one with the Countess on the cover. That was real cute.

Frame Twelve Analysis

The action continues forward. Each jockeys for status position.

May uses the Countess to win the round.

Frame Thirteen Text

(*Pause.*)

EDDIE. All right.

MAY. All right, what. (*He turns to go.*) Where are you going.

EDDIE. Just to get my stuff outa' the truck. I'll be right back.

MAY. What're you movin' in now or something?

EDDIE. Well, I thought I'd spend the night if that's okay.

MAY. Are you kidding?

EDDIE. Then I'll just leave I guess.

Frame Thirteen Analysis

The action rises.

Eddie presumes the game is over. Will he do what he always does? Will the game end as it always has?

Both call the bluff of the other's status position.

Frame Fourteen Text

MAY. (*She stands.*) Wait. (*They stand there facing each other for a while. They cross slowly to each other. Pause as they look at each other. They embrace. Long, tender kiss. They are very soft with each other. She suddenly knees him in the groin with tremendous force. Eddie doubles over and drops like a rock. She stands over him. Pause.*) You can take it, right? You're a stuntman. (*She exits into bathroom, Stage Right. Slams the door behind her. The door is amplified with microphones and a resonator hidden in the frame so that each time an actor slams it, the door booms loud and long. Same is true for Stage Left door. Eddie remains on the floor holding his stomach in pain.*)

Frame Fourteen Analysis

Crescendo of the action. May seems to adopt low status position. The fantasy/game seems to be ending as it always does. Then May wins by a sexual knock-out.

Frame Fifteen Text

(*Stage lights drop to half their intensity as a spot rises softly on The Old Man. He speaks directly to Eddie.*)

THE OLD MAN. I thought you were supposed to be a fantasist. Isn't that basically the deal with you? You dream things up. Isn't that true?

EDDIE. (*Stays on floor.*) I don't know.

THE OLD MAN. You don't know. Well, if you don't know I don't know who the hell else does. I wanna' show you somethin'. Somethin' real, okay? Somethin' actual.

EDDIE. Sure.

THE OLD MAN. Take a look at that picture on the wall over there. (*He points to wall Stage Right. There is no picture but Eddie stares at the wall.*) Ya' see that? Take a look at that. Ya' see it?

EDDIE. (*Staring at wall.*) Yeah.

THE OLD MAN. Ya' know who that is?

EDDIE. I'm not sure.

THE OLD MAN. Barbara Mandrell. That's who that is. Barbara Mandrell. You heard a' her?

EDDIE. Sure.

THE OLD MAN. Well, would you believe me if I told ya' I was married to her?

EDDIE. (*Pause.*) No.

THE OLD MAN. Well, see, now that's the difference right there. That's realism. I am actually married to Barbara Mandrell in my mind. Can you understand that?

EDDIE. Sure.

THE OLD MAN. Good. I'm glad we have an understanding. (*The Old Man drinks from his cup. Spot slowly fades to black as stage lights come back up full.*)

Frame Fifteen Analysis

The perspective of the action shifts to the outside "reality."

The Old Man has seen this all before. He got out of an irresolvable, foolish game of love; he has made his own fantasy his "reality" instead of making his reality work. He is married to Barbara Mandrell in his mind. That is a stable "reality."

Thought: "Lying is when you believe it's true. If you already know it's a lie, it's not lying" (p. 29).

You can believe anything if it stays in your mind: that's reality; the rest is fantasy.

Is this the main action/theme of the play? That there is more reality in the fantasy of the mind than in the shifting, uncertain fantasy of life? If you take no action your fantasy stays real in your head; otherwise love is an unfinished sexual boxing matched played by fools.

Is love a cruel and foolish fantasy? We cannot live with it or without it— are we forever sexually trapped in the cell of a transient motel/boxing ring?

Throughout, the doors boom and reverberate in the space. Use them to emphasize the crescendo in the action—make them a reverberation of doom? Also, the doors always slam in Eddie and May's faces as they attempt to get together.

The noise is like a bell at the end of the round in a boxing match.

REHEARSAL 1: *SHAPE*

In the first rehearsal focus on establishing the boundaries and framework of the relationship between the characters. You also will focus on finding the physical shape of the character mask.

Start the rehearsal by reading the entire play aloud. Sit at a table facing one another. Make eye contact with your partner whenever possible. Read the play with a sense of action and purpose. Focus on offering and accepting. Stay flexible in your responses to your partner. Listen to each other.

After the first read, talk about the play as you understand it. What are the themes of *Fool for Love*?—what is its core, its central dramatic focus and action? How do Eddie and May and the Old Man shape, influence, reflect, or in some way carry forward the heart of the play's intent?

Focus on the relationship between Eddie and May. What are the most significant factors in their relationship? How long have they been apart? What are they like when they're together? Who are they to each other and what do you think they want from each other?

Also discuss the possibilities of intent and action. Do they want to stay apart or do they want to stay together? What attracts them to each other? What are the possible hurdles that keep them apart? What do they have to overcome in order to get together?

What is the play's "punch line"? What moment is the action driving towards—what is the play's thematic "point"? This "point" does not have to be intellectual—it may be emotional or intuitively perceived by the audience. How does this first scene work to "set up" the punch line? How much information should we know about Eddie and May from the beginning of the scene to get us to the end of the scene? What history in the endowments affects and conditions the relationship?

Structurally, what is the balance in the Eddie/May relationship at the beginning of the scene and at the end of the scene? Is it a Mini or a Maxi Gap, or does it have elements of both? Is one the cover for the other?

How does the balance shift and change as the scene progresses? When and where do the changes happen in the text? How many "frames" of action do you move through in the scene? How do the frames link up in terms of their magnets?

Read just the first scene. As you read, stop at the end of each potential frame. Give each frame a name or title that describes the action within the frame. Be specific about when the frame begins and when it ends.

Read the scene again, and make each frame specific in terms of its action. Each frame must have a beginning, a middle, and an end. In each frame you must initiate an action, engage in the action, and complete the action. The frame changes when the action has been completed.

Was this reading any different from the first? Is the action within the scene clearer or more specific? Has your initial impression of the scene changed now that you are working with your partner? Has the discussion with your partner about the scene triggered your imagination or changed your perception of what happens in the scene? Is the relationship clearer to you?

Leave the table and move to the playing space. Begin to work on transforming your impressions from image into action by shaping the mask of the character. Work to investigate your impressions and images by giving them physical form and substance. Remember, this is a starting point where the MAP begins, not where it ends.

Move around the playing space. Start with a Parallel and Perpendicular walk. As you walk, focus on your image and impressions of the character. Gradually transform the parallel into a sagittal line—lean slightly forward or backwards—and transform the perpendiculars by adding horizontals, to tilt in one direction. As you continue to walk, become aware of moving as either a table, wheel, or door. Change into another type. Change again into the third type. Explore all three types before determining which type you are.

Move directly into the most appropriate body type. Follow the lead of one part of your body. Use that lead as your key into body shape. Once you've determined the lead, focus on which body part the mask withholds. Have one active center within your body and an inert center. How do they make you respond? How does your shape influence your perception? Let the mask take over as you move.

Focus on direction in space. Work with direct focus; everything you do, everywhere you move, has a clear and defined target. Do the opposite. Everything is indirect. Lead with your eyes. Flick your focus up and down, and change your focus continually. Which seems appropriate for the character—direct or indirect?

Add weight to the mask. Make everything you do strong. Work either strong and direct or strong and indirect. Work light. Either light and direct or light and indirect. Which seems most appropriate for the character?

Now add time to the effort of the mask. Work quick. Do the opposite and work sustained. Add time to weight and direction in space. Are you a presser, puncher, flicker, dabber, slasher, wringer, floater, or glider? Which action seems most appropriate and true for the mask?

Stop. In front of you is an imaginary mirror. Next to the mirror there is a table with invisible putty. Mold a putty mask onto your face and body. Create your musculature and body shape with the putty. When you have finished turn behind you. On an imaginary chair you will find your clothes laid out for you. Put the clothes on and examine yourself in the mirror. Turn to look at yourself from all angles. Once you have a complete picture of yourself dressed and in body shape, turn away from the mirror and walk around the playing space again. Let the walk transform. Respond to the new image of who you are.

As you walk, begin to talk to yourself on a whisper. Talk about your history—where and when you were born, how you grew up, your relationship with your brother/sister. Knowing you are going to meet your brother/sister again, what might you want from them this time? Begin to imagine the meeting, and use "this or that" to define what might happen at the encounter. If you do this, that will happen; if that, this will happen. Thinking aloud, define for yourself the possibilities and alternatives of action that lie before you in confronting your sibling for the first time.

Stop. Turn to each other. Examine one another. Endow one another with status. Your partner is either master or servant. In turn, you are either master or servant to your partner. Determine your relationship through status and adjust yourself physically to match the status.

Standing opposite one another, begin to speak. Build your history together with Remember When. One of you initiates the memory by offering Remember When we.... Accept the offer by saying yes, elaborating on the memory and then offer back with And Then You.... Collaborate on the memory until it is complete. Move on to build another one. Build three memories together.

Move around the playing space, side by side. Do not speak. Stay within the mask, the shape, the status. Stop and turn to one another. Using physical and sound leads, endow one another with You Always. Accept each endowment with "yes, that's true, but You Always...." Play rapidly and use the leads with every acceptance.

Change the endowment pattern by using You Never. Accept the offers using leads and offer back. Transform the playing pattern a third time by combining You Always and You Never.

Separate from one another. Move rapidly around the playing space. Return to your mirror. Take off the mask's clothes. Then peel off the putty mask. Return to your own body.

Turn away from the mirror and move quick and light through the playing space. Change your dynamic and energy. Stop. Use Balloon Breathing to recharge and energize.

Move back to the table. Without talking, sit and read the scene one more time. Look at one another whenever possible. See if the playing transforms. Is the relationship between you more specific, and how does that affect the quality of the playing?

Take a few moments at the end of this first rehearsal to evaluate what you have just done. In what ways has your approach to the text changed? Do you have a stronger sense of who you are in the scene? Of who your partner is to you? Of how your shared history brings you together to this point in time and space? How that history influences what you want from each other? How has the physical work triggered your imagination? Do you feel you have the beginnings of a solid foundation to build a relationship with your partner throughout the scene? How has the information you have gathered in preparation been transformed into concrete physical images?

Remember, the physical mask will continue to transform as you work. You will want this transformational process to continue. Where you begin is not where you end. You are creating the first stepping stones with each other in the rehearsal process to unlock, discover, and create the score of action collaboratively.

You have begun to translate your initial impressions into physical form and shape. You have begun to bridge to your partner by endowing, offering, and accepting. You've started to create agreements and boundaries for the working process and for the relationship between the characters. You've also begun to create a working environment for yourself in which it is possible to experiment without fear of judgment or destructive criticism. You will continue and advance this process in the second rehearsal, when you will focus your attention on the structure of the action.

REHEARSAL 2: *STRUCTURE*

In the second rehearsal you will continue to focus on owning the text by discovering the inner structure of the scene. You will work with status and narrative structure to determine the specific patterns of transformation within Eddie and May's relationship, and how these patterns can be adapted and translated into space. In addition, you will begin to name and define the targets and hurdles that shape each frame by creating action cycles.

Begin your second rehearsal with a physical warm-up: start with Blind Offers and then progress to Kinetic Sculpture. Play both games within the perimeters and context of the characters in *Fool for Love*.

In Blind Offers what type of physical offers does Eddie make to May and May to Eddie? What do you say once the offer has been made? Does each offer clarify or illuminate the nature of your relationship? What are the perimeters that determine which type of offer is appropriate and which isn't? Are those perimeters determined by the text?

Use Kinetic Sculpture to begin to define the nature of the reach space in your relationship. Do the two of you feel comfortable in near or intermediate or far space? Does one spatial quality seem more appropriate than the other? Does the quality of the space depend on the nature of the transaction between the two of you? How do you react and adapt when your partner changes the reach space?

After the warm-up, return to the table and read the scene. Does it seem any different to you since the first rehearsal? What are your impressions of the characters and the nature of the relationship? Define, in your own words, who the characters are to each other.

Work through the text frame by frame. Agree on the yields, the blocks, and the shelves within each frame—the moves that create and determine the action cycle within the frame. Do you yield to the content or the intent of your partner's offer? Are you blocking content or intent? Discuss the possible intent of each offer—what you want to do to your partner to make him/ her change. Begin to name your targets in each frame. Make sure the target is in the form of a verb—"I want you to take care of me.... I want to buffalo you..." Each target should trigger your imagination with the possibility of action, of doing something to help you get what you want.

How do the targets create a pattern of action that changes your relationship? Make sure you have a target for each frame in the scene. Remember that the name for the targets may change as you begin to physicalize the action. This form of table work is merely preparation for the playing of the scene. It creates a boundary for you, a specific point of attention that will guide and trigger your imagination. The targets will transform and become more specific as you work on the scene.

Prepare to play a Parallel and Paraphrase.

Agree on a parallel situation, one which mirrors the context of the scene, but is closer to your own life experience. Determine for yourself a parallel relationship, one that you can use to substitute for the Eddie/May relationship in the play. For the parallel use the image of someone you want to see yet who has the potential to hurt, disappoint, or abandon you. Keep this person's identity as your secret. Endow your partner with the qualities of this person and use the endowment throughout the scene to define your relationship to one another.

Agree on a where—one that parallels the text—a setting that feels like a boxing arena. It must have a sense of independence to it, yet be neutral enough for both of you to claim ownership. Agree on all of the specifics that will affect and color your meeting in this space—the last time you met, the nature of the final meeting, the last words you said to one another.

Play the scene in your own words. Parallel the scene frame by frame. Play each Yield, Block, or Shelve in sequence. Call each other by character name, but keep the substituted parallel alive in your imagination. Use it to define for yourself the changing nature of your relationship with your partner from frame to frame within the scene.

When you finish the Parallel and Paraphrase briefly discuss the exercise. Did you skip any frames? If so, which ones and why? How did the relationship transform? Did you chart the progression of the transformation through the pattern of the Yield, Block, and Shelve? Do you have a clear bridge to your partner—do you know who you are to one another from frame to frame? Is the sequence of the pattern of action clear to you?

Now return to your mask and use your key to slip inside the mask and wear the character's shape. Move around the playing space and use the outer to trigger your inner. Engage your spine and pelvis in the shape. Focus on your partner and verbalize your inner voice as you move around one another.

Endow each other with status. Begin the Parallel and Paraphrase again, wearing the mask. Parallel the Yield, Block, and Shelve. But this time, play the Parallel and Paraphrase as master and endow your partner as servant. Play the scene through to the end. Sustain your status in the scene, even if it feels wrong to you. Use the status to deliberately provoke your imagination and create a strong bridge with your partner.

Play the scene again. Reverse status roles. Deliberately play the scene as servant, even if that feels wrong to you. How might this status position lead you into action? How do you fulfill the obligation of Yield, Block, and Shelve playing the lower position in the scene?

Play the scene a third time and continually shift and transform your status. Play either master or servant from frame to frame, and endow your partner with their role. Be specific and deliberate with your physical transformation from high to low status from frame to frame. Focus on transforming the roles and finding the balance in the relationship with each Yield, Block, and Shelve.

What do you do to your partner to get what you want? How does the doing affect and change the target you've selected for yourself? Is your focus on checking and landing action on your partner or on yourself?

Work with script in hand. On your feet, incorporate the text into your action. Use your own words when you need to as a bridge into the text, but begin to rely on the text more and your own words less. If the Parallel and Paraphrase has worked for you your thinking patterns will be clear from frame to frame, and the script will help make the thinking even more specific.

Use the text to affect the status transformations from frame to frame. How do you make the language active as you Yield, Block, and Shelve? Are you staying on target from frame to frame? Does your positioning in space—your use of direction, level, and reach space—accurately mirror the nature of your relationship as it progresses and changes?

Return to the table and evaluate the exercise. Do you agree or disagree on the status transactions from frame to frame? If you disagree, you will need to continue to explore the possibilities of action within the frame until you reach a consensus. How do the frames link up to take you forward? Do you have a clear image of what you do structurally within each frame—how the Seesaw works and how the Yield, Block, and Shelve works to create pattern and sequence?

Does your target pull you forward to the end of each frame? If you don't get what you want at the end of the frame, do you change your action and continue the pursuit in the next frame? Does each pursuit of the target result in a shift in your relationship? How does the text support your pursuit of the target through the action? Does your mask adjust and adapt from frame to frame?

The focus of the work in this rehearsal is on experiencing the pursuit of the target. You named the target in the beginning of the session to create a boundary and perimeter for your imagination. Once you were on your feet and working physically, did you surrender to the impulse of the moment and respond to your partner? This is how change and discovery happens in rehearsal. Be willing to throw away all of your homework at any moment and say yes to your partner. Code the experience of the action into your body and then connect up with it, through insight, after the playing.

You can always discard any choice once you have experienced it. But you may not predetermine your choices and stay inflexible or rigid to the possibilities of interaction in rehearsal.

You now are ready to memorize the text. You've built up a series of associations and images of the text by working with your partner script in hand. By working the Parallel and Paraphrase you've absorbed the structure and sequence of events into your body and found a way to bridge into the text. Learn the text by building on this series of physical associations and images. Connect and associate physical action, intent, and language. Once you've memorized the text you can look into your partner's eyes and begin to truly play the scene.

In the third rehearsal you will continue and advance the work on structure by physicalizing the structure in space.

REHEARSAL 3: *PHYSICALIZING STRUCTURE AND PLAYING ACTION*

In the third rehearsal you will focus on transforming the structure of the scene into a physical score of action, one that accurately mirrors the intent of your mask and the changing nature of the Seesaw. At the same time you will focus your attention on translating the contextual endowments of time, place, and mask history into physical/effort factors that will color, tone, and condition the quality of your playing.

Use the Plastique as a warm-up for this rehearsal. Run through the scene using the Plastique as a language substitute for the text. Play each frame fully; focus your attention on initiating, engaging in, and completing each frame of action. Vary the effort dynamics from frame to frame and engage your pelvis as you work. Change the spatial relationship with your partner from frame to frame; move into and away from one another, work directly and indirectly, work front to back, back to front, and sideways.

When you finish working through the scene with the Plastique, repeat the exercise. This time play with sustained effort—withhold the impulse to work quickly. Justify the need for sustained effort. Continue to trigger your partner with each offer and accept every offer made to you.

When you finish working with sustained effort, repeat the scene for a third time, using very quick effort. Justify the need for quick effort. Continually change the space between you, keeping it dynamic, alive, and charged with action.

When you finish this round of playing take a moment and evaluate the exercise. The challenge of playing the scene with the Plastique shifts your focus from the intellectual pursuit of the target onto the physical pursuit—what do you do and how do you do it to make your partner respond to you.

The physicality of the playing and the full integration of body parts will help trigger insight into the basic nature of the action itself and the sequencing of the action—how A leads to B leads to C. As you clarify each frame you are establishing your "points" within the scene—the targets you aim to hit at the end of each frame. The shifts in the Seesaw—the pattern of how the relationship changes from frame to frame—is built into the score of action.

Once you have established the structure of the score, it is inviolate. It must be played in the same sequence and in the same order every time you play. The playing is physical; the experience of the action cycle exists within your body. Engage your mind in justifying or motivating the pursuit, but keep the playing physical.

You will continually refine the score of action, moving from the general to the specific in the pursuit of each target. While the sequence of the score is fixed, how you play the score is not; the how will continue to transform as you work. Focus your attention on translating the endowments into effort factors that will tune, condition, and tone the quality of your playing.

Work together to create a where for the scene. In order to release physically, you must have a secure sense of environment and know your relationship to the environment. Your body doesn't lie; you must be comfortable in space at every moment within the scene.

Agree on the placement of the bed, the doors, the window, the table. Stand at the front door and at the window and describe what you see—accept every description and build upon it, as in Gift Giving. Describe the parking lot, the number of cars parked, their year, model, and make. Describe the landscape beyond the parking lot. The colors, smells, temperature, time of day, quality of light—all of the sensory elements in your environment.

Move to the bathroom and open the medicine cabinet above the sink. Describe the contents of the medicine cabinet to one another, building on each other's suggestions as in the Yes Game. Turn and describe the rest of the bathroom to one another—the color of the walls and floor; the look, size, and shape of the shower or tub; the coolness of the tiles; etc. Again, build the sensory environment together and overload your imagination with detail.

Does the room have a "fourth wall"—a wall separating you from the audience and making the room a truly dimensional space rather than a theatrical one? Though the context of the play is theatrical—the Old Man is present throughout the play's action—the motel room is your sole reality. What is on the fourth wall? Move around the room until you are comfortable in every corner of it. Don't be afraid to stand against the fourth wall with your back to the audience. Focus on making the space real for yourself and allow your body to release into the space.

Move to separate parts of the room—do you "own" the room or are you a visitor here? Whose territory is it and how comfortable do you feel in the space? Does your relationship/status with the room ever change in the course of the scene? Does the room seem to shrink or expand in size as the scene progresses?

As you move around the space, use your physical key to trigger your body and move into your mask. Wear the mask as an Invisible Envelope and allow it to take over. Engage your face in the mask as well as your spine and pelvis. Move around the room and talk to yourself as you move. Remember one important event in the history of your relationship—the event in which you made a promise to yourself about the other character. Recall the promise as you make eye contact with your partner.

Move apart from one another. Improvise the beginning of the scene—the moment when Eddie knocks on the door of May's room. Play this scene straight through and aim at moving into the first lines of the scene.

When you reach your target, play the scene through once, using the text as written. Play the score of action as you understand it through the text. Move in the space whenever you feel the impulse to move. Each move will affect your partner and affect the Seesaw.

When you reach the end of the scene, freeze. Immediately return to the beginning of the scene. Repeat your physical score of action as you start the scene. Use your physical pattern as a means of graphing and charting the progression of the relationship as it Seesaws and changes. Attend to the moments when you are close to one another and when you are apart. When do you use direct or indirect focus? When you use direct focus, are you playing with your pelvises toward one another, or are you opening up and pulling apart?

Maintain the integrity of the physical score this second time through. You will amend or change the score the third time through, to clarify your intent and the nature of your relationship from frame to frame. Each time you work through the score, you'll make your targets more specific.

When do you feel secure and certain of what you are doing and when do you feel you are drifting in the scene? When you drift, do you feel isolated in space, or are you connected with your partner? What feels comfortable to you physically, and what doesn't? How can you adjust in space to one another to clarify your intent and make the playing more specific? Does one frame flow into the next, or do the links feel unnecessarily abrupt? Most importantly, are you developing a sense of inner flow in the course of the scene? When are you self-conscious and when are you released?

As you rehearse continually look for ways to heighten your involvement in the playing of the action of the scene, ways that will help you forget about the presence of the audience and allow you to surrender to the intensity of your relationship with your partner.

Remember that the score involves shifting the balance in the master/servant relationship. At times you both may be master, trying to make the other servant; at times you may both be servant trying to please master. Or you may deliberately play the role of servant in order to manipulate your partner with a false sense of master. The stronger and more specific you can make the moves of the seesaw within the scene, the easier the scene will be to play. The more specific the seesaw pattern is in space, the more comfortable you will feel as the work progresses.

Focus on any frame that does not feel comfortable. Work through the frame from beginning to end, and adjust and adapt to one another until you have found a comfortable solution in space for the frame. Work to clarify intent and place the intent in space through body relationship. Work through any other frames which seem uncomfortable.

Now repeat the entire score of action a third time with the new and adjusted frames. See how they affect the nature and quality of the the flow within the scene. As you play this time, vary the effort factors; play one frame strong and sustained, another quick and strong. Respond immediately to each offer and the way it was sent. Do not think too much as you work.

Play each frame to hit your target—remember that the target always rests within your partner. Change the effort from frame to frame, and use the changes in effort to connect the outside with the inside, as you drilled in the transformational work. Make sure each action is fully supported internally—use the effort of the outer to connect with the effort of the inner. As you connect, you may want to transform and modify how you play the outer.

Take a moment and talk about the shape and design of the scene. Do you ever press, punch, flick, dab, slash, wring, float, or glide? What is your central effort core? How do you go about getting what you want? What effort pattern does the mask use as its neutral base?

Now repeat the score one final time, but play the scene as a Silent Movie. Play the scene fully. Stay within the boundaries of the score of action, adding the effort factors. Do not use sound, though you do talk to one another in the scene. Just play with the volume turned down.

When you finish the scene, evaluate the work. When were you in sync with one another, when apart? How does your partner's relationship in space affect you? Can you justify the changes of effort in the course of the scene by the history you have created with one another? Or by the history and nature of the mask? Does the scene have a sense of flow to it?

As you have worked through this rehearsal, how has the scene transformed? Is it different now than when you began? Have you been able to work with a clear and defined focus every time you've run through the scene? Have you been able to stay within the perimeters of that focus, or did your focus change? Do you feel yourself responding completely to the impulse of the moment and connecting the outer with the inner?

When the connect-up happens, integrate the impulse into the score of action. This is how the score transforms and grows, by the consistent and specific incorporation of discoveries as you work with your partner. When the two of you are in a heightened state of flow, your intuition will guide you. Remember and incorporate the physical changes you played spontaneously into the score of action. Work to continually play as if for the first time, as if you are discovering the impulse for the action of each frame for the first time.

In the fourth rehearsal you will continue the process of refining the playing of the score of action by focusing on the language—both the verbal and the nonverbal language of the scene—to heighten and intensify the quality of the play.

REHEARSAL 4: *PLAYING THE ACTION*

The focus of the fourth rehearsal is on adding stakes to the playing by using rewards, penalties, and overloads to heighten and intensify the quality of the playing. As the hurdles integrate into the score, the intent of the inner flow will transform once again to have greater clarity and specificity.

Use Energy Ball as a warm-up for the rehearsal. Play quickly. Use sound. Move from gestural to postural action—receive and send with the center of your body, not just your arms and hands.

As you continue to play, gradually focus on your mask, and begin to play Energy Ball as the mask. Focus on using full body effort to affect your partner. Use the outer to trigger your imagination and connect with your inner. You may touch one another, but never with your hands.

Now build the where together, silently. Stay very aware of one another as you construct the space. Play within the mask and focus on justifying the Silent Tension.

As soon as the where is completed, play the scene straight through. Play with Silent Tension. Never break eye contact with your partner. Talk only when necessary. Use the language to continually build the tension rather than release it. Take as much time as you need to play the scene. Do not rush; do not feel obligated to "perform." Find the impulse to speak through your partner. Keep your inner voice active and alive.

Without talking or taking a break, play the scene a second time. Add Touch and Talk. Even if it feels arbitrary, speak only when your partner touches you and only as long as you maintain or sustain physical contact. Try to touch one another without using your hands.

Evaluate the exercise. Did you surrender control to your partner? Did the endowments and relationship change as the scene progressed? How do you justify the silence in the scene? How does the silence and the tension—even if it is artificially induced at first—trigger your imagination? Does the silence change the nature of the endowments in the scene? How does that affect the quality of your effort? Does it change what you do to one another, or how you do it?

Repeat the scene a third time. Focus on the quality of the tension and flow within the score of action. Incorporate any changes into the score. Add silence when it seems appropriate. Add Silent Tension when it seems appropriate. If the playing changes in space, incorporate the adjustments into your physical score of action. Set the sequence of the score for yourself, so you don't have to think about what you do. Focus merely on the doing of it, from frame to frame.

Repeat the scene again. This time use a language substitute: A/B. Play the scene through, from frame to frame, using A or B, A-B, or B-A in place of the dialogue. Play the scene as if you were paraphrasing in a different language. The intent of each line is exactly the same and the target within each frame is exactly the same. Only the "words" are different. Take as much time as you need to play the scene.

When you've finished, evaluate the process. Is your intent from target to target more specific? Did the hurdle of the language substitute force you into adjusting and adapting the quality of your play? Did you offer in a more physical manner or less? Is your outer changing? Does the shift in the outer—in what you do and how you do it—trigger any new insight or transform the quality of your playing?

Repeat the scene again, using the text as written. Incorporate insights and discoveries from the language substitute into the score of action. Make sure they are justified and motivated. You still must have an outward focus. You must target, affect, and change your relationship with your partner. Do the words have any different meaning or value to you now than they did before? Is your relationship with your partner any different?

Repeat the scene once again. As you play, eliminate action. Use only the operative words of the text—the verbs and the nouns. Discard everything else. Play the full intent of the line with only those words. Maintain and sustain the silent tension as well as the physical patterns in space. The physical score of action must stay intact at all times. How do you justify using only these words? Do they carry your intent? Or do you need to adjust and adapt your playing physically to help clarify your intent?

Without taking a break, play the scene one final time. Use the full text. Integrate and incorporate the operatives into the text; let them inform the quality of your play. Play the scene "full out." Add a silent penalty every time your partner does not respond to you as you want; make the playing of the next frame more and more important until you finally get what you want from your partner. If and when you do, repeat the process with the next frame. Continue to raise the stakes by making your partner's response more and more crucial to the quality of your playing. Use the language to sharpen and hone your intent and hit your target from frame to frame.

Evaluate the scene. Has the Eddie/May relationship changed in the course of the rehearsal? How has your playing transformed? Have the hurdles made the playing any more difficult, dangerous, or exciting? What happened when you overloaded with the language substitute? Did you find yourself playing with more physicality? Did you use greater effort to overcome the hurdle? How can you retain and incorporate these changes into the score of action? Do they change what's at stake? Is what's at stake connected to your partner, or are you manufacturing the stakes yourself?

If the scene feels "slow" at this point, do not speed up. Do the opposite; slow down and focus more intensely on your partner. Adjust and increase your involvement in the action of the scene through your inner flow rather than trying to adjust the outer flow. When the scene feels slow, you are out of sync with one another; your focus of attention is split and you are not engaging or deepening your connection with your partner.

To intensify the flow within the scene and help you reconnect, use a sound lead. Respond to every offer from your partner with an open, emotive sound—work with vowel sounds and let them grow and develop as you are triggered into responding. Let the sound lead you into your line. Do not jump. Go wherever the sound takes you. As you re-sync with your partner, you can eliminate the sound leads. Whenever you feel the connection waning, add the leads again. Incorporate any insights and changes they may trigger into your score of action.

By the end of this fourth rehearsal the score of action will have physical shape, dynamic tension, and forwardness. You will have discovered the action of the scene through your partner. You are now working to surrender control and responsibility for the playing of the scene. Release into the playing of the scene by intensifying the rewards and penalties that are a part of the rules of your relationship. You'll discover the rules by playing them first in a physical manner and then adjusting and adapting your effort. Then connect the effort with its intent.

As you work from the outside in connect the two; as your physical action triggers your imagination, transform, adjust, adapt, and change the target or your aim at the target. This is how the score evolves. At this stage of the process, you are fine tuning the score.

In the fifth rehearsal you will focus on elements of design as you approach performing the action. You will give the score greater musicality, dynamic, and drive as you focus on increasing the forwardness of the action.

REHEARSAL 5: *PERFORMING THE ACTION*

In this rehearsal you will add design elements to deliberately provoke new ways of looking at the shape, structure, and score of action within the scene. You will focus on increasing the spontaneity of your playing by giving the entire score greater musicality, physicality, and drive.

Begin the rehearsal by playing The Hunter and the Hunted in character. Use May's hotel room as your playing space. Change your tactics often as you play. Play two or three rounds, switching roles with each round. Deepen the endowments during each round of playing to raise the stakes.

Add more furniture to create more hurdles.

When you've finished the last round of The Hunter and the Hunted stand back to back. Play the scene silently graphing, using pressure and touch against your partner's back as your form of communication. Play the scene with full intent. Work from frame to frame and make your partner respond to you.

Repeat this variation of Graphing a second time, and change your dynamics and effort from line to line. Even if the changes feel arbitrary or artificial, respond in a different way to your partner. Continually try to throw your partner off balance by being unpredictable. Deliberately break whatever dynamic patterns you have established to make your partner "listen" to you. Change your physical level as you play. Work to strengthen the sense of flow and synchronicity with your partner.

Repeat the exercise a third time. Add the dialogue. Make the words and the action "fit." As you speak, connect the verbal life with the physical life—if you are "punching" physically, punch verbally as well. Connect the outer and the inner as well as the physical and the verbal in the endeavor.

Evaluate the exercises. Do you feel tuned into and in sync with one another? Does your playing of the score have clarity of intent and consistency of attack? Are you completing each frame and hitting your target? Do you feel comfortable adjusting and adapting to one another as you play the score?

If you feel there are gaps in the score—disconnected moments when the seesaw is not specific or the endowments do not condition the action, focus on them now. Target and work those moments until you physically feel comfortable in space during the frame. Then run through the scene once, maintaining the integrity and sequence of the score of action. Play full out. Work frame to frame, and link all the frames together with the magnet to give the playing forwardness.

Repeat the scene a second time. Play using Go. Eliminate all pauses. Overlap the ends of lines. Do not anticipate or jump; play the full score of action, but think quickly. Justify the quick tempo of the scene. Add endowments that make playing at this tempo necessary and logical.

As you repeat the Go one more time add Crescendos and Cascades. As the frames link up, eliminate all down endings in the sentences. Play the intent of the target through to the end of the line and land each target with a sustained or rising end. Let the frames build in tension and dynamic with a crescendo, or diminish with a cascade. Build the Crescendos and Cascades together.

Continue to use the same sense of physicality you discovered at the beginning of this rehearsal, graphing back to back. Continue to justify the changes in shape and design of the score by adjusting and adapting the endowments of the relationship to the expanding context of the scene. Every time you change the outer, adjust the inner. Play with as many links and changes as possible.

Evaluate the changes in the scene. Does the playing feel more "forward"? Does it have a greater sense of urgency and drive to it? Are there frames when the playing is too fast or not fast enough? Do the Cascades and Crescendos help punctuate the action? Are there elements of this new shape you wish to incorporate or discard as you continue playing the scene?

Repeat the scene. Is there a style of music that seems appropriate for the scene? Country and Western? Opera? Rhythm and Blues? Decide on the style of music, and play the scene in the manner of that style. Play the entire score As If it were a piece of music meant to be sung/spoken in rhythm. Play the score entirely for its musical rhythm and lyric sensibility. When you finish, repeat the scene again, using a different musical style. Play it as the Blues or Rock 'n Roll. Again, adjust and adapt the inner to suit the new form of the outer.

Play the scene one last time. Incorporate as many elements of the rehearsal into the run as possible: the physicality of the graphing, the danger and intensified endowments of The Hunter and the Hunted, the forwardness of the Go, the continuously changing shapes of the Crescendos and Cascades, the inner intensity and drive of the musical style.

At the same time, continue to play the structure of the score of action: play the narrative patterns of the Yield, Block, and Shelve, the pattern of changing relationships in the Seesaw, the direct or indirectness of aiming your targets and using hurdles to intensify your effort. Continue to work with the sensory endowments of time and place that affect, condition, and color your effort. Continue to use the physical keys that unlock the shape and form of the mask.

By the end of this rehearsal you should feel comfortable in space with one another, able to adjust and adapt to any mode or form of playing. By working in this rehearsal to continually throw your partner off balance by adding new dynamics you reopen the channels of communication. You had to look at one another and listen to one another from frame to frame, because nothing was as it was before. The score of action was the same, the sequence of events was the same, but the approach and the launch into action were different.

By adding musicality, and imposing external musical styles on the scene, you test your ability to play the scene without thinking. When you no longer have to think about what comes next or what you are supposed to do or say, you can react spontaneously to your partner and are free to act and ready to perform.

Performing the scene for the first time is a major hurdle. Once you've moved through that hurdle, you are released from the obligation to "perform" and can return to the ongoing process of structuring, shaping, and playing the action.

When you perform, you offer your work to the judgment of the causal observer. When you perform a scene for the first time, you move into a heightened state of awareness. Fear triggers your chemical balance and you start to pump out adrenalin—it's part of the fight or flight mechanism when you are confronted by anything new, anything that causes you to respond with terror. Because of the adrenalin, all of your senses are wide open and you see, hear, feel, touch, and taste as if for the first time. You expand your awareness, unlock your intuition and play with a directness and immediacy you rarely experience in ordinary life.

Unfortunately, you also tend to forget what has happened because you are in an agitated, chemically induced state of flow. It comes and goes and is then gone, seemingly forever. This is when repetition as a technique and discipline becomes important. Go back and incorporate the discoveries you made in performance, as you remember them. Do not attempt to play the scene as you played it before. Rather, approach the scene as if for the first time. Focus on playing the scene frame by frame with your newfound awareness, and focus on uncovering the impulse for action.

Use the experience of working with an objective observer to focus your attention on your partner. Use the sensory endowments to help "ground" you in the world of the scene. Take a moment to breathe before you begin the scene. Make sure you breathe throughout the playing of the scene. Work to deepen your connection with your partner by offering and accepting, adjusting and adapting to one another.

When you finish the scene, evaluate the experience. Were you in your body in the scene or did your attention wander? Do you recall the scene or is it just a blur? What felt connected and what unconnected? What went as planned and what was new or different? What would you like to incorporate into the score of the scene, now that you've done it once?

As a performer, you are vulnerable in the most expected, and sometimes unexpected, ways. Criticism, especially right after you have performed, can seem unduly brutal or unreasonable. Being open to criticism means you are willing to listen and hear other points of view. You don't have to agree with them, but you must acknowledge that other points of view exist. Sometimes they are valid, sometimes not. Assume that each criticism is an offer; accept every offer. Forget your defensive posture for a moment and listen. Later, as you replay the mental tape of the critique, you can decide if you wish to incorporate the adjustments or not. Keep the possibility of growth alive, even in the harshest of moments.

Go back into rehearsal after performing the scene and incorporate any changes you wish to make into the scene. Work to tune the targets and adjust the playing of the score. Incorporate any notes or suggestions from the trainer into the playing of the scene and work to sharpen your attention to detail.

Use the MAP to continue experimenting with the score by focusing your attention every time you work. Have a clear rehearsal target every time you get up to work. Always start with a warm-up that fosters a sense of flow between you and your partner. Always work by repeating the scene in threes to discover the pattern, repeat the pattern, and then play the pattern. Connect the outer with the inner to release and focus your imagination. Always use an outer focus to bridge with your partner. Accept every offer. Work first, talk after.

The Duchess of Malfi, 1993 production at the American Conservatory Theater, San Francisco, California.

Photograph © 1993 by Ken Friedman.

CODA

This, as a basic acting book, stops where style begins. Well, it doesn't really, because everything has its own style. In theater, however, we tend to apply "style" to those plays with nonrealistic tendencies: heightened language; exaggerated, or simply noncontemporary clothes and manners; and an absent fourth wall that probably reveals anything but a sitting room or the kitchen sink.

As we quoted in our book *Acting With Style,* John Gielgud has described style as "knowing what kind of play you are in." This simply reinforces what we stated about everything having its own style, which Gielgud suggested you have to be able to recognize from the given circumstances of the play. In our earlier book, for ease of distinction, we spoke of a play having intrinsic qualities—those that the playwright gave it, its structure and sensibility, so to speak—and extrinsic qualities—those that could be interpolated by the director for instance, to bring a more contemporary look to an old classic. The intrinsic–extrinsic perspective is still significantly true, and a useful tool for analysis. You will approach style by learning to edit your choices for consistency and synchronicity with the world of the play as you have chosen to present it. But we might now have to adapt Sir John's succinct phrase to add "knowing what kind of a play you *want* to be in." The intrinsic qualities of a play no longer are seen to be as specific or exclusive. As was suggested in the prologue, style is no longer seen as such an absolute; it has changed its focus, perspective, and sometimes its face.

What we then called extrinsic qualities are now largely known under the postmodern term of deconstruction, and a more dominant partner in the intrinsic–extrinsic structure. This is significantly due to the world changes that were discussed in the prologue and don't need to be recapitulated here. The basic principles of *Basic Acting: The Modular Acting Process* are similar to *Acting With Style*—based upon action, mask, and play, rather than purely inner process—and thus the basic process is consistent with the demands of and bridges over to the playing of style as examined in *Acting With Style:* the playing of physical actions and creation of a mask of character that is consistent with the demands of the text; the journey taken by the actors through the map of the text, from whatever chosen starting point.

What *Basic Acting: The Modular Acting Process* does to expand this idea is to present a process that can deal with the multifaceted masks, multilayered action, and multicultural sensibilities of the future, and also the deconstructive perspective possible to take on the past repertory. It is still, however, a basic training process that can deal with the discrete mask of realism while providing a bridge to the diverse range of styles now available to the actor and director. It is a process by which actors and directors can create for themselves their particular comment upon the world in which they live.

All periods will see life through their own lens. As Jonathan Miller has said, "Life is a constantly changing fiction, based upon a similar theme." An actor will capture his or her sense of the action of the play and present it through the filter of the current time for the engagement of the contemporary audience. The job is to make the action interesting, engaging and contemporary; not fixed, sterile, and immutable.

There are at least two ways of approaching style through *Basic Acting: The Modular Acting Process.* As a means of illustration, consider Noel Coward. An African-American actor can know as much about the realities of the 1920s and 1930s culture as an English or white American knows about the 16th and 17th century of Shakespeare. In both instances the actor can learn to speak the rhythm of Coward's language and the manners of his movement. There is absolutely no reason why a Coward play acted by African-American, Hispanic, or Asian actors cannot work on its own terms. On the other hand, a multiracial cast could deconstruct the play, making some kind of social or political comment upon its presumptions of upper-class distinctions and superiority. The action could be turned upon its head, but still be the core of the play.

Basic Acting: The Modular Acting Process can train you to do this work either way. It all depends upon how you enter the map, cover all the modules, and arrange them in whatever order or shape fits the look of the production; whatever journey through the map you set out to take or discover as you deal with its problems.

As suggested with one or two productions quoted in the prologue, theater has been slouching towards the Bethlehem of such a process for the last several years. There have been all–African-American productions of *The Death of a Salesman,* there has been an all female production of *Romeo and Juliet,* there has been a female Falstaff, and most of Shakespeare's plays have had multiracial productions. Action still drives the plays. And if the action is correctly "modulated," then it can be clothed in many forms and still communicate the validity of its essence, even through the social and cultural kaleidoscope of 400 years or more. Culture is not defined by color. And, as we have said, action is basically raceless and genderless.

Patterning the play is the core of *Basic Acting: The Modular Acting Process*. It shows the actor how, from any starting point, patterns of action may be uncovered, and by permutating any element of action (module) with any other, different maps are achieved. It is a flexible process, reflecting today's fractured world, which allows the actor to choose any point of entry into the action and create either an entirely consistent pattern from that point or a pattern of consistent inconsistencies. It gives an actor an enormous range of choices. Mapping is the bridge from the creation of patterns of action to the creation of the mask of character consistent with those patterns of action, i.e., contours of the map text, required by the performance. Exploring the contours of the journey through the text reveals the impulses to action that create for the actor the mask required by the map of the text. Text is a map to action and the mask is a map of action—the physical shape of the action will be the style of the performance.

Art operates within the same system of physics that we all do. Chaos theory allows us many possible dynamics, but finally returns us to our balance in the human system in which we exist. All the differences add up to a whole: chaos finally has to have its own order. One thing changes, something else changes; this does not mean that there is no ultimate form, or that "anything goes." It is a movement towards a freedom that allows many shapes within this final structure. It is a movement towards the multifaceted and multicultural world of the next century.

Basic Acting: The Modular Acting Process, because of its many entry points into the map of action and modular flexibility, works as well for naturalism as it does for Dada, deconstruction, and all the many aspects of postmodernism. But it does not lock you into any of them. Like the childlike vision of play, which is yet to be preconditioned, the process contains the possibilities of a lot of emotional velocity and risk, just as a child may make many shapes and happy accidents out of his or her modular games. The modular process is flexible and nonprescriptive, but at the same time will have the form and focus the actors give each individual piece by the sum and arrangement of their choices. Finally, we all partake of the same balance of chaos—its gravity holds us together, if in increasingly various forms and styles.

While a protean self emerges from the many dislocations of the twentieth century, we have, at the same time, escaped from the rigid exaggerated individualism of our particular present. Our selves are not our property alone, but are created in relationship with all other peoples and cultures. And when we know what the action requirements are of any theatre piece and have explored their possible endowments, we will have the style of the piece, i.e., the shape and sensibility of the communication between the society of actors and the society of the audience it wants to reflect.

While *Basic Acting: The Modular Acting Process* will work for naturalism and a consistent throughline, classical texts still speak to us across the ages in terms of the problems of race, gender, and class with which contemporary naturalism tries to deal in miniature. The much-maligned "canon" can, however, still fire a relevant broadside today. Though a play's style may no longer be absolutely recognizable to its original audience, when performed today its action and the resonances of that action for humanity, will.

As Walt Whitman has said, we "contain multitudes" (*Song of Myself*, 1.50), and we may be sure that Stanislavski would agree. What *Basic Acting: The Modular Acting Process* does is to set those multitudes free to explore and create whatever styles of theater speak to a contemporary audience.

SOME SUGGESTED
PLAYS FOR SCENES

A Boy's Life, Howard Korder
Album, David Rimer
And Miss Reardon Drinks a Little, Paul Zindel
Come Back to the Five and Dime Jimmie Dean, Ed Graczyk
Courtship, Horton Foote
Did You Ever Go to PS 43, Michael Schulman
Fool for Love, Sam Shepard
Hurly Burly, David Rabe
Isn't It Romantic, Wendy Wasserstein
Ladies at the Alamo, Paul Zindel
Loose Ends, Michael Weller
Ludlow Fair, Lanford Wilson
Our Town, Thornton Wilder
Painting Churches, Tina Howe
Sexual Perversity in Chicago, David Mamet
Speed the Plough, David Mamet
Streamers, David Rabe
The Ballad of the Sad Cafe, Carson McCullers
The Effect of Gamma Rays on Man-in-the-Moon Marigolds, Paul Zindel
The Girl on the Via Flaminia, Alred Hayes
The Great Nebula in Orion, Lanford Wilson
The Miss Firecracker Contest, Beth Henley
The Wager, Mark Medoff
The Woolgatherer, William Mastrosimone
Uncommon Women and Others, Wendy Wasserstein

BIBLIOGRAPHY

Anderson, Walter Truett. *Reality Isn't What It Used To Be*. New York: Harper and Row, 1990.

Chekhov, Michael. *To the Actor*. New York: Harper and Row, 1953.

De Bono, Edward. *Lateral Thinking, a Textbook of Creativity*. London: Penguin Books, 1970.

Harrop, John. *Acting*. London: Routledge, 1992.

Harrop, John, and Sabin Epstein. *Acting With Style*. New Jersey: Prentice Hall, 1987.

Johnstone, Keith. *Impro*. New York: Theatre Arts Books, 1979.

Laban, Rudolf. *The Mastery of Movement*. London: Macdonald and Evans, 1960.

Lewis, Robert. *Method or Madness*. New York: Samuel French, 1958.

Marowitz, Charles. *Directing the Action*. New York: Applause Books, 1986.

Munk, Erica (ed.). *Stanislavski and America*. Greenwich, Conn: Fawcett, 1967.

Shlain, Leonard. *Art and Physics*. New York: William Morrow, 1991.

Spolin, Viola. *Improvisations for the Theatre*. Evanston, Ill.: Northwestern University Press, 1963.

Stanislavski, Konstantin. *An Actor Prepares*. (Elizabeth Reynolds Hapgood, trans.) New York: Theatre Arts Books, 1930.

——*My Life in Art*. (G. Ivanov-Mumjiev, trans.) Moscow: Foreign Languages Publishing House, 1925.

INDEX

GUIDE TO EXERCISES

The letter *f* following a page number indicates an illustration.